AF669644

CLASSIC TEXTS SERIES

A SCHOOL GEOMETRY

HS HALL & FH STEVENS

arihant

SUCCESS AND NOTHING LESS

arihant
SUCCESS AND NOTHING LESS

ARIHANT PRAKASHAN (Series), MEERUT

卐 **Administrative & Production Offices**

Regd. Office

'Ramchhaya' 4577/15, Agarwal Road, Darya Ganj, New Delhi -110002
Tele: 011- 47630600, 43518550

卐 **Head Office**

Kalindi, TP Nagar, Meerut (UP) - 250002
Tel: 0121-7156203, 7156204

卐 **Sales & Support Offices**

Agra, Ahmedabad, Bengaluru, Bareilly, Chennai, Delhi, Guwahati, Hyderabad, Jaipur, Jhansi, Kolkata, Lucknow, Nagpur & Pune.

卐 **PRICE** ₹140.00

卐 **PO No :** TXT-59-T065546-06-25

Published by Arihant Publications (India) Ltd.

For further information about the books published by Arihant, log on to www.arihantbooks.com or e-mail at info@arihantbooks.com

Follow us on

PREFACE

The present work provides a course of Elementary Geometry based on the recommendations of the Mathematical Association and on the schedule recently proposed and adopted at Cambridge.

The principles which governed these proposals have been confirmed by the issue of revised schedules for all the more important Examinations, and they are now so generally accepted by teachers that they need no discussion here. It is enough to note the following points:

(i) We agree that a pupil should gain his first geometrical ideas from a short preliminary course of a practical and experimental character. A suitable introduction to the present book would consist of Easy Exercises in Drawing to illustrate the subject matter of the Definitions; Measurements of Lines and Angles; Use of Compasses and Protractor; Problems on Bisection; Perpendiculars and Parallels; Use of Set Squares; The Construction of Triangles and Quadrilaterals. These problems should be accompanied by informal explanation, and the results verified by measurement. Concurrently, there should be a series of exercises in Drawing and Measurement designed to lead inductively to the more important Theorems of Part I [Euc. I. 1-34].* While strongly advocating some such introductory lessons, we may point out that our book, as far as it goes, is complete in itself, and from the first is illustrated by numerical and graphical examples of the easiest types. Thus, throughout the whole work, a graphical and experimental course is provided side by side with the usual deductive exercises.

(ii) Theorems and Problems are arranged in separate but parallel courses, intended to be studied *pari passu*. This arrangement is made possible by the use, now generally sanctioned, of *Hypothetical Constructions*. These, before being employed in the text, are carefully specified, and referred to the Axioms on which they depend.

(iii) The subject is placed on the basis of *Commensurable Magnitudes*. By this means, certain difficulties which are wholly beyond the grasp of a young learner are postponed, and a wide field of graphical and numerical illustration is opened. Moreover, the fundamental

* *Such an introductory course is now furnished by our Lessons in Experimental and Practical Geometry.*

Theorems on Areas (hardly less than those on Proportion) may thus be reduced in number, greatly simplified, and brought into line with practical applications.

(iv) An attempt has been made to curtail the excessive body of text which the demands of Examinations have hitherto forced as "bookwork" on a beginner's memory. Even of the Theorems here given a certain number (which we have distinguished with an asterisk) might be omitted or postponed at the discretion of the teacher. And the formal propositions for which—as such—teacher/and pupil are held responsible, might perhaps be still further limited to those which make the landmarks of Elementary Geometry. Time so gained should be used in getting the pupil to *apply* his knowledge; and the working of examples should be made as important a part of a lesson in Geometry as it is so considered in Arithmetic and Algebra.

Though we have not always followed Euclid's order of Propositions, we think it desirable for the present, in regard to the subject matter of Euclid Book I to preserve the essentials of his logical sequence. Our departure from Euclid's treatment of Areas has already been mentioned; the only other important divergence in this section of the work is the position of I. 26 (Theorem 17), which we place after I. 32 (Theorem 16), thus getting rid of the tedious and uninstructive *Second Case*. In subsequent Parts a freer treatment in respect of logical order 'has been followed.

As regards the presentment of the propositions, we have constantly kept in mind the needs of that large class of students, who, without special aptitude for mathematical study, and under no necessity for acquiring technical knowledge, may and do derive real intellectual advantage from lessons in pure deductive reasoning. Nothing has as yet been devised as effective for this purpose as the Euclidean form of proof; and in our opinion no excuse is needed for treating the earlier proofs with that fulness which we have always found necessary in our experience as teachers.

The examples are numerous and for the most part easy. They have been very carefully arranged, and are distributed throughout the text in immediate connection with the propositions on which they depend. A special feature is the large number of examples involving graphical or numerical work. The answers to these have been printed on perforated pages, so that they may easily be removed if it is found that access to numerical results is a source of temptation in examples involving measurement.

We are indebted to several friends for advice and suggestions. In particular we wish to express our thanks to Mr. H. C. Playne and Mr. H. C. Beaven of Clifton College for the valuable assistance they have rendered in reading the proof sheets and checking the answers to some of the numerical exercises.

H. S. HALL
F. H. STEVENS

PREFATORY NOTE TO THE SECOND EDITION

IN the present edition some further steps have been taken towards the curtailment of bookwork by reducing certain less important propositions (e.g. Euclid I. 22, 43, 44) to the rank of exercises. Room has thus been found for more numerical and graphical exercises, and experimental work such as that leading to the Theorem of Pythagoras.

Theorem 22 (page 62), in the shape recommended in the Cambridge Schedule, replaces the equivalent proposition given as *Additional Theorem* A (page 60) in previous editions.

In the case of a few problems (e.g. Problems 23, 28, 29) it has been thought more instructive to justify the construction by a preliminary analysis than by the usual formal proof.

H.S. HALL
F.H. STEVENS

CONTENTS

PART I

Parallels

Triangles Continued

PART II

Areas

Problems on Areas

Axes of Reference. Coordinates

PART III

PART IV

PART I
AXIOMS

ALL mathematical reasoning is founded on certain simple principles, the truth of which is so evident that they are accepted without proof. These self-evident truths are called Axioms.

For instance:

Things which are equal to the same thing are equal to one another.

The following axioms, corresponding to the first four Rules of Arithmetic, are among those most commonly used in geometrical reasoning.

Addition. *If equals are added to equals, the sums are equal.*

Subtraction. *If equals are taken from equals, the remainders are equal.*

Multiplication. *Things which are the same multiples of equals are equal to one another.*

For instance: *Doubles of equals are equal to one another.*

Division. *Things which are she same parts of equals are equal to one another.*

For instance: *Halves of equals are equal to one another.*

The above Axioms are given as instances, and not as a complete list, of those which will be used. They are said to be *general*, because they apply equally to magnitudes of all kinds. Certain special axioms relating to geometrical magnitudes only will be stated from time to time as they are required.

DEFINITIONS AND FIRST PRINCIPLES

Every beginner knows in a general way what is meant by a point, a line, and a surface. But in geometry these terms are used in a strict sense which needs some explanation.

1. A point has position, but is said to have *no magnitude*.

   This means that we are to attach to a point no idea of size either as to *length* or *breadth*, but to think only where it is situated. A dot made with a sharp pencil may be taken as roughly representing a point; but small as such a dot may be, it still has *some* length and breadth, and is therefore not actually a geometrical point. The smaller he dot however, the nearly it represents a point.

2. A line has length, but is said to have *no breadth*.

   A line is traced out by a moving point. If the point of a pencil is moved over a sheet of paper, the trace left represents a line. But such a trace, however finely drawn, has some degree of breadth, and is therefore not itself a true geometrical line. The finer the trace left by the moving pencil-point, the more nearly will it represent a line.

3. Proceeding in a similar manner from the idea of a line to the idea of a surface, we say that

A surface has length and breadth, but *no thickness*. And finally,

A solid has length, breadth, and thickness.

Solids, surfaces, lines and points are thus related to one another:

(i) A solid is bounded by surfaces.

(ii) A surface is bounded by lines; and surfaces meet in lines.

(iii) A line is boundedk (or terminated) by points; and lines meet in points.

4. A line may be straight or curved.

A straight line has the same direction from point to point throughout its whole length.

A curved line changes its direction continually from point to point.

AXIOM. *There can be only one straight line joining two given points*: that is,

Two straight lines cannot enclose a space.

5. A plane is a *flat* surface, the test of flatness being that if any two points are taken in the surface, the straight line between them lies wholly in that surface.

6. When two straight lines meet at a point,they are said to form an angle. The straight lines are called the arms of the angle; .the point at which they meet is its vertex.

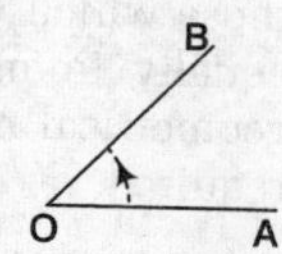

The magnitude of the angle may be thus explained:

Suppose that the arm **OA** is fixed, and that **OB** *turns about the point* **O** (as shown by the arrow). Suppose also that **OB** began its turning from the position **OA**. Then the size of the angle **AOB** is measured by the *amount of turning* required to bring the revolving arm from its first position **OA** into its subsequent position **OB**.

Observe that the size of an angle does not in any way depend on the length of its arms.

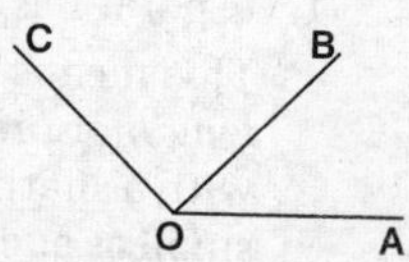

Angles which lie on either side of a common arm are said to be adjacent.

For example, the angles **AOB, BOC**, which have the common arm **OB**, are adjacent.

When two straight lines such as **AB, CD** cross one another at **O**, the angles **COA, BOD** are said to be vertically opposite. The angles **AOD, COB** are also vertically opposite to one another.

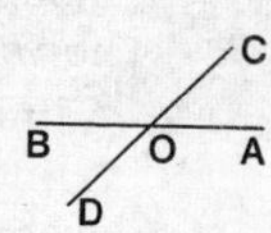

7. When one straight line stands on another so as to make the adjacent angles equal to one another, each of the angles is called a right angle; and each line is said to be perpendicular to the other.

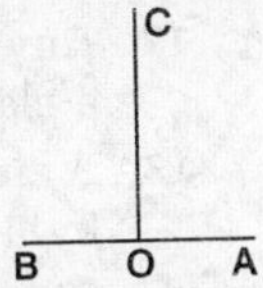

AXIOMS. (i) *If* **O** *is a point in a straight line* **AB**, *then a line* **OC**, *which turns about* **O** *from the position* **OA** *to the position* **OB** *must pass through one position, and only one, in which it is perpendicular to* **AB**.

(ii) *All right angles are equal.*

A right angle is divided into 90 equal parts called degrees (°); each degree into 60 equal parts called minutes (′); each minute into 60 equal parts called seconds (″).

In the above figure, if **OC** revolves about **O** from the position **OA** into the position **OB**, it turns through *two right angles*, or 180°.

If **OC** makes a *complete revolution* about **O**, starting from **OA** and returning to its original position, it turns through *four right angles*, or 360°.

8. An angle which is less than one right angle is said to be acute.

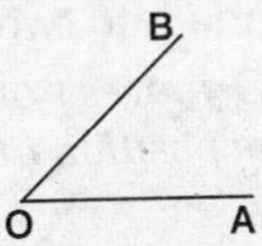

That is, an acute angle is less than 90°.

9. An angle which is greater than *one* right angle, but less than *two* right angles, is said to be obtuse. That is, an obtuse angle lies between 90° and 180°.

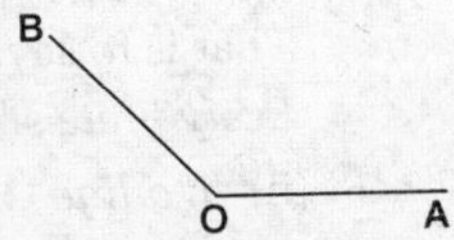

10. If one arm **OB** of an angle turns until it makes *a straight line* with the other arm **OA**, the angle so formed is called a straight angle.

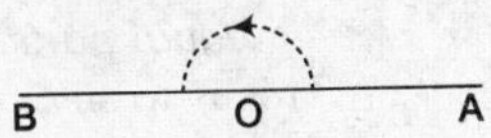

A straight angle = 2 right angles = 180°.

11. An angle which is greater than *two* right angles, but less that *four* right angles, is said to be reflex.

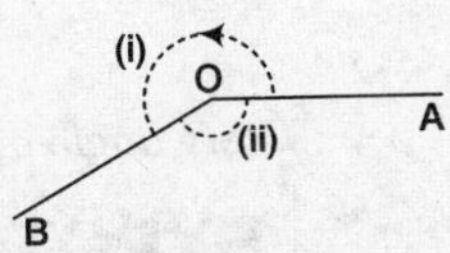

That is, a reflex angle lies between 180° and 360°.

NOTE. When two straight lines meet, *two* angles are formed, one greater, and one less than two right angles. The first arises by supposing **OB** to have revolved from the position **OA** the longer way round, marked (i); the other by supposing **OB** to have revolved the shorter way round, marked (ii). Unless the contrary is stated, the angle between two straight lines will be considered to be that which is less than two right angles.

12. Any portion of a plane surface bounded by one or more lines is called a plane figure.

13. A circle is a plane figure contained by a line traced out by a point which moves so that its distance from a certain fixed point is always the same.

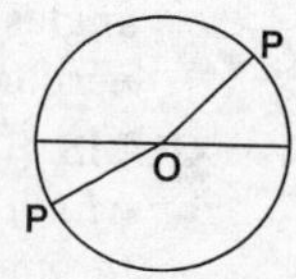

Here the point **P** moves so that its distance from the fixed point **O** is always the same.

The fixed point is called the centre, and the bounding line is called the circumference.

14. A radius of a circle is a straight line drawn from the centre to the circumference. It follows that all radii of a circle are equal.

15. A diameter of a circle is a straight line drawn through the centre, and terminated both ways by the circumference.

16. An arc of a circle is any part of the circumference.

17. A semi-circle is the figure bounded by a diameter of a circle and the part of the circumference cut off by the diameter.

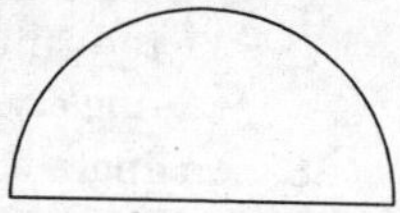

18. To bisect means to divide into two *equal* parts.

AXIOMS. (i) *If a point* **O** *moves from* **A** *to* **B** *along the straight line* **AB**, *it must pass through one position in which it divides* **AB** *into two equal parts.*

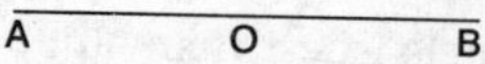

That is to say:

Every finite straight line has a point of bisection.

(ii) *If a line* **OP**, *revolving about* **O**, *turns from* **OA** *to* **OB**, *it must pass through one position in which it divides the angle* **AOB** *into two equal parts.*

This is to say :

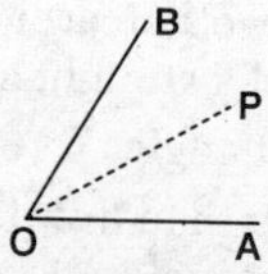

Every angle may be supposed to have a line of bisection.

HYPOTHETICAL CONSTRUCTIONS

From the Axioms attached to Definitions 7 and 18, it follows that we may suppose.

(i) *A straight line to drawn perpendicular to a given straight line from any point in it.*

(ii) *A finite straight line to be bisected at a point.*

(iii) *An angle to be bisected by a line.*

SUPERPOSITION AND EQUALITY

AXIOM. *Magnitudes which can be made to coincide with one another are equal.*

This axiom implies that any line, angle, or figure, may be taken up from its position, and without change in size or form, laid down upon a second line, angle, or figure, for the purpose of comparison, and it states that two such magnitudes are equal when one can be exactly placed over the other without overlapping. This process is called superposition, and the first magnitude is said to be applied to the other.

POSTULATES

In order to draw geometrical figures certain instruments are required. These are, for the purposes of this book, (i) *a straight ruler,* (ii) *a pair of compasses.* The following Postulates (or requests) claim the use of these instruments, and assume that with their help the processes mentioned below may be duly performed.

Let it be granted:

1. *That a straight line may be drawn from any one point to any other point.*
2. *That a* FINITE (*or terminated*) *straight line may be* PRODUCED (*that is, prolonged*) *to any length in that straight line.*
3. *That a circle may be drawn with any point as centre and with a radius of any length.*

NOTES. (i) Postulate 3, as stated above, implies that we may adjust the compasses to the length of any straight line **PQ**, and with a radius of this length draw a circle with any point **O** as centre. That is to say, the compasses may be used to *transfer distances* from one part of a diagram to another.

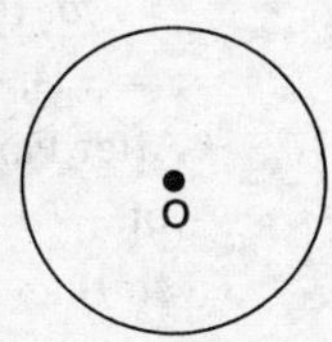

(ii) *Hence from* **AB**, *the greater of two straight lines, we may cut off a part equal to* **PQ** *the less.*

For if with centre **A**, and radius equal to **PQ**, we draw an arc of a circle cutting **AB** at **X**, it is obvious that **AX** is equal to **PQ**.

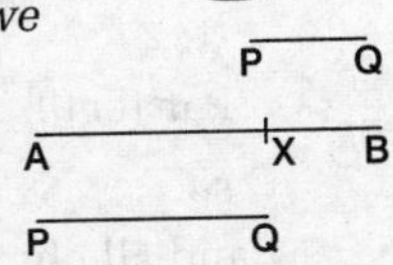

INTRODUCTORY

1. Plane geometry deals with the properties of such lines and figures as may be drawn on a plane surface.
2. The subject is divided into a number of separate discussions, called propositions.

   Propositions are of two kinds, Theorems and Problems.

   A Theorem proposes to prove the truth of some geometrical statement.

A Problem process to perform some geometrical construction, such as to draw some particular line, or to construct some required figure.

3. A Proposition consists of the following parts:

The General Enunciation, the Particular Enunciation, the Construction, and *the Proof.*

(i) The General Enunciation is a preliminary statement, describing in general terms the purpose of the proposition.

(ii) The Particular Enunciation repeats in special terms the statement already made, and refers it to a diagram, which enables the reader to follow the reasoning more easily.

(iii) The Construction then directs the drawing of such straight lines and circles as may be required to effect the purpose of a problem, or to prove the truth of a theorem.

(iv) The Proof shows that the object proposed in a problem has been accomplished, or that the property stated in a theorem is true.

4. The letters Q.E.D. are appended to a theorem, and stand for Quod erat Demonstrandum, *which was to be proved.*

5. A Corollary is a statement the truth of which follows readily from an established proposition; it is therefore appended to the proposition as an inference or deduction, which usually requires no further proof.

6. The following symbols and abbreviations are used in the text of this book.

In Part I.

∴ *for* therefore,	∠ *for* angle,
= ,, is, or are, equal to,	Δ ,, triangle.

After Part I.

pt.	*for* point,	perp.	*for* perpendicular,
st. line	,, straight line,	par^{m}	,, parallelogram,
rt. ∠	,, right angle,	rectil	,, rectilineal,
Par^{l} (or ||)	,, parallel,	⊙	,, circle,
sq.	,, square,	$○^{ce}$	,, circumference;

and all obvious contractions of commonly occurring words, such as opp., adj., diag., etc., *for* opposite, adjacent, diagonal, etc.

[For convenience of oral work, and to prevent the rather common abuse of contractions by beginners, the above code of signs has been introduced gradually, and at first somewhat sparingly.]

In numerical examples the following abbreviations will be used.

m.	*for* metre,	cm.	*for* centimetre,
mm.	,, millimetre,	dm.	,, decimetre,
l.	,, *litre.*	*km.*	,, *kilometre.*

kg. *for* kilogram.

ON LINES AND ANGLES

THEOREM 1. [Euclid I. 13]

The adjacent angles which one straight line makes with another straight line on one side of it, are together equal to two right angles.

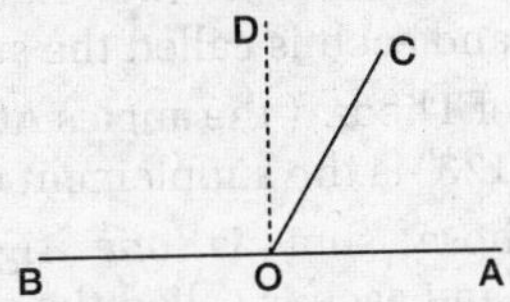

Let the straight line **CO** make with the straight line **AB** the adjacent $\angle^s$ **AOC, COB.**

It is required to prove that the $\angle^s$ **AOC, COB** *are together equal to two right angles.*

Suppose **OD** is at right angles to**BA**.

Proof. Then the $\angle^s$ **AOC, COB** together = the three $\angle^s$ **AOC, COD, DOB**

Also the $\angle^s$ **AOD, DOB** together = the three $\angle^s$ **AOC, COD, DOB.**

$\therefore$the $\angle^s$ **AOC, COB** together = the $\angle^s$ **AOD, DOB** = two right angles. Q.E.D.

PROOF BY ROTATION

Suppose a straight line revolving about **O** turns from the position **OA** into the position **OC**, and thence into the position **OB**; that is, let the revolving line turn in succession through the $\angle^s$ **AOC, COB.**

Now in passing from its first position **OA** to its final position **OB**, the revolving line turns through two right angles, for **AOB** is a straight line.

Hence the $\angle^s$ **AOC, COB** together = two right angles.

COROLLARY 1. *If two straight lines cut one another, the four angles so formed are together equal to four right angles.*

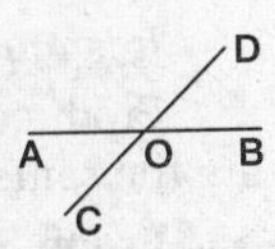

For example,

$$\angle BOD + \angle DOA + \angle AOC + \angle COB = 4 \text{ right angles.}$$

COROLLARY 2. *When any number of straight lines meet at a point, the sum of the consecutive angles so formed is equal to four right angles.*

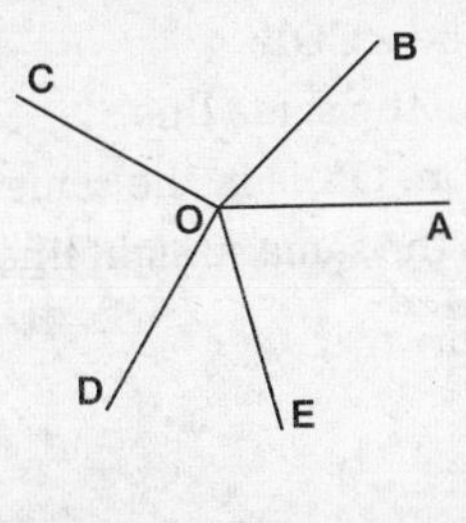

For a straight line revolving about **O**, and turning in succession through the $\angle^s$**AOB, BOC, COD, DOE, EOA,** will have made one complete revolution, and therefore turned through four right angles.

DEFINITIONS

(i) Two angles whose sum is *two* right angles, are said to be supplementary; and each is called the supplement of the other.

Thus in the Fig. of Theor. 1 the angles **AOC, COB** are supplementary. Again the angle 123° is the supplement of the angle 57°.

(ii) Two angles whose sum is *one* right angle are said to be complementary; and each is called the complement of the other.

Thus in the Fig. of Theor. 1 the angle **DOC** is the complement of the angle **AOC**. Again angles of 34° and 56° are complementary.

COROLLARY 3. (i) *Supplements of the same angle are equal.*

(ii) *Complements of the same angle are equal.*

THEOREM 2. [Euclid I. 14]

If, at a point in a straight line, two other straight lines, on opposite sides of it, make the adjacent angles together equal to two right angles, then these two straight lines are in one and the same straight line.

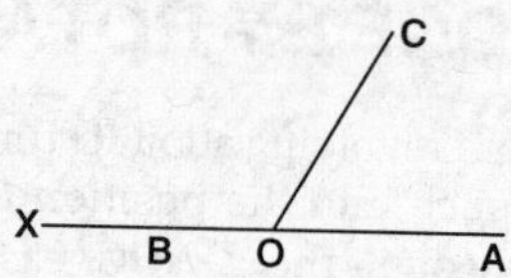

At **O** in the straight line **CO** let the two straight lines **OA, OB,** on opposite sides of **CO**, make the adjacent $\angle^s$**AOC, COB** together equal to two right angles; (that is, let the adjacent $\angle^s$**AOC, COB** be supplementary).

It is required to prove that **OB** *and* **OA** *are in the same straight line.*

Produce **AO** beyond **O** to any point **X** : it will be shown that **OX** and **OB** are the same line.

Proof. Since by construction **AOX** is a straight line,

∴ the ∠**COX** is the supplement of the ∠**COA**. *Theor.* 1.

But, by hypothesis,

the ∠**COB** is the supplement of the ∠**COA**.

∴ the ∠**COX** = the ∠**COB**;

∴ **OX** and **OB** are the same line.

But, by construction, **OX** is in the same straight line with **OA**; hence **OB** is also in the same straight line with **OA**. **Q.E.D.**

EXERCISES

1. Write down the supplements of *one-half* of a right angle, *four-thirds* of a right angle; also of 46°,149°,83°,101°15′.
2. Write down the complement of *two-fifths* of a right angle; also of 27°, 38° 16′, and 41° 29′ 30″.
3. If two straight lines intersect forming four angles of which one is known to be a right angle, *prove that* : the other three are also right angles.
4. In the triangle **ABC** the angles **ABC, ACB** are given equal. If the side **BC** is produced both ways, show that the exterior angles so formed are equal.
5. In the triangle **ABC** the angles **ABC, ACB** are given equal. If **AB** and **AC** are produced beyond the base, show that the exterior angles so formed are equal.

DEFINITION. The lines which bisect an angle and the adjacent angle made by producing one of its arms are called the internal and external bisectors of the given angle.

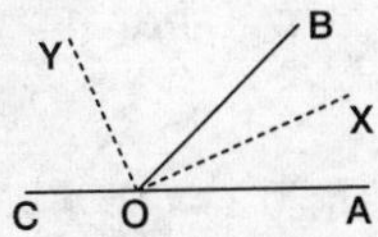

Thus in the diagram, **OX** and **OY** are the internal and external bisectors of the angle **AOB.**

6. Prove that the bisectors of the adjacent angles which one straight line makes with another contain a right angle. That is to say, *the internal and external bisectors of an angle are at right angles to one another.*
7. Show that the angles **AOX** and **COY** in the above diagram are complementary.
8. Show that the angles **BOX** and **COX** are supplementary; and also that the angles **AOY** and **BOY** are supplementary.
9. If the angle **AOB** is 35°, find the angle **COY**.

THEOREM 3. [Euclid I . 15]

If two straight lines cut one another, the vertically opposite angles are equal.

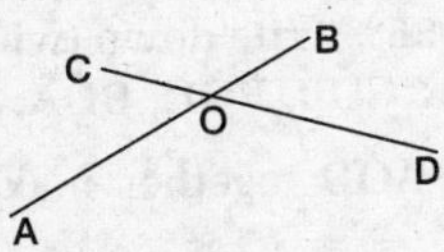

Let the straight lines **AB**, **CD** cut one another at the point **O.**

It is required to prove that

(i) *the* ∠**AOC** = *the* ∠**DOB** ;

(ii) *the* ∠**COB** = *the* ∠**AOD.**

Proof. Because **AO** meets the straight line **CD,**

∴ the adjacent $\angle^s$ **AOC, AOD** together = two right angles; that is, the $\angle$**AOC** is the supplement of the $\angle$**AOD.**

Again because **DO** meets the straight line **AB,**

∴ the adjacent $\angle^s$ **DOB, AOD** together = two right angles; that is, the $\angle$**DOB** is the supplement of the $\angle$**AOD.**

Thus each of the $\angle^s$ **AOC, DOB** is the supplement of the $\angle$**AOD** .

∴ the $\angle$**AOC** = the $\angle$**DOB.**

Similarly, the $\angle$**COB** = the $\angle$**AOD.** **Q. E.D.**

PROOF BY ROTATION

Suppose the line **COD** to revolve about **O** until **OC** turns into the position **OA**. Then at the same moment **OD** must reach the position **OB** (for **AOB** and **COD** are *straight*):

Thus the same amount of turning is required to close the $\angle$**AOC** as to close the $\angle$**DOB.**

∴ the $\angle$**AOC** = the $\angle$**DOB.**

EXERCISES ON ANGLES

(*Numerical*)

1. Through what angle does the minute-hand of a clock turn in (i) 5 minutes, (ii) 21 minutes, (iii) $43\frac{1}{2}$ minutes, (iv) 14 min. 10 sec.? And how long will it take to turn through (v) 66°, (vi) 222°?

2. A clock is started at noon : through what angles will the hour-hand have turned by (i) 3.45, (ii) 10 minutes past 5? And what will be the time when it has turned through $172\frac{1}{2}^\circ$?

3. The earth makes a complete revolution about its axis in 24 hours. Through what angle will it turn in 3 hrs. 20 min., and how long will it take to turn through 130°?

4. In the diagram of Theorem 3

(i) If the $\angle$**AOC** = 35°, write down (without measurement) the value of each of the $\angle^s$**COB, BOD, DOA.**

(ii) If the $\angle^s$**COB, AOD** together make up 250°, find each of the $\angle^s$**COA, BOD.**

(iii) If the $\angle^s$ **AOC, COB, BOD** together make up 274°, find each of the four angles at **O**.

(*Theoretical*)

5. If from **O** a point in **AB** two straight lines **OC, OD** are drawn on opposite sides of **AB** so as to make the angle **COB** equal to the angle **AOD** ; show that **OC** and **OD** are in the same straight line.
6. Two straight lines **AB, CD** cross at **O**. If **OX** is the bisector of the angle **BOD**, prove that **XO** produced bisects the angle **AOC**.
7. Two straight lines **AB, CD** cross at **O**. If the angle **BOD** is bisected by **OX**, and **AOC** by **OY**, prove that **OX, OY** are in the same straight line.
8. If **OX** bisects an angle **AOB**, show that, by folding the diagram about the bisector, **OA** may be made to coincide with **OB**.
   How would **OA** fall with regard to **OB**, if
   (i) the $\angle$**AOX** were greater than the $\angle$**XOB**;
   (ii) the $\angle$**AOX** were less than the $\angle$**XOB** ?
9. **AB** and **CD** are straight lines intersecting at right angles at **O**; show by folding the figure about **AB**, that **OC** may be made to fall along **OD**.
10. A straight line **AOB** is drawn on paper, which is then folded about **O**, so as to make **OA** fall along **OB**; show that the crease left in the paper is perpendicular to **AB**.

ON TRIANGLES

1. Any portion of a plane surface bounded by one or more lines is called a plane figure.
   The sum of the bounding lines is called the perimeter of the figure.
   The amount of surface enclosed by the perimeter is called the area.
2. Rectilineal figures are those which are bounded by straight lines.
3. A triangle is a plane figure bounded by *three* straight lines.
4. A quadrilateral is a plane figure bounded by *four* straight lines.
5. A polygon is a plane figure bounded by more than four straight lines.
6. A rectilineal figure is said to be
   equilateral, when all its sides are equal;
   equiangular, when all its angles are equal;
   regular, when it is both equilateral and equiangular.

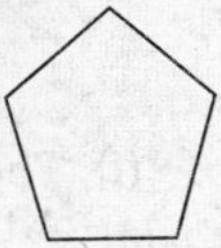

7. Triangles are thus classified with regard to their sides:
   A triangle is said to be
   equilateral, when *all* its sides are equal;
   isosceles, when *two* of its sides are equal;
   scalene, when its sides are all unequal.

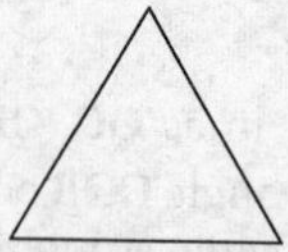
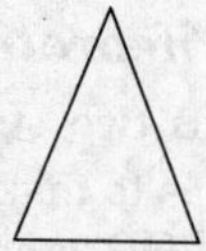
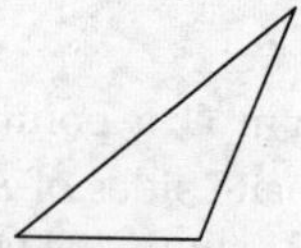

Equilateral Triangle. Isosceles Triangle. Scalene Triangle.

In a triangle **ABC**, the letters **A, B, C** often denote the *magnitude* of the several angles (as measured in degrees); and the letters a, b, c the *lengths* of the opposite sides (as measured in inches, centimetres, or some other unit of length).

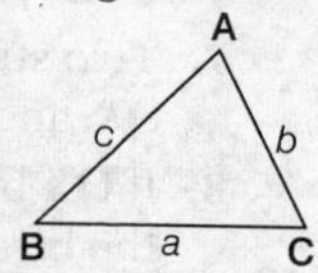

Any one of the angular points of a triangle may be regarded as its vertex; and the opposite side is then called the base.

In an *isosceles* triangle the term *vertex* is usually applied to the point at which the equal sides intersect; and the vertical angle is the angle included by them.

8. Triangles are thus classified with regard to their angles:

A triangle is said to be

right-angled, when one of its angles is a right angle;
obtuse-angled, when one of its angles is obtuse;
acute-angled, when *all three* of its angles are acute.

[It will be seen hereafter (Theorem 8. Cor. 1) *that every triangle must have at least two acute angles.*]

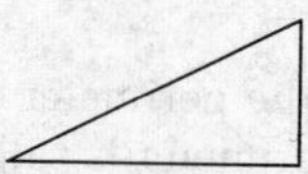
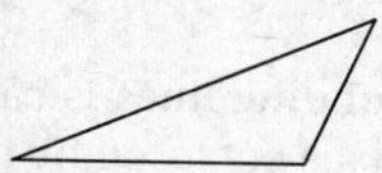
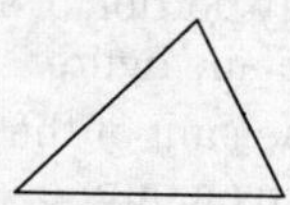

Right-angled Triangle. Obtuse-angled Triangle. Acute-angled Triangle.

In a right-angled triangle the side opposite to the right angle is called the hypotenuse.

9. In any triangle the straight line joining a vertex to the middle point of the opposite side is called a median.

THE COMPARISON OF TWO TRIANGLES

(i) The three sides and three angles of a triangle are called its six parts. A triangle may also be considered with regard of its area.

(ii) Two triangles are said to be equal in all respects, when one may be so placed upon the other as to exactly coincide with it; in which case each part of the first triangles is equal to the corresponding part (namely that with which it coincides) of the other; and the triangles are equal in area.

In two such triangles corresponding sides are *opposite to equal angles,* and corresponding angles are *opposite to equal sides.*

Triangles which may thus be made to coincide by superposition are said to be identically equal or congruent.

THEOREM 4. [Euclid I. 4]

If two triangles have two sides of the one equal to two sides of the other each to each, and the angles included by those sides equal, then the triangles are equal in all respects.

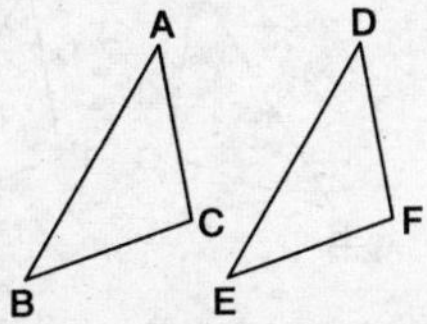

Let **ABC, DEF** be two triangles in which **AB** = **DE**, **AC** = **DF**, and the included angle **BAC** = the included angle **EDF**.

It is required to prove that the **ΔABC** = *the* **ΔDEF** *in all respects.*

Proof. Apply the **ΔABC** to the **ΔDEF**,

so that the point **A** falls on the point **D**,

and the side **AB** along the side **DE**.

Then because **AB** = **DE**,

∴ the point **B** must coincide with the point **E**.

And because **AB** falls along **DE**,

and the ∠**BAC** = the ∠**EDF**,

∴ **AC** must fall along **DF**.

And because **AC** = **DF**,

∴ the point **C** must coincide with the point **F**.

Then since **B** coincides with **E**, and **C** with **F**.

∴ the side **BC** must coincide with the side **EF**.

Hence the **ΔABC** coincides with the **ΔDEF**,

and is therefore equal to it in all respects. **Q.E.D.**

Obs. In this Theorem we must carefully observe what is *given* and what is *proved*.

Given that { **AB** = **DE**, **AC** = **DF**, and the ∠**BAC** = the ∠**EDF**.

From these data we prove that the triangles coincide on superposition.

Hence we *conclude* that { **BC** = **EF**, the ∠**ABC** = the ∠**DEF**, and the ∠**ACB** = the ∠**DEF**;

also that the triangles are equal in area.

Notice that the angles which are proved equal in the two triangles are opposite to sides which were given equal.

NOTE. The adjoining diagram shows that in order to make two congruent triangles coincide, it may be necessary to *reverse*, that is, turn over one of them before superposition.

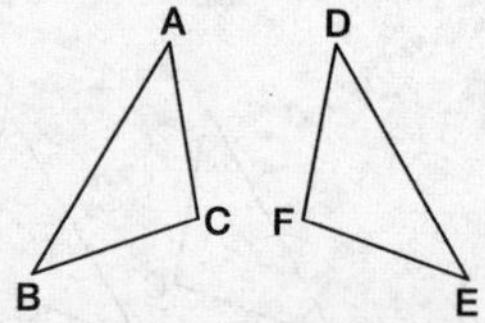

EXERCISES

1. *Show that the bisector of the vertical angle of an isosceles triangle*
   (i) *bisects the base,* (ii) *is perpendicular to the base.*
2. *Let* **O** *be the middle point of a straight line* **AB**, *and let* **OC** *be perpendicular to it. Then if* **P** *is any point in* **OC**, *prove that* **PA = PB.**
3. Assuming that the four sides of a square are equal, and that its angles are all right angles, prove that in the square **ABCD**, the diagonals **AC, BD** are equal.
4. **ABCD** is a square, and **L, M,** and **N** are the middle points of **AB, BC,** and **CD** : prove that
   (i) **LM = MN.** (ii) **AM = DM.**
   (iii) **AN = AM.** (iv) **BN = DM.**
   [Draw a separate figure in each case.]
5. **ABC** is an isosceles triangle : from the equal sides **AB, AC** two equal parts **AX, AY** are cut off, and **BY** and **CX** are joined. Prove that **BY = CX.**

THEOREM 5. [Euclid I. 5]

The angles at the base of an isosceles triangle are equal.

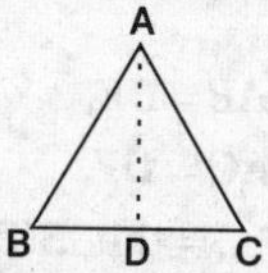

Let **ABC** be an isosceles triangle, in which the side **AB** = the side **AC.**

It is required to prove that the ∠**ABC** = *the* ∠**ACB.**

Suppose that **AD** is the line which bisects the ∠**BAC**, and let it meet **BC** in **D**

1st Proof. Then in the Δ **BAD, CAD,**

because { **BA** = **CA,**
AD is common to both triangles,
and the included ∠**BAD** = the included ∠**CAD;**

∴ the triangles are equal in all respects; *Theor.* **4.**
so that the ∠ **ABD** = the ∠ **ACD**. **Q.E.D.**

2nd Proof. Suppose the Δ **ABC** to be folded about **AD**.

Then since the ∠**BAD** = the ∠**CAD**,

∴ **AB** must fall along **AC**.

And since **AB** = **AC**,

∴ **B** must fall on **C**, and consequently **DB** on **DC**.

∴ the ∠ **ABD** will coincide with the ∠ **ACD**, and is therefore equal to it.

Q.E.D.

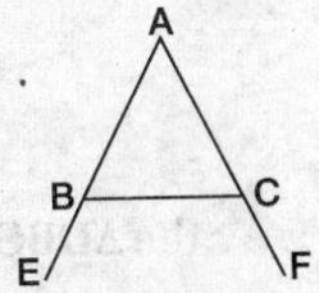

COROLLARY 1. *If the equal sides* **AB**, **AC** *of an isosceles triangle are produced, the exterior angles* **EBC**, **FCB** *are equal; for they are the supplements of the equal angles at the base.*

COROLLARY 2. *If a triangle is equilateral, it is also equiangular.*

DEFINITION. A figure is said to be symmetrical about a line when, on being folded about that line, the parts of the figure on each side of it can be brought into coincidence.

The straight line is called an **axis of symmetry**.

That this may be possible, it is clear that the two parts of the figure must have the same size and shape, and must be similarly placed with regard to the axis.

EXERCISES

1. **ABCD** is a four–sided figure whose sides are all equal, and the diagonal **BD** is drawn : show that
   (i) the angle **ABD** = the angle **ADB**;
   (ii) the angle **CBD** = the angle **CDB**;
   (iii) the angle **ABC** = the angle **ADC**.
2. **ABC**, **DBC** are two isosceles triangles drawn on the same base **BC**, but on *opposite* sides of it: prove (by means of Theorem 5) that the angle **ABD** = the angle **ACD**.
3. **ABC**, **DBC** are two isosceles triangles drawn on the same base **BC** and on *the same* side of it : employ Theorem 5 to prove that the angle **ABD** = the angle **ACD**.
4. **AB**, **AC** are the equal sides of an isosceles triangle **ABC**; and **L**, **M**, **N** are the middle points of **AB**, **BC**, and **CA** respectively:
   prove that (i) **LM** = **NM**. (ii) **BN** = **CL**.
   (iii) the angle **ALM** = the angle **ANM**.

THEOREM 6. [Euclid I. 6]

If two angles of a triangle are equal to one another, then the sides which are opposite to the equal angles are equal to one another.

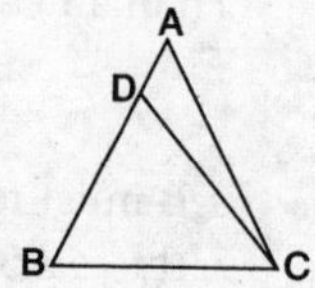

Let **ABC** be a triangle in which the ∠**ABC** = the ∠**ACB**.

It is required to prove that the side **AC** = *the side* **AB**.

If **AC** and **AB** are not equal, suppose that **AB** is the greater.

From **BA** cut off **BD** equal to **AC** Join **DC**.

Proof. Then in the Δ**DBC**, **ACB**,

because { **DB** = **AC**,
BC is common to both,
and the included ∠**DBC** = the included ∠**ACB**;

∴the Δ**DBC** = the Δ **ACB** in area, ***Theor.*** **4.**

the part equal to the whole; which is absurd.

∴ **AB** is not unequal to **AC** ;

that is, **AB** = **AC**. **Q.E.D.**

COROLLARY. *An equiangular triangle is also equilateral.*

In Theorem 6 we employ an *indirect method of proof* frequently used in geometry. It consists in showing that the theorem *cannot be untrue*; since, if it were, we should be led to some *impossible conclusion*. This form of proof is known as **Reduction and Absurdum**.

NOTE ON THEOREMS 5 AND 6

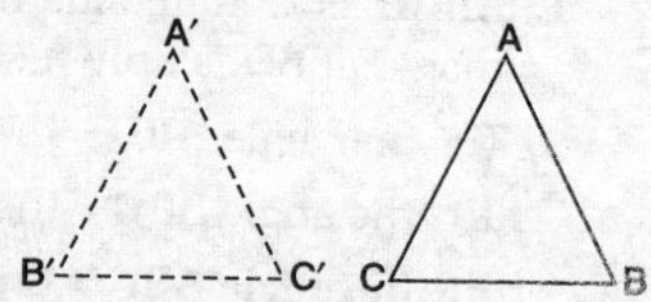

Theorems 5 and 6 may be verified experimentally by cutting out the given Δ **ABC**, and, after turning it over. fitting it *thus reversed* into the vacant space left in the paper.

Suppose **A′ B′ C′** to be the original position of the Δ **ABC**, and let **ACB** represent the triangle when reversed.

In Theorem 5, it will be found on applying **A** to **A′** that **C** may be made to fall on **B′**, and **B** on **C′**.

In Theorem 6, on applying **C** to **B′** and **B** to **C′** we find that **A** will fall on **A′**.

In either case the given triangle *reversed* will coincide with its own "trace," so that the side and angle on the *left* are respectively equal to the side and angle on the *right*.

NOTE ON A THEOREM AND ITS CONVERSE

The enunciation of a theorem consists of two clauses. The first clause tells us what we are to *assume*, and is called the **hypothesis**; the second tells us what *it is required to prove*, and is called the **conclusion**.

For example, the enunciation of Theorem 5 assumes that in a certain triangle **ABC** *the side* **AB** = *the side* **AC**: this is the *hypothesis*.

From this it is required to prove that *the angle* **ABC** = *the angle* **ACB**; this is the *conclusion*.

If we interchange the hypothesis and conclusion of a theorem.

we enunciate a new theorem which is called the **converse of the first**.

For example, in Theorem 5

it is *assumed* that **AB** = **AC**:

it is *required to prove* that the angle **ABC** = the angle **ACB**.

Now in Theorem 6

it is *assumed* that the angle **ABC** = the angle **ACB**;

it is *required to prove* that **AB** = **AC**.

Thus we see that Theorem 6 is the converse of Theorem 5; for the *hypothesis of each is the conclusion of the other*.

It must not however be supposed that if a theorem is true, its converse is *necessarily* true. [See p. 25.]

THEOREM 7. [Euclid I. 8]

If two triangles have the three sides of the one equal to the three sides of the other, each to each, they are equal in all respects.

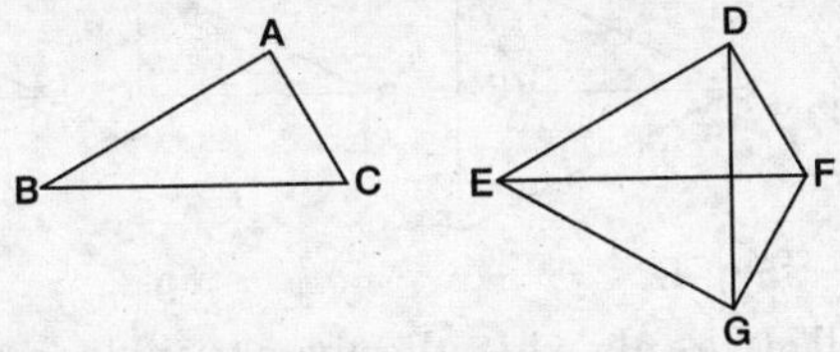

Let **ABC**, **DEF** be two triangles in which

AB = **DE**,

AC = **DF**,

BC = **EF**.

It is required to prove that the triangles are equal in all respects.

Proof. Apply the Δ **ABC** to the Δ **DEF**,

so that **B** falls on **E**, and **BC** along **EF**, and

so that **A** is on the side of **EF** opposite to **D**.

Then because **BC** = **EF**, **C** must fall on **F**.

Let **GEF** be the new position of the Δ **ABC**.

Join **DG**.

Because **ED = EG,**

∴ the $\angle$**EDG** = the $\angle$**EGD.** ***Theor.* 5.**

Again, because **FD = FG,**

∴ the $\angle$**FDG** = the $\angle$**FGD.**

Hence the whole $\angle$**EDF** = the $\angle$**EGF;**

that is, the $\angle$**EDF** = the $\angle$**BAC.**

Then in the Δ **BAC, EDF;**

because { **BA = ED,** and **AC = DF,**
and the included $\angle$**BAC** = the included $\angle$**EDF;**

∴ the triangles are equal in all respects. ***Theor.* 4.**

Obs. In this Theorem **Q.E.D.**

it is *given* that **AB = DE, BC = EF, CA = FD;**

and we *prove* that $\angle$**C** = $\angle$**F**, $\angle$**A** = $\angle$**D**, $\angle$**C** = $\angle$**E.**

Also the triangles are equal in area.

Notice that the angles which are proved equal in the two triangles are opposite to sides which were given equal.

NOTE 1. We have taken the case in which **DG** falls within the **ΔEDF, EGF.**

Two other cases might arise :

(i) **DG** might fall outside the **ΔEDF, EGF** [as in Fig. 1.]

(ii) **DG** might coincide with **DF, FG** [as in Fig. 2.]

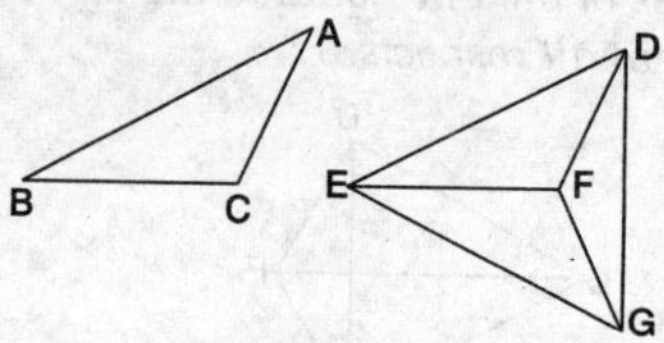

Fig. 1.

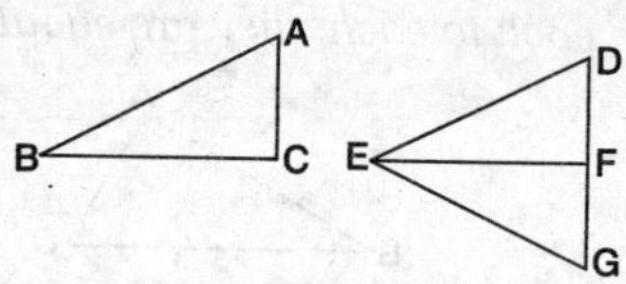

fig. 2.

These cases will arise only when the given triangles are obtuse angled or right-angled; and (as will be seen hereafter) not even then. if we begin by choosing for superposition the *greatest* side of the **ΔABC**, as in the diagram of page 24.

NOTE 2. Two triangles are said to be equiangular to one another when the angles of one are respectively equal to the angles of the other.

Hence if two triangles have the three sides of one severally equal to the three sides of the other, the triangles are equiangular to one another.

The student should state the converse theorem, and show by a diagram that the converse is not necessarily true.

. *At this stage Problems* 1-5 *and* 8 *[see page* 70*] may conveniently be taken, the proofs affording good illustrations of the Identical Equality of Two Triangles.*

EXERCISES

ON THE IDENTICAL EQUALITY OF TWO TRIANGLES

THEOREMS 4 AND 7 (*Theoretical*)

1. Show that the straight line which joins the vertex of an isosceles triangle to the middle point of the base,

    (i) bisects the vertical angle;

    (ii) is perpendicular to the base.

2. If **ABCD** is a rhombus, that is, an equilateral foursided figure; show, by drawing the diagonals **AC**, **BD**, that

    (i) the angle **ABC** = the angle **ADC**;

    (ii) **AC** bisects each of the angles **BAD**, **BCD**.

    (iii) the diagonals bisect one another at right angles.

3. If in a quadrilateral **ABCD** the opposite sides are equal, namely **AB** = **CD** and **AD** = **CB**; prove that the angle **ADC** = the angle **ABC**.

4. If **ABC** and **DBC** are two isosceles triangles drawn on the same base **BC**, prove (by means of Theorem 7) that the angle **ABD** = the angle **ACD**, taking (i) the case where the triangles are on the *same* side of **BC**, (ii) the case where they are on *opposite* sides of **BC**.

5. If **ABC**, **DBC** are two isosceles triangles drawn on opposite sides of the same base **BC**, and if **AD** be joined, prove that each of the angles **BAC**, **BDC** will be divided into two equal parts.

6. Show that the straight lines which join the extremities of the base of an isosceles triangle to the middle points of the opposite sides are equal to one another.

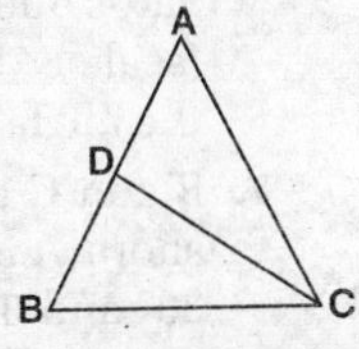

7. Two given points in the base of an isosceles triangle are equidistant from the extremities of the base; show that they are also equidistant from the vertex.

8. Show that the triangle formed by joining the middle points of the sides of an equilateral triangle is also equilateral.

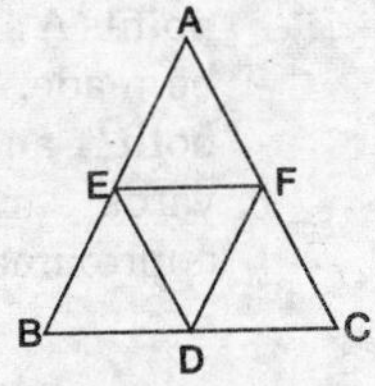

9. **ABC** is an isosceles triangle having **AB** equal to **AC**; and the angles at **B** and **C** are bisected by **BO** and **CO**; show that

    (i) **BO** = **CO** ;

    (ii) **AO** bisects the angle **BAC**.

10. The equal sides **BA, CA** of an isosceles triangle **BAC** are produced beyond the vertex **A** to the points **E** and **F**, so that **AE** is equal to **AF**; and **FB, EC** are joined: show that **FB** is equal to **EC**.

EXERCISES ON TRIANGLES

(Numerical and Graphical)

1. Draw a triangle **ABC**, having given $a = 2 \cdot 0''$, $b = 2 \cdot 1''$, $c = 1 \cdot 3''$. Measure the angles, and find their sum.

2. In the triangle **ABC**, $a = 7 \cdot 5$ cm, $b = 7 \cdot 0$ cm, $c = 6 \cdot 5$ cm. Draw and measure the perpendicular from **B** on **CA**.

3. Draw a triangle **ABC**, in which $a = 7$ cm, $b = 6$ cm., **C** $= 65°$.

How would you prove theoretically that any two triangles having these parts are alike in size and shape? Invent some experimental illustration.

4. Draw a triangle from the following data : $b = 5.1$ cm; **C** $= 5.1$ cm; **A** $= 57°$; and measure a, **B** and **C**.

Draw a second triangle, using as data the values just found for a, **B**, **C**; and measure b, **C** and **A**. What conclusion do you draw?

5. When the sun is 42° above the horizon, a vertical pole casts a shadow 30 ft. long. Represent this on a diagram (scale 1'' to 10 ft.); and find by measurement the approximate height of the pole.

6. From a point **A** a surveyor goes 150 yards due East to **B**; then 300 yards due North to **C**; finally 450 yards due West to **D**. Plot his course (scale 1'' to 100 yards); and find roughly how far **D** is from **A**. Measure the angle **DAB**, and say in what direction **D** bears from **A**.

7. **B** and **C** are two points, known to be 260 yards apart, on a straight shore. **A** is a vessel at anchor. The angles **CBA**, **BCA** are observed to be 33° and 81° respectively. Find graphically the approximate distance of the vessel from the points **B** and **C**, and from the nearest point on shore.

8. In surveying a park it is required to find the distance between two points **A** and **B**; but as a lake intervenes, a direct measurement cannot be made. The surveyor therefore takes a third point **C**, from which both **A** and **B** are accessible, and he finds **C A** $= 245$ yards, **CB** $= 320$ yards, and the angle **ACB** $= 42°$. Ascertain from a plan the approximate distance between **A** and **B**.

THEOREM 8. [Euclid I. 16]

If one side of a triangle is produced, then the exterior angle is greater than either of the interior oposite angles.

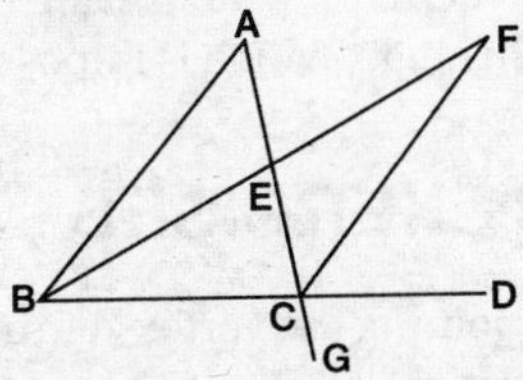

Let **ABC** be a triangle, and let **BC** be produced to **D**.

It is required to prove that the exterior ∠**ACD** *is greater than either of the interior opposite* ∠**ABC, BAC**.

Suppose **E** to be the middle point of **AC**.

Join **BE**; and produce it to **F**, making **EF** equal to **BE** .

Join **FC**.

Proof. Then in the Δ**AEB, CEF**,

because { **AE** = **CE**, **EB** = **EF**, and the ∠**AEB** = the vertically opposite ∠**CEF** ;

∴ the triangles are equal in all respects ; ***Theor. 4.***

so that the ∠**BAE** = the ∠**ECF**.

But the ∠**ECD** is greater than the ∠**ECF**;

∴ the ∠**ECD** is greater than the ∠**BAE**;

that is, the ∠**ACD** is greater than the ∠**BAC**.

In the same way, if **AC** is produced to **G**, by supposing **A** to be joined to the middle point of **BC**, it may be proved that the ∠**BCG** is greater than the ∠**ABC**.

But the ∠**BCG** = the vertically opposite ∠**ACD**.

∴ the ∠**ACD** is greater than the ∠**ABC**. **Q.E.D.**

COROLLARY 1. *Any two angles of a triangle are together less than two right angles.*

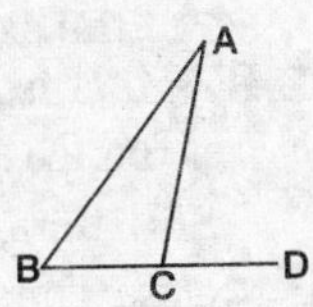

For the ∠**ABC** is less than the ∠**ACD** : *Proved.*

to each add the ∠**ACB**.

Then the ∠**ABC**, ∠**ACB** are less than the ∠**ACD**, ∠**ACB**, therefore, less than two right angles.

COROLLARY 2. *Every triangle must have at least two acute angles.*

For if one angle is obtuse or a right angle, then by Cor. 1 each of the other angles must be less than a right angle.

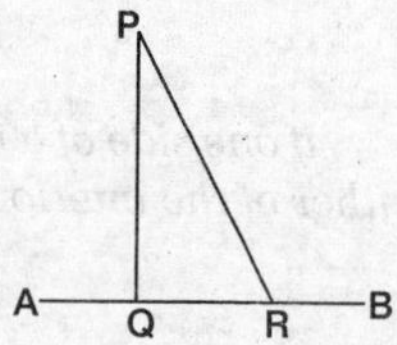

COROLLARY 3. *Only one perpendicular can be drawn to a straight line from a given point outside it.*

If two perpendiculars could be drawn to **AB** from **P**, we should have a triangle **PQR** in which each of the $\angle^s$**PQR, PRQ** would be a right angle, which is impossible.

EXERCISES

1. Prove Corollary 1 by joining the vertex *A* to any point in the base **BC**.
2. **ABC** *is a triangle and* **D** *any point within it. If* **BD** *and* **CD** *are joined, the angle* **BDC** *is greater than the angle* **BAC**. Prove this
   (i) by producing **BD** to meet **AC**.
   (ii) by joining **AD**, and producing it towards the base.
3. If any side of a triangle is produced both ways, the exterior angles so formed are together greater than two right angles.
4. To a given straight line there cannot be drawn from a point outside it more than two straight lines of the same given length.
5. If the equal sides of an isosceles triangle are produced, the exterior angles must be obtuse.

THEOREM 9. [Euclid I. 18]

If one side of a triangle is greater than another, then the angle opposite to the greater side is greater than the angle opposite to the less.

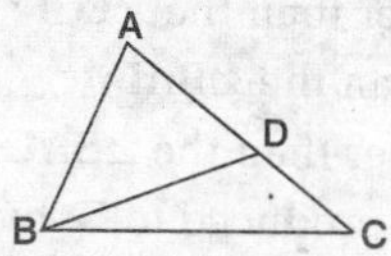

Let **ABC** be a triangle, in which the side **AC** is greater than the side **AB**.

It is required to prove that the $\angle$**ABC** *is greater than the* $\angle$**ACB**.

From **AC** cut off **AD** equal to **AB**. Join **BD**.

Proof. Because **AB** = **AD**,

∴ the $\angle$**ABD** = the $\angle$**ADB**. *Theor.* **5.**

But the exterior $\angle$**ADB** of the Δ**BDC** is greater than the interior opposite $\angle$**DCB**; that is, greater than the $\angle$**ACB**.

∴ the $\angle$**ABD** is greater than the $\angle$**ACB**.

Still more then is the $\angle$**ABC** greater than the $\angle$**ACB**. **Q.E.D.**

Obs. The mode of demonstration used in the following Theorem is known as the **Proof by Exhaustion**. It is applicable to cases in which *one* of certain suppositions must necessarily be true; and it consists in shewing that each of these suppositions is false *with one exception* : hence the truth of the remaining supposition is inferred.

THEOREM 10. [Euclid I. 19]

If one angle of a triangle is greater than another, then the side opposite to the greater angle is greater than the side opposite to the less.

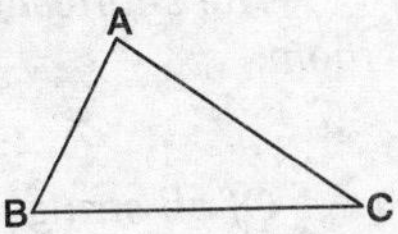

Let **ABC** be a triangle, in which the ∠**ABC** is greater than the ∠**ACB**.

It is required to prove that the side **AC** *is greater than the side* **AB**.

Proof. If **AC** is not greater than **AB**,

it must be either equal to, or less than **AB**.

Now if **AC** were equal to **AB**,

then the ∠**ABC** would be equal to the ∠**ACB**; *Theor*. 5.

but, by hypothesis, it is not.

Again, if **AC** were less than **AB**,

then the ∠**ABC** would be less than the ∠**ACB**; *Theor.* 9.

but, by hypothesis, it is not.

That is, **AC** is neither equal to, nor less than **AB**.

∴ **AC** is greater than **AB**. Q.E.D.

[For Excercises on Theorems 9 and 10 see page 34.]

Theorem 11. [Euclid I. 20]

Any two sides of a triangle are together greater than the third side.

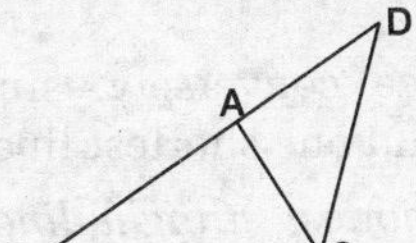

Let **ABC** be a triangle.

It is required to prove that any two of its sides are together greater than the third side.

It is enough to shew that if **BC** is the greatest side, then **BA**, **AC** are together greater than **BC**.

Produce **BA** to **D**, making **AD** equal to **AC**. Join **DC**.

Proof. Because **AD** = **AC**,

∴ the ∠**ACD** = the ∠**ADC**. *Theor.* 5.

But the ∠**BCD** is greater than the ∠**ACD**;

∴ the ∠**BCD** is greater than the ∠**ADC**,

that is, than the ∠**BDC**.

Hence from the Δ**BDC**,

BD is greater than **BC**. *Theor.* 10.

But **BD** = **BA** and **AC** together;

∴ **BA** and **AC** are together greater than **BC**. Q.E.D.

NOTE. This proof may serve as an exercise, but the truth of the Theorem is really self-evident. For to go from **B** to **C** along the straight line **BC** is clearly shorter than to go from **B** to **A** and then from **A** to **C**. In other words

The shortest distance between two points is the straight line which joins them.

THEOREM 12

Of all straight lines drawn from a given point to a given straight line the perpendicular is the least.

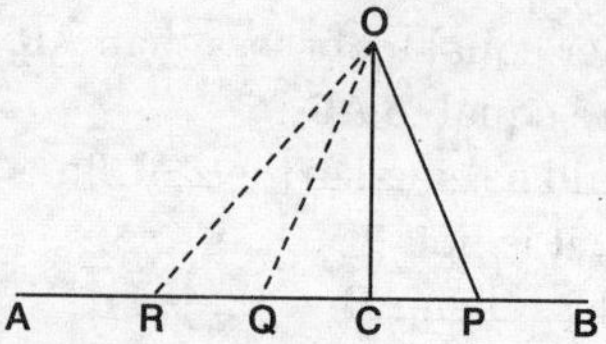

Let **OC** be the perpendicular, and **OP** *any* oblique, drawn from the given point **O** to the given straight line **AB**.

It is required to prove that **OC** *is less than* **OP**.

Proof. In the ΔOCP, since the ∠OCP is a right angle,

∴ the ∠**OPC** is less than a right angle; ***Theor.* 8. *Cor.***

that is, the ∠**OPC** is less than the ∠**OCP**.

∴ **OC** is less than **OP**. ***Theor.* 10.**

Q.E.D.

COROLLARY 1. Hence conversely, since there can be only one perpendicular and one shortest line from **O** to **AB**,

If **OC** *is the shortest straight line from* **O** *to* **AB**, *then* **OC** *is perpendicular to* **AB**.

COROLLARY 2. *Two obliques* **OP**, **OQ**, *which cut* **AB** *at equal distances from* **C**, *the foot of the perpendicular, are equal.*

The ΔOCP, ΔOCQ may be shewn to be congruent by Theorem 4; hence **OP** = **OQ**.

COROLLARY 3. *Of two obliques* **OQ**, **OR**, *if* **OR** *cuts* **AB** *at the greater distance from* **C**, *the foot of the perpendicular, then* **OR** *is greater than* **OQ**.

The ∠**OQC** is acute, ∴ the ∠**OQR** is obtuse;

∴ the ∠**OQR** is greater than the ∠**ORQ**;

∴ **OR** is greater than **OQ**.

EXERCISES ON INEQUALITIES IN A TRIANGLE

1. *The hypotenuse is the greatest side of a right-angled triangle.*
2. *The greatest side of any triangle makes acute angles with each of the other sides.*
3. *If from the ends of a side of a triangle, two straight lines are drawn to a point within the triangle, then these straight lines are together less than the other two sides of the triangle.*
4. **BC**, the base of an isosceles triangle **ABC**, is produced to any point **D**, shew that **AD** is greater than either of the equal sides.
5. If in a quadrilateral the greatest and least sides are opposite to one another, then each of the angles adjacent to the least side is greater than its opposite angle.
6. In a triangle **ABC**, if **AC** is not greater than **AB**, shew that any straight line drawn through the vertex **A** and terminated by the base **BC**, is less than **AB**.
7. **ABC** is a triangle, in which **OB**, **OC** bisect the angles **ABC**, **ACB** respectively: show that, if **AB** is greater than **AC**, then **OB** is greater than **OC**.
8. The difference of any two sides of a triangle is less than the third side.
9. The sum of the distances of any point from the three angular points of a triangle is greater than half its perimeter.
10. **ABC** is a triangle and the vertical angle **BAC** is bisected by line which meets **BC** in **X**; shew that **BA** is greater than **BX**, and **CA** greater than **CX**. Hence obtain a proof of Theorem II.
11. The sum of the distances of any point within a triangle from its angular points is less than the perimeter of the triangle.
12. The sum of the diagonals of a quadrilateral is not greater than the sum of the four straight lines drawn from the angular points to any given point. In what case are these sums equal?
13. *In a triangle any two sides are together greater than twice the median which bisects the remaining side.*

    [Produce the median, and complete the construction after the manner of Theorem 8.]
14. *In any triangle the sum of the medians is less than the perimeter.*

PARALLELS

DEFINITION. Parallel straight lines are such as, being in the same plane, do not meet however far they are produced beyond both ends.

NOTE. Parallel lines must be *in the same plane*. For instance, two straight lines, one of which is drawn on a table and the other on the floor, would never meet if produced; but they are not for that reason necessarily parallel.

AXIOM. *Two intersecting straight lines cannot both be parallel to a third straight line.*

In other words:

Through a given point there can be only one straight line parallel to a given straight line.

This assumption is known as *Playfair's Axiom.*

DEFINITION. When two straight lines **AB, CD** are met by a third straight line *EF*, *eight* angles are formed, to which for the sake of distinction particular names are given.

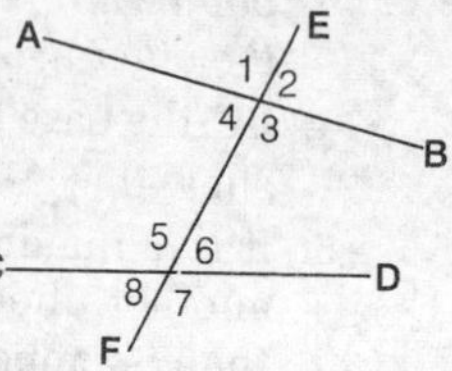

Thus in the adjoining figure,

1, 2, 7, 8 are called **exterior** angles,

3, 4, 5, 6 are called **interior** angles,

4 and 6 are said to be **alternate** angles;

so also the angles 3 and 5 are alternate to one another.

Of the angles 2 and 6, 2 is referred to as the **exterior** angle, and 6 as the **interior opposite** angle on the same side of **EF**. Such angles are also known as **corresponding angles.**

Similarly 7 and 3, 8 and 4, 1 and 5 are pairs of corresponding angles.

THEOREM 13. [Euclid I. 27 and 28]

If a straight line cuts two other straight lines so as to make

(i) *the alternate angles equal,*

or (ii) *an exterior angle equal to the interior opposite angle on the same side of the cutting line,*

or (iii) *the interior angles on the same side equal to two right angles;*

then in each case the two straight lines are parallel.

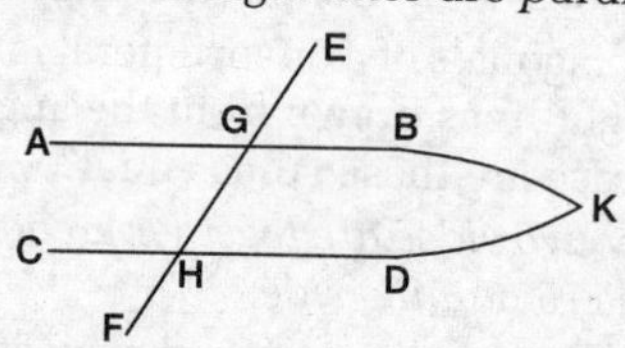

(i) Let the straight line **EGHF** cut the two straight lines **AB, CD** at **G** and *H* so as to make the alternate ∠*s* **AGH, GHD** equal to one another.
It is required to prove that **AB** *and* **CD** *are parallel.*
Proof. If *AB* and **CD** are not parallel, they will meet, if produced, either towards **B** and **D** or towards **A** and **C**.
If possible, let **AB** and **CD**, when produced, meet towards **B** and **D**, at the point **K**.
Then **KGH** is a triangle, of which one side **KG** is produced to **A**;
∴ the exterior ∠**AGH** is greater than the interior opposite ∠**GHK**; but, by hypothesis, it is not greater.
∴ **AB** and **CD** cannot meet when produced towards **B** and **D**.

Similarly it may be shewn that they cannot meet towards **A** and **C**:
∴ **AB** and **CD** are parallel.

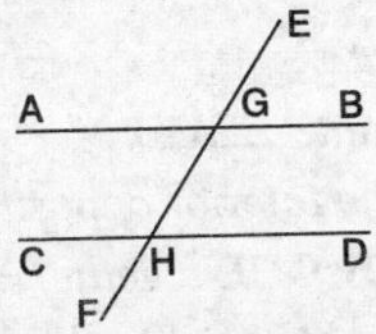

(ii) Let the exterior ∠**EGB** = the interior opposite ∠**GHD**.
It is required to prove that **AB** *and* **CD** *are parallel.*
Proof. Because the ∠**EGB** = the ∠**GHD**,
and the ∠**EGB** = the vertically opposite ∠**AGH**;
∴ the ∠**AGH** = the ∠**GHD**;
and these are alternate angles;
∴ **AB** and **CD** are parallel.

(iii) Let the two interior ∠*s***BGH**, **GHD** be together equal to two right angles.
It is required to prove that **AB** *and* **CD** *are parallel.*
Proof. Because the ∠*s* **BGH, GHD** together = two right angles;
and because the adjacent ∠*s***BGH**, **AGH** together = two right angles;
∴ the ∠*s***BGH, AGH** together = ∠*s* **BGH, GHD.**
From these equals take the ∠**BGH** ;
then the remaining ∠**AGH** = the remaining ∠**GHD** :
and these are alternate angles;
∴ **AB** and **CD** are parallel. **Q.E.D.**

DEFINITION. A straight line drawn across a set of given lines is called a **transversal**.

For instance, in the above diagram the line **EGHF**, which crosses the given lines **AB, CD**, is a transversal.

THEOREM 14. [Euclid I. 29]

If a straight line cuts two parallel lines, it makes
(i) *the alternate angles equal to one another;*
(ii) *the exterior angle equal to the interior opposite angle on the same side of the cutting line;*
(iii) *the two interior angles on the same side together equal to two right angles.*

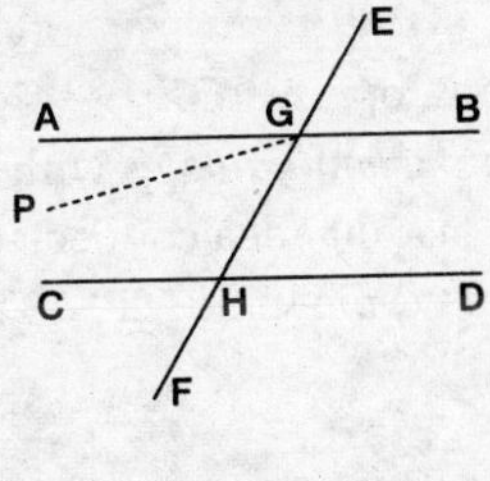

Let the straight lines **AB**, **CD** be parallel, and let the straight line **EGHF** cut them.

It is required to prove that

(i) *the* ∠**AGH** = *the alternate* ∠**GHD**;

(ii) *the exterior* ∠**EGB** = *the interior opposite* ∠**GHD**;

(iii) *the two interior* ∠ˢ **BGH**, **GHD** *together* = *two right angles.*

Proof. (i) If the ∠**AGH** is not equal to the ∠**GHD**, suppose the ∠**PGH** equal to the ∠**GHD**, and alternate to it;

then **PG** and **CD** are parallel. ***Theor.* 13.**

But, by hypothesis, **AB** and **CD** are parallel;

∴ the two intersecting straight lines **AG**, **PG** are both parallel to **CD**: which is impossible. *Playfair's Axiom.*

∴ the ∠**AGH** is not unequal to the ∠**GHD**;

that is, the alternate ∠ˢ **AGH**, **GHD** are equal.

(ii) Again, because the ∠**EGB** = the vertically opposite ∠**AGH**;

and the ∠**AGH** = the alternate ∠**GHD**; *Proved.*

∴ the exterior ∠**EGB** = the interior opposite ∠**GHD**.

(iii) Lastly, the ∠**EGB** = the ∠**GHD**; *Proved.*

add to each the ∠**BGH**;

then the ∠ˢ **EGB**, **BGH** together = the angles **BGH**, **GHD**.

But the adjacent ∠ˢ **EGB**, **BGH** together = two right angles;

∴ the two interior ∠ˢ **BGH**, **GHD** together = two right angles. **Q.E.D.**

PARALLELS ILLUSTRATED BY ROTATION

The direction of a straight line is determined by the angle which it makes with some given line of reference.

Thus the direction of **AB**, relatively to the given line **YX**, is given by the angle **APX**.

Now suppose that **AB** and **CD** in the adjoining diagram are parallel; then we have learned that

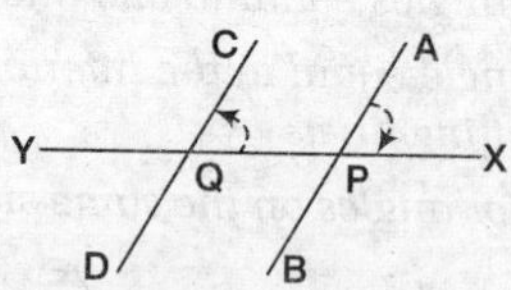

the ext. ∠**APX** = the int. opp. ∠**CQX**;

that is, **AB** and **CD** *make equal angles* with the line of reference **YX**.

This brings us to the leading idea connected with parallels:

Parallel straight lines have the same DIRECTION, *but differ in* POSITION.

The same idea may be illustrated thus:

Suppose **AB** to rotate about **P** through the ∠**APX**, so as to take the position **XY**. Hence let it rotate about **Q** *the opposite way* through the equal ∠**XQC**: it will now take the position **CD**. Thus **AB** may be brought into the position of **CD** by two rotations which, being equal and opposite, involve no final change of direction.

HYPOTHETICAL CONSTRUCTION. In the above diagram let **AB** be a fixed straight line, **Q** a fixed point, **CD** a straight line turning about **Q**, and **YQPX** any transversal through **Q**. Then as **CD** rotates, there must be one position in which the ∠**CQX** = the fixed ∠**APX**.

Hence through any given point we may assume a line to pass parallel to any given straight line.

Obs. If **AB** is a straight line, movements from **A** towards **B**, and from **B** towards **A** are said to be in opposite **senses** of the line **AB**.

THEOREM 15. [Euclid I. 30]

Straight lines which are parallel to the same straight line are parallel to one another.

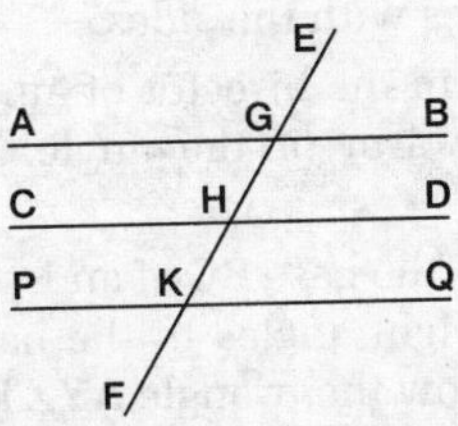

Let the straight lines **AB**, **CD** be each parallel to the straight line **PQ**.

It is required to prove that **AB** *and* **CD** *are parallel to one another.*

Draw a straight line **EF** cutting **AB**, **CD**, and **PQ** in the points **G**, **H**, and **K**.

Proof. Then because **AB** and **PQ** are parallel, and **EF** meets them

∴ the ∠**AGK** = the alternate ∠**GKQ**.

And because **CD** and **PQ** are parallel, and **EF** meets them,

∴ the exterior ∠**GHD** = the interior opposite ∠**GKQ**.

∴ the ∠**AGH** = the ∠**GHD**;

and these are alternate angles;

∴ **AB** and **CD** are parallel. **Q.E.D.**

NOTE. If **PQ** lies between **AB** and **CD**, the Proposition needs no proof; for it is inconceivable that two straight lines, which do not meet an intermediate straight line, should meet one another.

The truth of this Proposition may be readily deduced from Playfair's Axiom, of which it is the converse.

For if **AB** and **CD** were not parallel, they would meet when produced. Then there would be two intersecting straight lines both parallel to a third straight line: which is impossible.

Therefore **AB** and **CD** never meet; that is, they are parallel.

EXERCISES ON PARALLELS

1. In the diagram of the previous page, if the angle **EGB** is 55°, express in degrees each of the angles **GHC, HKQ, QKF.**
2. *Straight lines which are perpendicular to the same straight line are parallel to one another.*
3. *If a straight line meets two or more parallel straight lines, and is perpendicular to one of them, it is also perpendicular to all the others.*
4. *Angles of which the arms are parallel, each to each, are either equal or supplementary.*
5. Two straight lines **AB**, **CD** bisect one another at **O**. Show that the straight lines joining **AC** and **BD** are parallel.
6. Any straight line drawn parallel to the base of an isosceles triangle makes equal angles with the sides.
7. If from any point in the bisector of an angle a straight line is drawn parallel to either arm of the angle, the triangle thus formed is isosceles.
8. From **X**, a point in the base **BC** of an isosceles triangle **ABC** a straight line is drawn at right angles to the base, cutting **AB** in **Y**, and **CA** produced in **Z**: show the triangle **AYZ** is isosceles.
9. If the straight line which bisects an exterior angle of a triangle is parallel to the opposite side, show that the triangle is isosceles.
10. The straight line drawn from any point in the bisector of an angle parallel to the arms of the angle, and terminated by them, are equal; and the resulting figure is a quadrilateral having all its side equal.
11. **AB** and **CD** are two straight lines intersecting at **D**, and the adjacent angles so formed are bisected: if through any point **X** in **DC** a straight line **XYZ** is drawn parallel to **AB** and meeting the bisectors **Y** and **Z**, show that **XY** is equal to **XZ**.
12. Two straight rods **PA**, **QB** revolve about pivots at **P** and **Q**, **PA** making 12 complete revolutions a minute, and **QB** making 10. If they start parallel and pointing the same way, how long will it be before they are again parallel, (i) pointing opposite ways, (ii) pointing the same way ?

THEOREM 16. [Euclid I. 32]

The three angles of a triangle are together equal to two right angles.

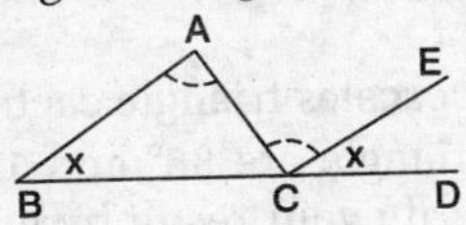

Let **ABC** be a triangle.

It is required to prove that three ∠^{s} **ABC, BCA, CAB** *together = two right angles.*

Produce **BC** to any point **D**; and suppose **CE** to be the line through **C** parallel to **BA**.

Proof. Because **BA** and **CE** are parallel and **AC** meets them,

∴ the ∠**ACE** = the alternate ∠**CAB**.

Again, because **BA** and **CE** are parallel, and **BD** meets them,

∴ the exterior ∠**ECD** = the interior opposite ∠**ABC**.

∴ *the whole exterior* ∠**ACD** = *the sum of the two interior opposite* ∠^{s}**CAB, ABC**.

To each of these equals add the ∠**BCA**;

then the ∠^{s}**BCA, ACD** together = the three ∠^{s}**BCA, CAB, ABC**.

But the adjacent ∠^{s}**BCA, ACD** together = two right angles.

∴ the ∠^{s}**BCA; CAB, ABC** together = two right angles. **Q.E.D.**

Obs. In the course of this proof the following most important property has been established.

If a side of a triangle is produced the exterior angle is equal to the sum of the two interior opposite angles.

Namely, the ext. ∠**ACD** = the ∠**CAB** + the ∠**ABC**.

INFERENCES FROM THEOREM 16

1. *If* **A, B,** *and* **C** *denote the number of degrees in the angles of a triangle, then* **A + B + C** = 180°.
2. *If two triangles have two angles of the one respectively equal to two angles of the other, then the third angle of the one is equal to the third angle of the other.*
3. *In any right-angled triangle the two acute angles are complementary.*
4. *If one angle of a triangle is equal to the sum of the other two, the triangle is right-angled.*
5. *The sum of the angles of any quadrilateral figure is equal to four right angles.*

EXERCISES ON THEOREM 16

1. Each angle of an equilateral triangle is two-thirds of a right angle, or 60°.
2. In a right-angled isosceles triangle each of the equal angles is 45°.
3. Two angles of a triangle are 36° and 123° respectively: deduce the third angle; and verify your result by measurement.
4. In a triangle **ABC**, the $\angle$**B** = 111°, the $\angle$**C** = 42°; deduce the $\angle$**A**, and verify by measurement.
5. One side **BC** of a triangle **ABC** is produced to **D**. If the exterior angle **ACD** is 134°; and the angle **BAC** is 42°; find each of the remaining interior angles.
6. In the figure of Theorem 16, if the $\angle$**ACD** = 118°, and the $\angle$**B** = 51°, find the $\angle^s$**A** and **C**; and check your results by measurement.
7. *Prove that the three angles of a triangle are together equal to two right angles by supposing a line drawn through the vertex parallel to the base.*
8. *It two straight lines are perpendicular to two other straight lines, each to each, the acute angle between the first pair is equal to the acute angle between the second pair.*

COROLLARY 1. *All the interior angles of any rectilinear figure, together with four right angles, are equal to twice as many right angles as the figure has sides.*

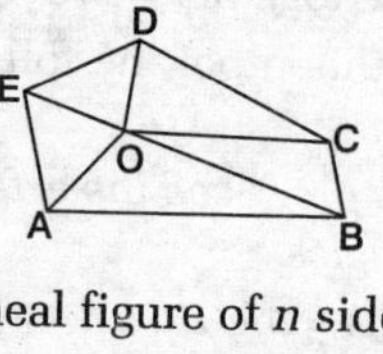

Let **ABCDE** be a rectilineal figure of *n* sides.

It is required to prove that all the interior angles + 4 rt. $\angle^s$ = *2n rt.* $\angle^s$.

Take any point **O** within the figure, and join **O** to each of its vertices.

Then the figure is divided into *n* triangles.

And the three $\angle^s$ of each Δ together = 2 rt. $\angle^s$.

Hence all the $\angle^s$ of *all* the Δ^s together = 2*n* rt. $\angle^s$.

But all the $\angle^s$ of all the Δ^s make up all the interior angles of the figure together with the angles at **O**, which = 4 rt. $\angle^s$.

$\therefore$ all the int. $\angle^s$ of the figure + 4rt. $\angle^s$ = 2*n*rt. $\angle^s$. **Q.E.D.**

DEFINITION. A **regular** polygon is one which has all its sides equal and all its angles equal.

Thus if **D** denotes the number of degrees in each angle of a *regular* polygon of *n* sides, the above result may be stated thus:

$$n\mathbf{D} + 360° = n.\ 180°.$$

EXAMPLE

Find the number of degrees in each angle of

(i) a regular hexagon (6 sides);

(ii) a regular octagon (8 sides);

(iii) a regular decagon (10 sides).

EXERCISES ON THEOREM 16

(Numerical and Graphical)

1. **ABC** is a triangle in which the angles at **B** and **C** are respectively double and triple of the angle at **A**: find the number of degrees in each of these angles.
2. Express in degrees the angles of an isosceles triangle in which
   (i) Each base angle is double of the vertical angle;
   (ii) Each base angle is four times the vertical angle.
3. The base of a triangle is produced both ways, and the exterior angles are found to be 94° and 126°; deduce the vertical angle. Construct such a triangle, and check your result by measurement.
4. The sum of the angles at the base of a triangle is 162°, and their difference is 60°: find all the angles.
5. The angles at the base of a triangle are 84° and 62°; deduce (i) the vertical angle, (ii) the angle between the bisectors of the base angles. Check your results by construction and measurement.
6. In a triangle **ABC**, the angles of **B** and **C** are 74° and 62°; if **AB** and **AC** are produced, deduce the angle between the bisectors of the exterior angles. Check your result graphically.
7. Three angles of a quadrilateral are respectively $114\frac{1}{4}°$, 50°, and $75\frac{1}{2}°$; find the fourth angle.
8. In a quadrilateral **ABCD**, the angles at **B**, **C**, and **D** are respectively equal to 2**A**, 3**A**, and 4**A**; find all the angles.
9. Four angles of an irregular pentagon (5 sides) are 40°, 78°, 122°, and 135°; find the fifth angle.
10. In any *regular* polygon of n sides, each angle contains $\frac{2(n-2)}{n}$ right angles.
    (i) Deduce this result from the Enunciation of Corollary 1.
    (ii) Prove it independently by joining one vertex **A** to each of the others (except the two immediately adjacent to **A**), thus dividing the polygon into $n-2$ triangles.
11. How many sides have the regular polygons each of whose angles is
    (i) 108°, (ii) 156°?

12. Show that the only *regular* figures which may be fitted together so as to form a plane surface are

(i) *equilateral triangles,* (ii) *squares,*

(iii) *regular hexagons.*

COROLLARY 2. *If the sides of a rectilineal figure, which has no reflex angle, are produced in order, then all the exterior angles so formed are together equal to four right angles.*

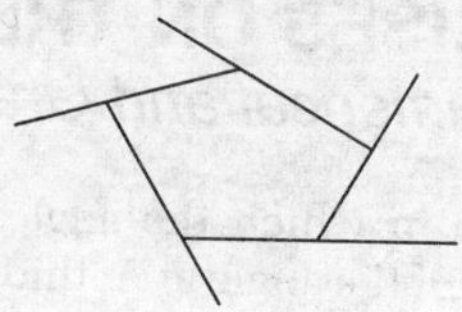

Ist proof. Suppose, as before, that the figure has n sides; and consequently n vertices.

Now at *each* vertex

the interior $\angle$ + the exterior $\angle = 2$ rt. $\angle^{s}$.

and there are n vertices,

$\therefore$ the sum of the int. $\angle^{s}$ + the sum of the ext. $\angle^{s} = 2n$ rt. $\angle^{s}$.

But by Corollary 1,

the sum of the int. $\angle^{s}$ + 4 rt. $\angle^{s} = 2n$ rt. $\angle^{s}$;

$\therefore$ the sum of the ext. $\angle^{s} = 4$ rt. $\angle^{s}$. **Q.E.D.**

2nd Proof.

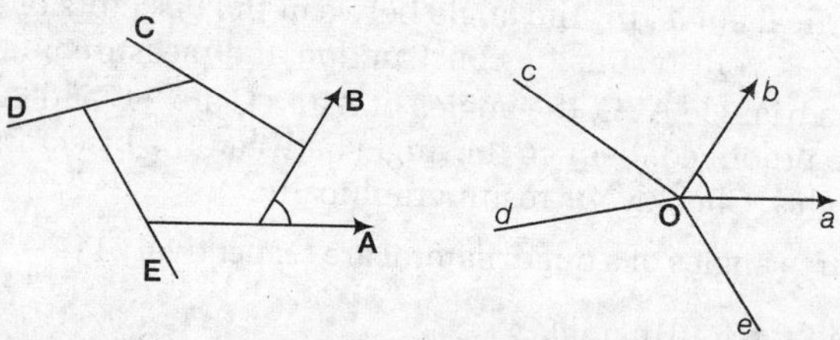

Take any point **O**, and suppose **O**a, **O**b, **O**c, **O**d, and **O**e are lines parallel to the sides marked, **A, B, C, D, E** (and drawn from **O** in the *sense* in which those sides were produced).

Then the exterior $\angle$ between the sides **A** and **B** = the $\angle a\mathbf{O}b$.

And the other exterior $\angle^{s}$ = the $\angle^{s}$ $b\mathbf{O}c$, $c\mathbf{O}d$, $d\mathbf{O}e$, $e\mathbf{O}a$, respectively.

$\therefore$ the sum of the ext. $\angle^{s}$ = the sum of the $\angle^{s}$ at **O** = 4 rt. $\angle^{s}$.

EXERCISES

1. If one side of a regular hexagon is produced, show that the exterior angle is equal to the interior angle of an equilateral triangle.
2. Express in degrees the magnitude of each *exterior* angle of (i) a regular octagon, (ii) a regular decagon.

3. How many sides has a regular polygon if each exterior angle is (i) 30°, (ii) 24°?
4. If a straight line meets two parallel straight lines, and the two interior angles on the same side are bisected, show that the bisectors meet at right angles.
5. If the base of any triangle is produced both ways, show that the sum of the two exterior angles *minus* the vertical angle is equal to two right angles.
6. In the triangle **ABC** the base angles at **B** and **C** are bisected by **BO** and **CO** respectively. Show that the angle $\mathbf{BOC} = 90° + \frac{A}{2}$.
7. In the triangle **ABC**, the sides **AB**, **AC** are produced, and the exterior angles are bisected by **BO** and **CO**. Show that the angle $\mathbf{BOC} = 90° - \frac{A}{2}$.
8. The angle contained by the bisectors of two adjacent angles of a quadrilateral is equal to half the sum of the remaining angles.
9. **A** is the vertex of an isosceles triangle **ABC**, and **BA** is produced to **D**, so that **AD** is equal to **BA**; if **DC** is drawn, show that **BCD** is a right angle.
10. The straight line joining the middle point of the hypotenuse of a right-angled triangle to the right angle is equal to half the hypotenuse.

EXPERIMENTAL PROOF OF THEOREM 16. [A+ B+ C= 180°]

In the Δ**ABC**, **AD** is perp. to **BC** the greatest side. **AD** is bisected at right angles by **ZY**; and **YP**, **ZQ** are perp^s. on **BC**.

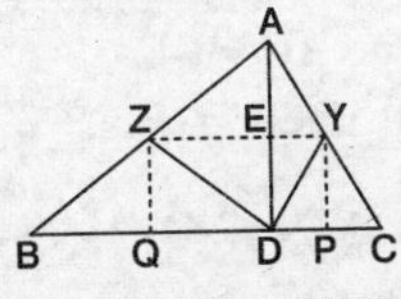

If now the Δ is folded about the three dotted lines, the $\angle^s$ **A**, **B**, and **C** will coincide with the $\angle^s$**ZDY**, **ZDQ**, **YDP**;

$\therefore$ their sum is 180°.

THEOREM 17. [Euclid I. 26]

If two triangles have two angles of one equal to two angles of the other, each to each, and any side of the first equal to the corresponding side of the other, the triangles are equal in all respects.

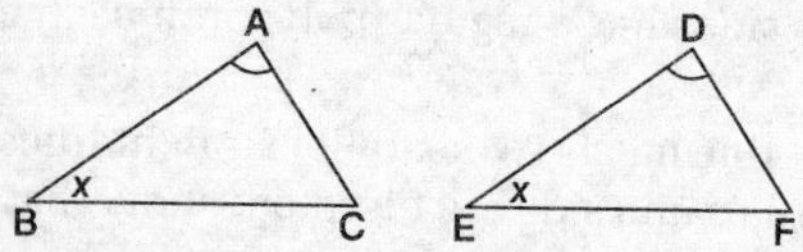

Let **ABC**, **DEF** to two triangles in which

the ∠**A** = the ∠**D**,

the ∠**B** = the ∠**E**,

also let the side **BC** = the corresponding side **EF**.

It is required to prove that the ∠ˢ**ABC** , **DEF** *are equal in all respects.*

Proof. The sum of the ∠ˢ**A**, **B** and **C**

= 2 rt. ∠ˢ *Theor. 16.*

= the sum of the ∠ˢ**D**, **E** and **F**;

and the ∠ˢ**A** and **B** = the ∠ˢ**D** and **E** respectively,

∴ the ∠**C** = the ∠**F**.

Apply the Δ**ABC** to the Δ**DEF**, so that **B** falls on **E**, and **BC** along **EF**.

Then because **BC** = **EF**,

∴ **C** must coincide with **F**.

And because the ∠**B** = the ∠**E**,

∴ **BA** must fall along **ED**.

And because the ∠**C** = the ∠**F**,

∴ **CA** must fall along **FD**.

∴ the point **A**, which falls both on **ED** and on **FD**, must coincide with **D**, the point in which these lines intersect.

∴ the Δ**ABC** coincides with the Δ**DEF**,

and is therefore equal to it in all respects.

So that **AB** = **DE**, and **AC** = **DF**;

and the Δ**ABC** = the Δ**DEF** in area. **Q.E.D.**

EXERCISES

ON THE IDENTICAL EQUALITY TRIANGLES

1. Show that the perpendiculars drawn from the extremities of the base of an isosceles triangle to the opposite sides are equal.
2. *Any point on the bisector of an angle is equidistant from the arms of the angle.*
3. Through **O**, the middle point of a straight line **AB**, any straight line is drawn, and perpendiculars **AX** and **BY** are dropped upon it from **A** and **B** : show that **AX** is equal to **BY**.

4. If the bisector of the vertical angle of a triangle is at right angles to the base, the triangle is isosceles.
5. If in a triangle the perpendicular from the vertex on the base bisects the base, then the triangle is isosceles.
6. If the bisector of the vertical angle of a triangle also bisects the base, the triangle is isosceles.

   [Produce the bisector, and complete the construction after the manner of Theorem **8.**]
7. The middle point of any straight line which meets two parallel straight lines, and is terminated by them, is equidistant from the parallels.
8. A straight line drawn between two parallels and terminated by them, is bisected; show that any other straight line passing through the middle point and terminated by the parallels, is also bisected at that point.
9. If through a point equidistant from two parallel straight lines, two straight lines are drawn cutting the parallels, the portions of the latter thus intercepted are equal.
10. In a quadrilateral, **ABCD**, if **AB** = **AD**, and **BC** = **DC** : show that the diagonal **AC** bisects each of the angles which it joins; and that **AC** is perpendicular to **BD**.
11. *A surveyor wishes to ascertain the breadth of a river which he cannot cross. Standing at a point* **A** *near the bank, he notes an object* **B** *immediately opposite on the other bank. He lays down a line* **AC** *of any length at right angles to* **AB**, *fixing a mark at* **O** *the middle point of* **AC**. *From* **C** *he walks along a line perpendicular to* **AC** *until he reaches a point* **D** *from which* **O** *and* **B** *are seen in the same direction. He now measures* **CD** : *prove that the result given him the width of the river.*

ON THE IDENTICAL EQUALITY OF TRIANGLES

Three cases of the congruence of triangles have been dealt with in Theorems 4, 7, 17, the results of which may be summarised as follows:

Two triangles are equal in all respects when the following three parts in each are severally equal :

1. *Two sides, and the included angle.* — *Theorem* 4.
2. *The three sides.* — *Theorem* 7.
3. *Two angles and one side, the side given is one triangle* CORRESPONDING *to that given in the other.* — *Theorem* 17.

Two triangles are not, however, necessarily equal in all respects when *any three parts* of one are equal to the corresponding parts of the other.

For example :

(i) When the *three angles* of one are equal to the *three angles* of the other, each to each, the adjoining diagram shows that the triangles need not be equal in all respects.

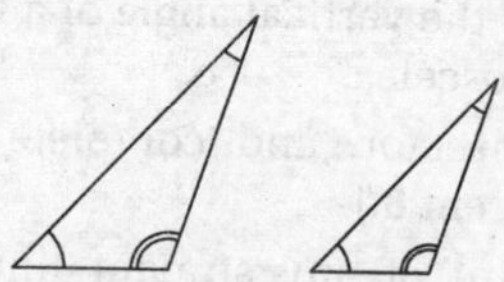

(ii) When *two sides and one angle* in one are equal to *two sides and one angle* of the other, the given angles being *opposite* to equal sides, the diagram below shows that the triangles need not be equal in all respects.

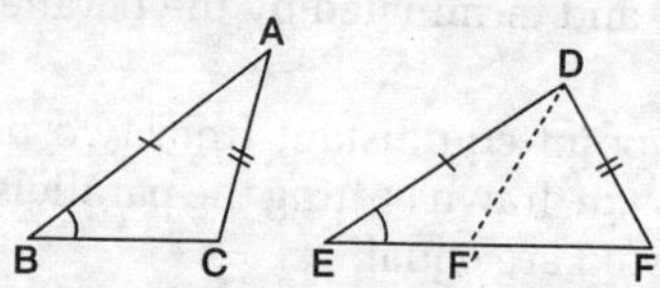

For if **AB** = **DE** and **AC** = **DF**, and the ∠**ABC** = the ∠**DEF**, it will be seen that the shorter of the given sides in the triangle **DEF** may lie in either of the positions **DF** or **DF′**.

NOTE. Fro these data it may be shown that the angles opposite to the equal sides **AB**, **DE** are either *equal* (as for instance the ∠**s** **ACB**, **DF′E**) or *supplementary* (as the ∠**s** **ACB**, **DFE**); and that in the former case the triangles are equal in all respects. This is called the ambiguous case in the congruence of triangles. [See Problem 9, p. 82.]

If the given angles at **B** and **E** are right angles, the ambiguity disappears. This exception is proved in the following Theorem.

THEOREM 18

Two **right-angled** *triangles which have their hypotenuses equal, and one side of one equal to one side of the other, are equal in all respects.*

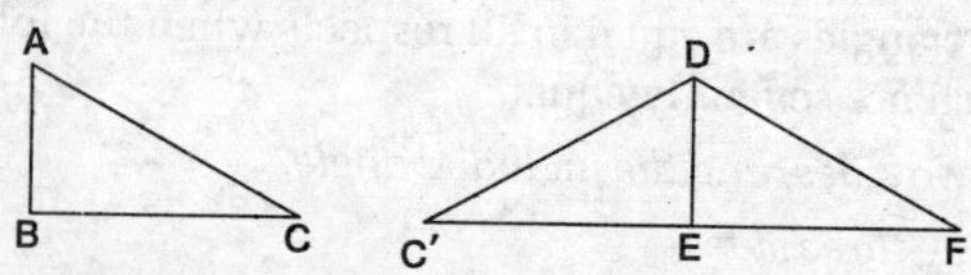

Let **ABC**, **DEF** be two **right-angled** triangles, in which

the ∠**s** **ABC**, **DEF** are right angles,

the hypotenuse **AC** = the hypotenuse **DF**,

and **AB** = **DE**.

It is required to prove that the Δ**s** **ABC**, **DEF** *are equal in all respects.*

Proof. Apply the Δ**ABC** to the Δ**DEF**, so that **AB** falls on the equal line **DE**, and **C** on the side of **DE** opposite to **F**.

Let **C′** be the point on which **C** falls.

Then **DEC′** represents the Δ**ABC** in its new position.

Since each of the $\angle^s$**DEF, DEC′** is a right angle,

∴ **EF** and **EC′** are in one straight line.

And in the Δ**C′ DF**, because **DF** = **DC′** (*i.e.* **AC**),

∴ the $\angle$**DFC′** = the $\angle$**DC′ F**. ***Theor. 5.***

Hence in the Δ^s**DEF, DEC′**,

because {
$\angle$**DEF** = the $\angle$**DEC′**, being right angles;
the $\angle$**DFE** = the $\angle$**DC′ E**, ***Proved.***
and the side **DE** is common.
}

∴ the Δ^s**DEF, DEC′** are equal in all respects; ***Theor. 17.***

that is, the Δ^s**DEF, ABC** are equal in all respects. **Q.E.D.**

*THEOREM 19. [Euclid I. 24]

If two triangles have two sides of the one equal to two sides of the other, each to each, but the angle included by the two sides of one greater than the angle included by the corresponding sides of the other; then the base of that which has the greater angle is greater than the base of the other.

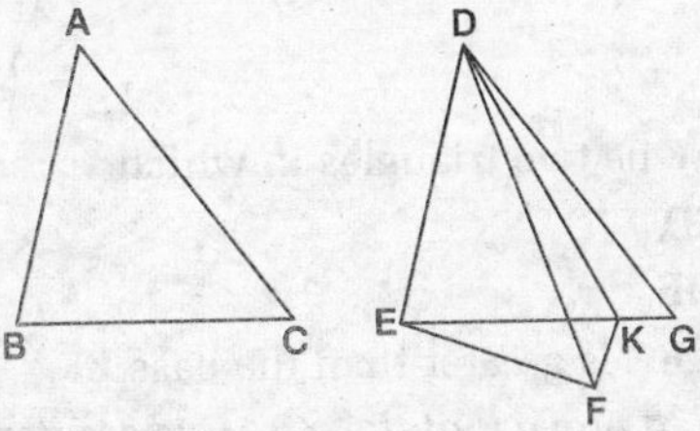

Let **ABC, DEF** be two triangles, in which

BA = **ED**,

and **AC** = **DF**,

but the $\angle$**BAC** is greater than the $\angle$**EDF**.

It is required to prove that the base **BC** *is greater than, the base* **EF**.

Proof. Apply the Δ**ABC** to the Δ**DEF**, so that **A** falls on **D**, and **AB** along **DE**.

Then because **AB** = **DE**, **B** must coincide with **E**.

Let **DG, GE** represent **AC, CB** in their new position.

Then if **EG** passes through **F**, **EG** is greater than **EF**;

that is, **BC** is greater than **EF**.

But if **EG** does not pass through **F**, suppose that **DK** bisects the ∠**FDG**, and meets **EG** in **K**. Join **FK**.

Then in the Δ[s] **FDK, GDK**,

because { **FD** = **GD**,
DK is common to both,
and the included ∠**FDK** = the included ∠**GDK**;

∴ **FK** = **GK**. ***Theor. 4.***

Now that the two sides **EK**, **KF** are greater than **EF**;
that is, **EK**, **KG** are greater than **EF**.
∴ **EG** (or **BC**) is greater than **EF**. **Q.E.D.**

Conversely, *if two triangles have two sides of the one equal to two sides of the other, each to each, but the base of one greater than the base of the other; then the angle contained by the sides of that which has the greater base, is greater than the angle contained by the corresponding sides of the other.*

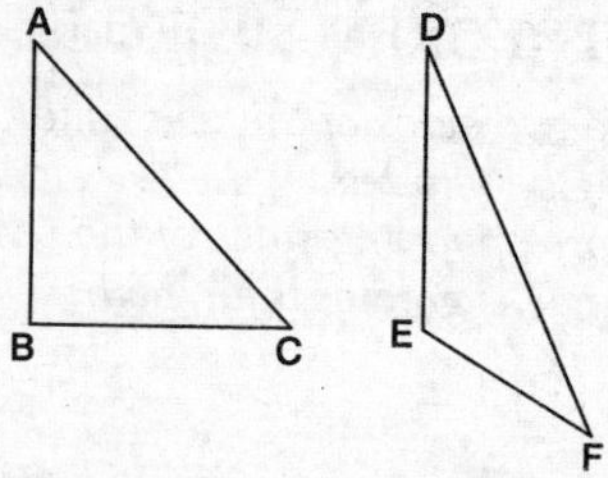

Let **ABC**, **DEF** be two triangles in which
BA = **ED**,
and **AC** = **DF**,
but the base **BC** is greater than the base **EF**.

It is required to prove that the ∠**BAC** *is greater than the* ∠**EDF**.

Proof. If the ∠**BAC** is not greater than the ∠**EDF**,
it must be either equal to, or less than the ∠**EDF**.
Now if the ∠**BAC** were equal to the ∠**EDF**,
then the base **BC** would be equal to the base **EF**; ***Theor. 4.***
but, by hypothesis, it is not.
Again, if the ∠**BAC** were less than the Δ**EDF**, then the base **BC** would be less than the base **EF**; ***Theor. 19.***
but, by hypothesis, it is not
That is, the ∠**BAC** is neither equal to, nor less than the ∠**EDF**;
∴ the ∠**BAC** is greater than ∠**EDF**. **Q.E.D**

* *Theorems marked with an asterisk may be omitted or postponed at the discretion of the teacher.*

REVISION LESSON ON TRIANGLES

1. State the properties of a triangle relating to

(i) the sum of its interior angles;

(ii) the sum of its exterior angles.

What property corresponds to (i) in a polygon of n sides? With what other figures does a triangle share the property (ii)?

2. Classify triangles with regard to their angles. Enunciate any Theorem or Corollary assumed in the classification.

3. Enunciate two Theorems in which from data relating to the sides a conclusion is drawn relating to the angles.

In the triangle **ABC**, if $a = 3.6$ cm., $b = 2.8$ cm., $c = 3.6$ cm., arrange the angles in order of their sizes (before measurement); and prove that the triangles is acute-angled.

4. Enunciate two Theorems in which from data relating to the angles a conclusion is drawn relating to the sides.

In the triangle **ABC**, if

(i) $\mathbf{A} = 48°$ and $\mathbf{B} = 51°$; find the third angle, and name the greatest side.

(ii) $\mathbf{A} = \mathbf{B} = 62\frac{1}{2}°$, find the third angle, and arrange the sides in order of their lengths.

5. From which of the conditions given below may we conclude that the triangles **ABC**, **A′B′C′** are identically equal? Point out where ambiguity arises; and draw the triangle **ABC** in each case.

(i) $\begin{cases} \mathbf{A} = \mathbf{A'} = 71° \\ \mathbf{B} = \mathbf{B'} = 46°. \\ a = a' = 3.7 \text{ cm.} \end{cases}$ (ii) $\begin{cases} a = a' = 4.2 \text{ cm.} \\ b = b' = 2.4 \text{ cm.} \\ \mathbf{C} = \mathbf{C'} = 81°. \end{cases}$

(iii) $\begin{cases} \mathbf{A} = \mathbf{A'} = 36°. \\ \mathbf{B} = \mathbf{B'} = 121°. \\ \mathbf{C} = \mathbf{C'} = 23°. \end{cases}$ (iv) $\begin{cases} a = a' = 3.0 \text{ cm.} \\ b = b' = 5.2 \text{ cm.} \\ c = c' = 4.5 \text{ cm.} \end{cases}$

(v) $\begin{cases} \mathbf{B} = \mathbf{B'} = 53°. \\ b = b' = 4.3 \text{ cm.} \\ c = c' = 5.0 \text{ cm.} \end{cases}$ (vi) $\begin{cases} \mathbf{C} = \mathbf{C'} = 90°. \\ c = c' = 5 \text{ cm.} \\ a = a' = 3 \text{ cm.} \end{cases}$

6. Summarise the results of the last question by stating generally under what conditions two triangles

(i) are necessarily congruent;

(ii) may or may not be congruent.

7. *If two triangles have their angles equal, each to each, the triangles are not necessarily equal in all respects, because the three data are not independent.* Carefully explain this statement.

(*Miscellaneous Examples*)

8. (i) *The perpendicular is the shortest line that can be drawn to a given straight line from a given point.*

   (ii) **Obliques** *which make equal angles with the perpendicular are equal.*

   (iii) *Of two obliques the less is that which makes the smaller angle with the perpendicular.*

9. *If two triangles have two sides of the one equal to two sides of the other, each to each, and have likewise the angles opposite to one pair of equal sides equal, then the angles opposite to the other pair of equal sides are either equal or supplementary, and in the former case the triangles are equal in all respects.*

10. **PQ** is a perpendicular (4 cm. in length) to a straight line **XY**. Draw through **P** a series of obliques making with **PQ** the angles 15°, 30°, 45°, 60°, 75°. *Measure* the lengths of these obliques, and tabulate the results.

11. **PAB** is a triangle in which **AB** and **AP** have constant lengths 4 cm and 3 cm. If **AB** is fixed, and **AP** rotates about **A**, trace the changes in **PB**, as ths angle **A** increases from 0° to 180°.

    Answer this question by drawing a series of figures, increasing **A** by increments of 30°. Measure **PB** in each case, and tabulate the results.

12. From **B** the foot of a flagstaff **AB** a horizontal line is drawn passing two points **C** and **D** which are 9 m. apart. The angles **BCA** and **BDA** are 65° and 40° respectively. Represents this on a diagram (scale 1 cm. to 3 m), and find by measurement the approximate height of the flagstaff.

13. From **P**, the top of a lighthouse **PQ**, two boats **A** and **B** are seen at anchor in a line due south of the lighthouse. It is known that **PQ** = 38.4 m., ∠**PAQ** = 57°, ∠**PBQ** = 33°; hence draw a plan in which 1 cm. represents 12 m., and find by measurement the distance between **A** and **B** to the nearest metre.

14. From a lighthouse **L** two ships **A** and **B**, which are 549 m. apart, are observed in directions S.W. and 15° East of South respectively. At the same time **B** is observed from **A** in a S.E. direction. Draw a plan (scale 1 cm. to 183 m), and find by measurement the distance of the lighthouse from each ship.

PARALLELOGRAMS

DEFINITIONS

1. **A quadrilateral** is a plane figure bounded by *four* straight lines.

   The straight line which joins opposite angular points in a quadrilateral is called a diagonal.

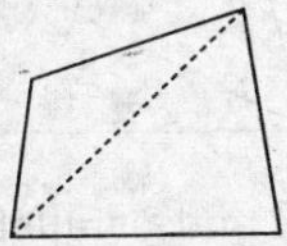

2. **A parallelogram** is a quadrilateral whose opposite sides are *parallel*.

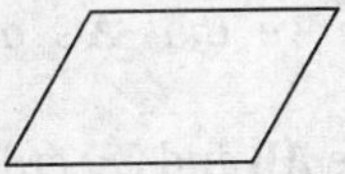

   [It will be proved hereafter that the opposite sides of a parallelogram are equal, and that its opposite angles are equal.]

3. **A rectangle** is a parallelogram which has one of its angles a right angle.

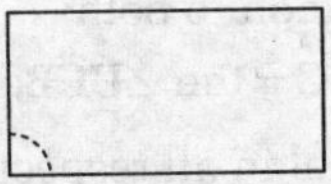

   [It will be proved hereafter that *all* the angles of a rectangle are right angles. See page 52]

4. **A square** is a rectangle which has two adjacent sides equal.

   [It will be proved that *all* the sides of a square are equal and all its angles right angles. See page 52.]

5. **A rhombus** is a quadrilateral which has all its sides equal, but its angles are not right angles.

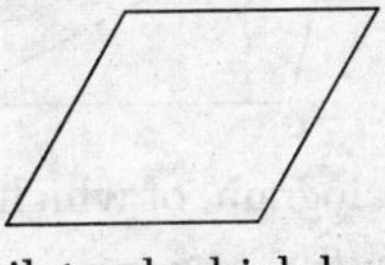

6. **A trapezium** is a quadrilateral which has *one* pair of parallel sides.

THEOREM 20. [Euclid I. 33]

The straight lines which join the extremities of two equal and parallel straight lines towards the same parts are themselves equal and parallel.

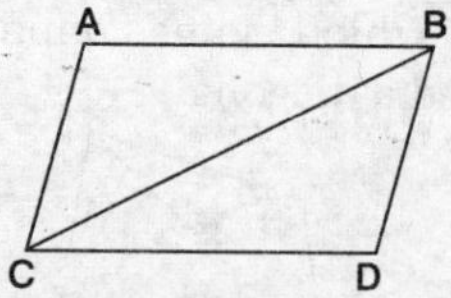

Let **AB** and **CD** be equal and parallel straight lines; and let them be joined towards the same parts by the straight lines **AC** and **BD**.

It is required to prove that **AC** *and* **BD** *are equal and parallel.*

Join **BC**.

Proof. Then because **AB** and **CD** are parallel, and **BC** meets them,

∴ the ∠**ABC** = the alternate ∠**DCB**.

Now in the Δ^s**ABC, DCB,**

because { **AB** = **DC**, **BC** is common to both; and the ∠**ABC** = the ∠**DCB**; } *Proved.*

∴ the triangles are equal in all respects;

so that **AC** = **DB**, ... (i)

and the ∠**ACB** = ∠**DBC**.

But these are alternate angles;

∴ **AC** and **BD** are parallel .... (ii)

That is, **AC** and **BD** are both equal and parallel. **Q.E.D.**

THEOREM 21. [Euclid I. 34]

The opposite sides and angles of a parallelogram are equal to one another, and each diagonal bisects the parallelogram.

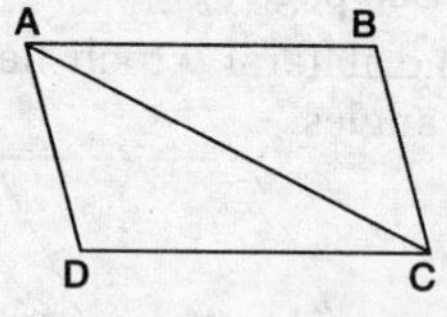

Let **ABCD** be a parallelogram, of which **BD** is a diagonal.

It required to prove that

(i) **AB** = **CD**, *and* **AD** = **CB**,

(ii) *the* ∠**BAD** = *the* ∠**DCB**,

(iii) *the* ∠**ADC** = *the* ∠**CBA**,

(iv) *the* Δ**ABD** = *the* Δ**CDB** *in area.*

Proof. Because **AB** and **DC** are parallel, and **BD** meets them,
∴ the ∠**ABD** = the alternate ∠**CBD**.
Again, because, **AD** and **BC** are parallel, and **BD** meets them,
∴ the ∠**ADB** = the alternate ∠**CDB**.
Hence in the ∆[s] **ABD**, **CDB**,

because { the ∠**ABD** = the ∠**CDB**, the ∠**ADB** = the ∠**CBD**, and **BD** is common to both; } *Proved.*

∴ the triangles are equal in all respects; ***Theor.* 17.**
so that **AB** = **CD**, and **AD** = **CB**; ... (i)
and the ∠**BAD** = the ∠**DCB** ; ...(ii)
and the ∆**ABD** = the ∆**CDB** in area. ... (iv)
And because the ∠**ADB** = the ∠**CBD**, *Proved.*
and the ∠**CDB** = the ∠**ABD**,
∴ the whole ∠**ADC** = the whole ∠**CBA**. ... (iii) **Q.E.D.**

COROLLARY 1. *If one angle of a parallelogram is a right angle, all its angles are right angles*
In other words : All the angles of a rectangle are right angles.
For the sum of two consecutive ∠[s] = 2 rt. ∠[s], *Theor.* 14.
∴ if one of these is a rt. angle, the other must be a rt. angle.
And the opposite angles of the par[m] are equal;
∴ all the angles are right angles.

COROLLARY 2. *All the sides of a square are equal; and all its angles are right angles.*

COROLLARY 3. *The diagonals of a parallelogram bisect one another.*
Let the diagonals **AC**, **BD** of the par[m] **ABCD** intersect at **O**.
To prove **AO** = **OC**, *and* **BO** = **OD**.
In the ∆[s] **AOB**, **COD**

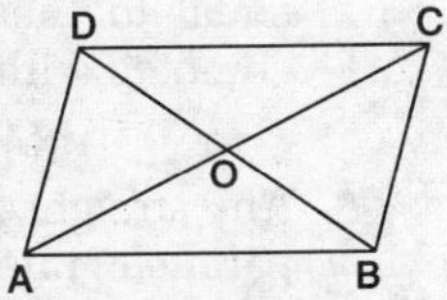

because { the ∠**OAB** = the alt. ∠**OCD**, the ∠**AOB** = vert. opp, ∆**COD**, and **AB** = the opp. side **CD**; }

∴**OB** = **OC**, and **OB** = **OD** *Theor.* 17.

EXERCISES

1. *If the opposite sides of a quadrilateral are equal, the figure is a parallelogram.*
2. *If the opposite angles of a quadrilateral are equal, the figure is a parallelogram.*

3. *If the diagonals of a quadrilateral bisect each other, the figure is a parallelogram.*
4. *The diagonals of a rhombus bisect one another at right angles.*
5. If the diagonals of a parallelogram are equal, all its angles are right angles.
6. In a parallelogram which is not rectangular the diagonals are unequal.

EXERCISES ON PARALLELS AND PARALLELOGRAMS
(*Symmetry and Superposition*)

1. Show that by folding a rhombus about one of its diagonals the triangles on opposite sides of the crease may be made to coincide. That is to say, prove that a rhombus is *symmetrical* about either diagonal.
2. Prove that the diagonals of a square are *axes of symmetry*. Name two other lines about which a square is symmetrical.
3. The diagonals of a rectangle divide the figure into two congruent triangles; is the diagonal, therefore, an axis of symmetry? About what two lines is a rectangle symmetrical?
4. Is there any axis about which an oblique parallelogram is symmetrical? Give reasons for your answer.
5. In a quadrilateral **ABCD**, **AB** = **AD** and **CB** = **CD**; but the sides are not all equal. Which of the diagonals (if either) is an axis of symmetry?
6. Prove by the method of superposition that
   (i) *Two parallelograms are identically equal if two adjacent sides of one are equal to two adjacent sides of the other, each to each, and one angle of one equal to one angle of the other.*
   (ii) *Two rectangles are equal if two adjacent sides of one are equal to two adjacent sides of the other, each to each.*
7. Two quadrilaterals **ABCD**, **EFGH** have the sides **AB**, **BC**, **CD**, **DA** equal respectively to the sides **EF**, **FG**, **GH**, **HE**, and have also the angle **BAD** equal to the angle **FEH**. Show that the figures may be made to coincide with one another.

(*Miscellaneous Theoretical Examples*)

8. Any straight line drawn through the middle point of a diagonal of a parallelogram and terminated by a pair of opposite sides, is bisected at that point.
9. In a parallelogram the perpendiculars drawn from one pair of opposite angles to the diagonal which joins the other pair are equal.
10. If **ABCD** is a parallelogram, and **X**, **Y** respectively the middle points of the sides **AD**, **BC**; show that the figure **AYCX** is a parallelogram.
11. **ABC** and **DEF** are two triangles such that **AB**, **BC** are respectively equal to and parallel to **DE**, **EF**; show that **AC** is equal and parallel to **DF**.

12. **ABCD** is a quadrilateral in which **AB** is parallel to **DC**, and **AD** equal but not parallel to **BC**; show that

(i) the $\angle$**A** + the $\angle$**C** = 180° = $\angle$**B** + the $\angle$**D**;

(ii) the diagonal **AC** = the diagonal **BD**;

(iii) the quadrilateral is *symmetrical* about the straight line joining the middle points of **AB** and **DC**.

13. **AP**, **BQ** are straight rods of equal length, turning at equal rates (both clockwise) about two fixed pivots **A** and **B** respectively. If the rods start parallel but pointing in opposite senses, show that

(i) they will always be parallel;

(ii) the line joining **PQ** will always pass through a certain fixed point.

(*Miscellaneous Numerical and Graphical Examples*)

14. Calculate the angles of the triangle **ABC**, having given:

int. $\angle$**A** = $\frac{3}{7}$ of ext. $\angle$**A** ; 3**B** = 4**C**.

15. A yacht sailing due East changes her course successively by 63° by 78°, by 119°, and by 64°, with a view to sailing round an island. What further change must be made to set her once more on an Easterly course?

16. If the sum of the interior angles of a rectilineal figure is equal to the sum of the exterior angles, how many sides has it, and why?

17. Draw, using your protractor, any five-sided figure **ABCDE**, in which

Δ**B** = 110°, $\angle$**C** = 115°, $\angle$**D** = 93°, $\angle$**E** = 152°.

Verify by a construction with ruler and compasses that **AE** is parallel to **BC**, and account theoretically for this fact.

18. **A** and **B** are two fixed points, and two straight lines **AP**, **BQ**, unlimited towards **P** and **Q**, are pivoted at **A** and **B**. **AP**, starting from the direction **AB**, turns about **A** clockwise at the uniform rate of $7\frac{1}{2}$° a second; and **BQ**, starting simultaneously from the direction **BA**, turns about **B** counter-clockwise at the rate of $3\frac{3°}{4}$ a second.

(i) How many seconds will elapse before **AP** and **BQ** are parallel?

(ii) Find graphically and by calculation the angle between **AP** and **BQ** twelve seconds from the start.

(iii) At what rate does this angle decrease?

THEOREM 22

If there are three or more parallel straight lines, and the intercepts made by them on any transversal are equal, then the corresponding intercepts on any other transversal are also equal.

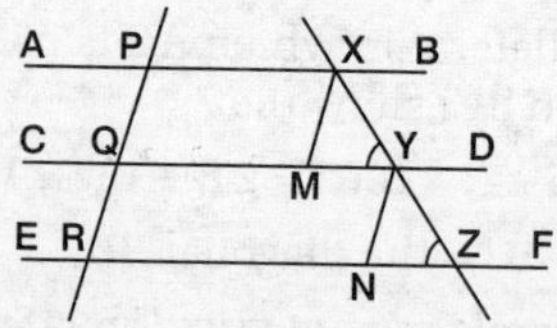

Let the parallels **AB**, **CD**, **EF** cut off equal intercepts **PQ**, **QR** from the transversal **PQR**; and let **XY**, **YZ** be the corresponding intercepts cut off from any other transversal **XYZ**.

It is required to prove that **XY = YZ**.

Through **X** and **Y** let **XM** and **YN** be drawn parallel to **PR**.

Proof. Since **CD** and **EF** are parallel, and **XZ** meets them,

∴ the ∠**XYM** = the corresponding ∠**YZN**.

And since **XM**, **YN** are parallel, each being parallel to **PR**,

∴ the ∠**MXY** = the corresponding ∠**NYZ**.

Now the figures **PM**, **QN** are parallelograms,

∴ **XM** = the opp. side **PQ**, and **YN** = the opp. side **QR**;

and since by hypothesis **PQ = QR**,

∴ **XM = YN**.

Then in the Δ^s **XMY**, **YNZ**,

because { the ∠**XYM** = the ∠**YZN**, the ∠**MXY** = the ∠**NYZ**, and **XM = YN**;

∴ the triangles are identically equal; ***Theor.*** **17.**

∴ **XY = YZ**. **Q.E.D.**

COROLLARY. In a triangle **ABC**, if a set of lines **P***p*, **Q***q*, **R***r*, ..., drawn parallel to the base, divide one side **AB** into equal parts, they also divide the other side **AC** into equal parts.

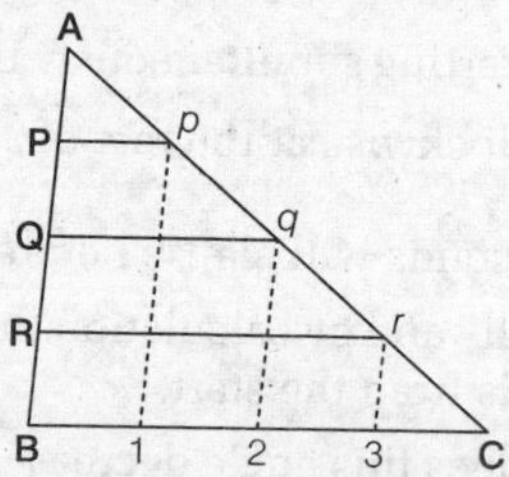

The lengths of the parallels **P***p*, **Q***q*, **R***r*, ... , may thus be expressed in terms of the base **BC**. Through *p*, *q* and *r* let *p*1, *q*2, *r*3 be drawn par[l] to **AB**.

Then, by Theorem 22, these par[ls] divide **BC** into *four* equal parts, of which **P***p* evidently contains *one*, **Q***q* *two*, and **R***r* *three*.

In other words, $\mathbf{P}p = \frac{1}{4} \cdot \mathbf{BC}$; $\mathbf{Q}q = \frac{2}{4} \cdot \mathbf{BC}$; $\mathbf{R}r = \frac{3}{4} \cdot \mathbf{BC}$.

Similarly if the given par[ls] divide **AB** into n equal parts,

$\mathbf{P}p = \frac{1}{n} \cdot \mathbf{BC}$, $\mathbf{Q}q = \frac{2}{n} \cdot \mathbf{BC}$, $\mathbf{R}r = \frac{3}{n} \cdot \mathbf{BC}$; and so on.

*** *Problem 7, p, 68, should now be worked.*

DEFINITION

If from the extremities of a straight line **AB** perpendiculars **AX, BY** are drawn to a straight line **PQ** of indefinite length, then **XY** is said to be the **orthogonal projection** of **AB** on **PQ**.

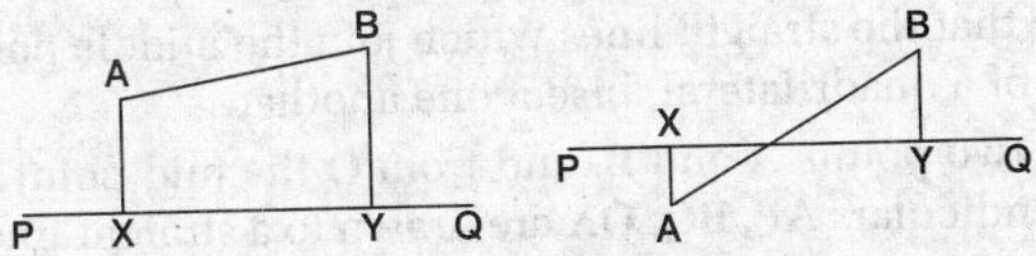

EXERCISES ON PARALLELS AND PARALLELOGRAMS

1. *The straight line drawn through the middle point of a side of a triangle, parallel to the base, bisects the remaining side.*

[This is an important particular case of Theorem 22.]

In the ΔABC, if **Z** is the middle point of **AB**, and **ZY** is drawn par[l] to **BC**, we have to prove that **AY = YC.**

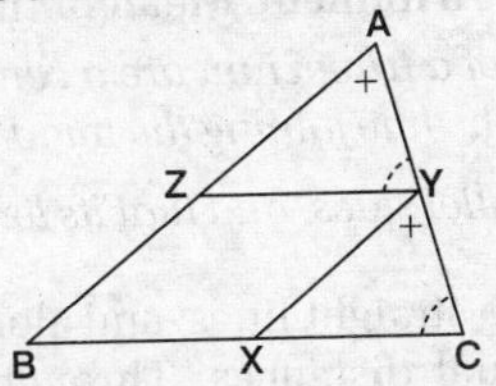

Draw **YX** par[l] to **AB**, and then prove the Δ[s] **ZAY, XYC** congruent.]

2. *The straight line which joins the middle points of two sides of a triangle is parallel to the third side*. [In the **ΔABC**, if **Z, Y** are the middle points of **AB, AC**, we have to prove **ZY** par[l] to **BC.**

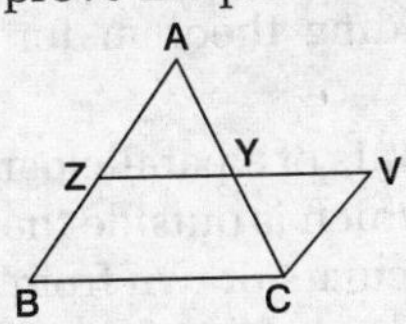

Produce **ZY** to **V**, making **YV** equal to **ZY**, and join **CV**. Prove the Δ[s] **AYZ, CYV** congruent; the rest follows at once.]

3. *The straight line which joins the middle points of two sides of a triangle is equal to half the third side.*
4. *Show that the three straight lines which join the middle points of the sides of a triangle, divide it into four triangles which are identically equal.*
5. *Any straight line drawn from the vertex of a triangle to the base is bisected by the straight line which joins the middle points of the other sides of the triangle.*
6. **ABCD** is a parallelogram, and **X**, **Y** are the middle points of the opposite sides **AD**, **BC**: show that **BX** and **DY** trisect the diagonal **AC**.
7. *If the middle points of adjacent sides of any quadrilateral are joined, the figure thus formed is a parallelogram.*
8. Show that the straight lines which join the middle points of opposite sides of a quadrilateral, bisect one another.
9. From two points **A** and **B**, and from **O** the mid-point between them, perpendiculars **AP**, **BQ**, **OX** are drawn to a straight line **CD**. If **AP**, **BQ** measure respectively 4.2 cm. and 5.8 cm., *deduce* the length of **OX**, and verify your result by measurement.

   Show that $\mathbf{OX} = \frac{1}{2}(\mathbf{AP} + \mathbf{BQ})$ or $\frac{1}{2}(\mathbf{AP} \sim \mathbf{BQ})$, according as **A** and **B** are on the *same* side, or on *opposite* sides of **CD**.
10. When three parallels cut off equal intercepts from two transversals, show that of three parallel lengths between the two transversals the middle one is the **Arithmetic Mean** of the other two.
11. *The parallel sides of a trapezium are a centimetres and b centimetres in length. Prove that the line joining the middle points of the oblique sides is parallel to the parallel sides, and that its length is* $\frac{1}{2}(a + b)$ *centimetres.*
12. **OX** and **OY** are two straight lines, and along **OX** five points 1, 2, 3, 4, 5 are marked at equal distances. Through these points parallels are drawn in any direction to meet **OY**. Measure the lengths of these parallels : take their average, and compare it with the length of the *third* parallel. Prove *geometrically* that the 3rd parallel is the mean of all five.

    State the corresponding theorem for any odd number $(2n + 1)$ of parallels so drawn.
13. From the angular points of a parallelogram perpendiculars are drawn to any straight line which is outside the parallelogram : show that the sum of the perpendiculars drawn from one pair of opposite angles is equal to the sum of those drawn from the other pair.

    [Draw the diagonals, and from their point of intersection suppose a perpendicular drawn to the given straight line.]

14. The sum of the perpendiculars drawn from any point in the base of an isosceles triangle to the equal sides is equal to the perpendicular drawn from either extremity of the base to the opposite side.

[It follows that the sum of the distances of *any* point in the base of an isosceles triangle from the equal sides is constant, that is, the same whatever point in the base is taken.] How would this property be modified if the given points were taken in the base *produced*?

15. The sum of the perpendiculars drawn from any point within an equilateral triangle to the three sides is equal to the perpendicular drawn from any one of the angular points to the opposite side, and is therefore constant.

16. Equal and parallel lines have equal projections on any other straight line.

DIAGONAL SCALES

Diagonal scales form an important application of Theorem 22. We shall illustrate their construction and use by describing a *Decimal Diagonal Scale to show Centimetres, Quarter.* (.25) *and Tenths of Quarters* (.025).

A straight line **AB** is divided (from **A**) into centimetres, and the points of division marked 0, 1, 2,..... The primary division 0**A** is subdivided into *quarter* (.25), these secondary divisions being numbered (from 0) 1, 2, 3, **A**. We may now read on **AB** *centimetres* and *quarters* (.25) of a centimetre.

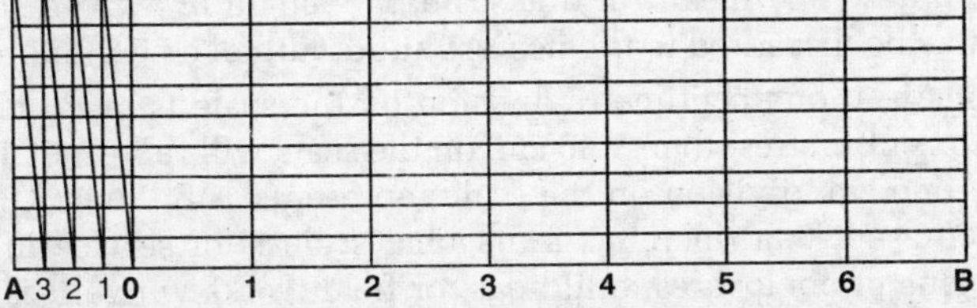

In order to read *tenths of quarters* (.025); ten lines are taken at any equal intervals parallel to **AB**; and perpendiculars are drawn through 0,1,2,... .

The primary (or centimetre) division corresponding to 0**A** on the tenth parallel is now subdivided into *four* equal parts; and diagonal lines are drawn, as in the diagram,

joining 0 to the *first* point of subdivision on the 10th parallel.

" 1 to the *second* " " " " " ;

" 2 to the *third* " " " " " ;

and so on.

The scale is now complete, and its use is shown in the following example.

Example. To take from the scale a length of 3.30 *centimetres.*

(i) Place one point of the dividers at 3 in **AB**, and extend them till the other point reaches 1 in the subdivided centimetre 0A.

We have now 3.25 centimetres in the dividers.

(ii) To get the remaining 0.05, move the right-hand point up the perpendicular through 3 till it reaches the 2nd parallel. Then extend the dividers till the left point reaches the diagonal through 1 also on the 2nd parallel. We have now 3.30 centimetres in the dividers.

REASON FOR THE ABOVE PROCESS

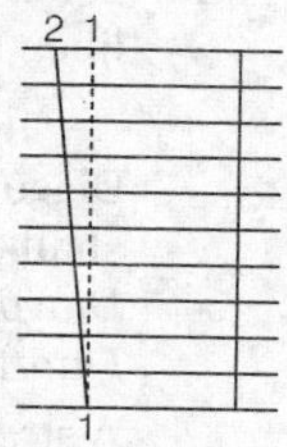

The first step needs no explanation. The reason of the second is found in the Corollary of Theorem 22.

Joining the point 1 to the corresponding point on the tenth parallel, we have a triangle 1, 1, 2, of which one side 1, 1 is divided into ten equal parts by a set of lines parallel to the base 1, 2.

Therefore the lengths of the parallels between 1, 1 and the diagonal 1, 2 are $\frac{1}{10}, \frac{2}{10}, \frac{3}{01}, \ldots$ of the base, which is .25 centimetre.

Hence these lengths are respectively .025, .050, .075 ... of 1 centimetre.

Similarly, by means of this scale, the length of a given straight line may be measured to the nearest hundredth of a centimetre.

Again, if one centimetre-division on the scale is taken to represent 10 centimetres, then 3.30 cm. on the scale will represent 33 cm. And if one cm. division on the scale represents 1 m,, then 3.30 cm. will represent 3.30 m. Thus a diagonal scale is of service in preparing plans of enclosures, buildings, or field-works where it is necessary that every dimension of the actual object must be represented by a line of proportional length on the plan.

NOTE The subdivision of a diagonal scale need not be *decimal.*

For instance we might construct a diagonal scale to read centimetres, millimetres, and *quarters* of a millimetre; in which case we should take *four* parallels to the line **AB**.

[For Exercises of Linear Measurements see the following page.]

EXERCISES ON LINEAR MEASUREMENTS

1. Draw straight lines whose lengths are 3.17 cm., 6.9 cm., 7.82 cm.
2. Find by measurement the equivalent of 3.15 inches in centimetres and millimetres. Hence calculate (correct to two decimal places) the value of 1 cm. in inches.
3. A distance of 50 km. is represented on a map by 1 cm. Draw lines to represent distances of 336 km. and 408 km.
4. If 2 cm. on a map represent 1 kilometre, draw lines to represent 850 metres, 2980 metres, and 1010 metres.
5. A plan is drawn to the scale of 1 cm. to 10 metres. Measure in centimetres and millimetres a line representing 91.74 metres.
6. Find to the nearest millimetre the length of a line which will represent 42.500 kilometres in a map drawn to the scale of 1 centimetre to 50 hectometres.
7. The distance from London to Oxford (in a direct line) in 88 km. If this distance is represented on a map by 5 cm., to what scale is the map drawn? That is, how many kilometres will be represented by 1 centimetre?
8. On a map of France drawn to the scale 1 cm. to 22.4 km., the distance from Paris to Calais is represent by 10.5 cm. Find the distance accurately in kilometres.
9. The distance from Exeter to Plymouth is 60 km., and appears on a certain map to be 6.3 cm.; and the distance from Lincoln to York is 88 km., and appears on another map to be 7 cm. Compare the scales of these maps.

PRACTICAL GEOMETRY

PROBLEMS

The following problems are to be solved with ruler and compasses only. No step requires the actual measurement of any line or angle; that is to say, the *constructions* are to be made without using either a graduated scale of length, or a protractor.

The problems are not merely to be studied as propositions; but the construction in every case is to be actually performed by the learner, great care being given to accuracy of drawing.

Each problem is followed by a *theoretical* proof; but the *results* of the work should always be verified by measurement, as a test of correct drawing. Accurate measurement is also required in applications of the problems.

In the diagrams of the problems lines which are inserted only for purposes of *proof* are dotted, to distinguish them from lines necessary to the construction.

For practical applications of the problems the student should be provided with the following instruments:

1. A flat ruler, one edge being graduated in centimetres and millimetres, and the other in inches and tenths.
2. Two set squares; one with angles of 45°, and the other with angles of 60° and 30°.
3. A pair of pencil compasses.
4. A pair of dividers, preferably with screw adjustment.
5. A semi-circular protractor.

PROBLEM 1

To bisect a given angle

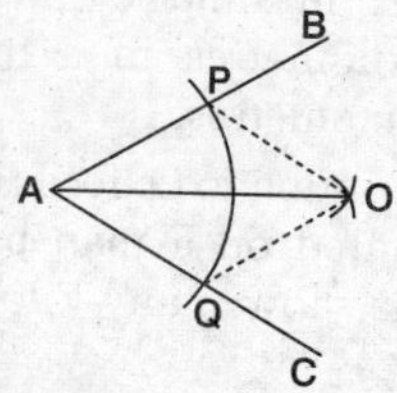

Let **BAC** be the given angle to be bisected.

Construction. With centre **A**, and any radius, draw an arc of a circle cutting **AB**, **AC** at **P** and **Q**.

With centres **P** and **Q**, and radius **PQ**, draw two arcs cutting at **O**.

Join **AO**.

Then the ∠**BAC** is bisected by **AO**.

Prdjofn PO, QO

In the Δ^s **APO, AQO,**

because { **AP** = **AQ**, being radii of a circle,
PO = **QO**, being radii of equal circles,
and **AO** is common;

∴ the triangles are equal in all respects; *Theor.* 7.

so that the ∠**PAO** = the ∠**QAO**;

that is, the ∠**BAC** is bisected by **AO**.

NOTE. **PQ** has been taken as the radius of the arcs drawn from the centres **P** and **Q**, and the intersection of these arcs determines the point **O**. *Any* radius, however, may be used instead of **PO**, provided that it is great enough to secure the intersection of the arcs.

PROBLEM 2

To bisect a given straight line

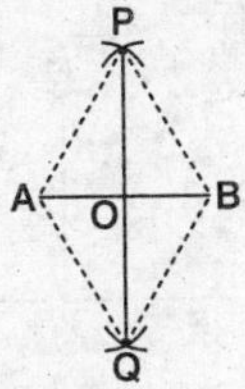

Let **AB** be the line to be bisected.

Construction. With centre **A**, and radius **AB**, draw two arcs, one on each side of **AB**.

With centre **B**, and radius **BA**, draw two arcs, one on each side of **AB**, cutting the first arcs at **P** and **Q**.

Join **PQ**, cutting **AB** at **O**.

Then **AB** is bisected at **O**.

Proof. Join **AP,AQ, BP, BQ.**

In the Δ^s **APQ, BPQ,**

because { **AP** = **BP**, being radii of equal circles. **AQ** = **BQ**, for the same reason, and **PQ** is common;

∴ the ∠**APQ** = the ∠**BPQ**. *Theor.* 7.

Again in the Δ^s **APO, BPO,**

because { **AP** = **BP**, **PO** is common, and the ∠**APO** = the ∠**BPO**;

∴ **AO** = **OB**; *Theor.* 4.

that is, **AB** is bisected at **O**.

NOTES. (i) **AB** was taken as the radius of the arcs drawn from the centres **A** and **B**, *any* radius may be used provided that it is great enough to secure the intersection of the arcs which determine the points **P** and **Q**.

(ii) From the congruence of the Δ^s **APO**, **BPO** it follows that the ∠**AOP** = the ∠**BOP**. As these are adjacent angles, it follows that **PQ** *bisects* **AB** *at right angles*.

PROBLEM 3

To draw a straight line perpendicular to a given straight line at a given point in it.

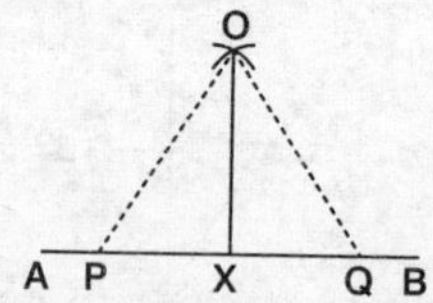

Let **AB** be the straight line, and **X** the point in it at which a perpendicular is to be drawn.

Construction. With centre **X** cut off from **AB** any two equal parts **XP, XQ.**

With centres **P** and **Q**, and radius **PQ**, draw two arcs cutting at **O.**

Join **XO.**

Then **XO** is perp. to **AB.**

Proof. Join **OP, OQ.**

In the Δ^s**OXP, OXQ,**

because { **XP** = **XQ**, by construction,
OX is common,
and **PO** = **QO**, being radii of equal circles;

∴ the ∠**OXP** = the ∠**OXQ**. ***Theor.*** **7.**

And these being adjacent angles, each is a right angle;

that is, **XO** is prep. to **AB**

Obs. If the point **X** is near one end of **AB** , one or other of the alternative construction on this page should be used.

PROBLEM 3. SECOND METHOD

Construction. Take any point **C** outside **AB.**

With centre **C**, and radius **CX**, draw a circle cutting **AB** at **D.**

Join **DC**, and produce it to meet the circumference of the circle at **O.**

Join **XO.**

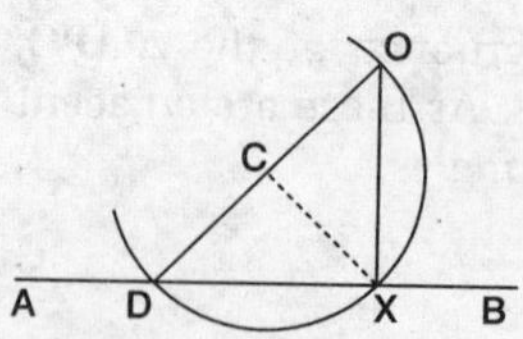

Then **XO** is prep. to **AB.**

Proof. Join **CX.**

Because **CO** = **CX**; ∴ the ∠**CXO** = the ∠**COX**;
and because **CD** = **CX**; ∴ the ∠**CXD** = the ∠**CDX**.
∴ the whole ∠**DXO** = the ∠**XOD** + the ∠**XDO**

$$= \frac{1}{2} \text{ of } 180° = 90°.$$

∴ **XO** is perp. to **AB**.

PROBLEM 3. THIRD METHOD

Construction. With centre **X** and any radius, draw the arc **CDE**, cutting **AB** at **C**.
With centre **C**, and with the same radius, draw an arc, cutting the first arc at **D**.
With centre **D**, and with the same radius, draw an arc, cutting the first arc at **E**.

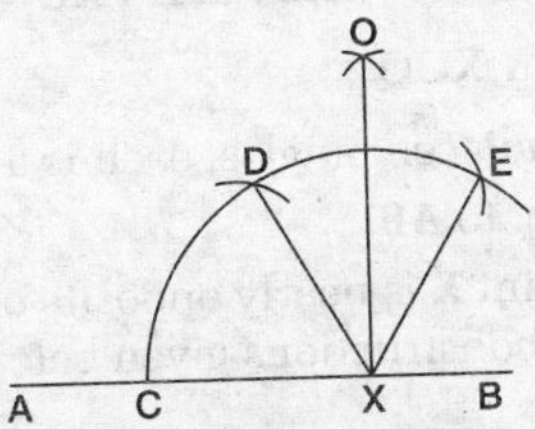

Bisect the ∠**DXE**by **XO**. *Prob.* **1.**
Then **XO** is prep. to **AB**.

Proof. Each of the ∠^s^**CXD, DXE** may be proved to be 60°;
and the ∠ **DXO** is half of the ∠ **DXE**;
∴ the ∠ **CXO** is 90°. That is, **XO** is prep. to **AB**.

PROBLEM 4

To draw a straight line perpendicular to a given straight line from a given external point.

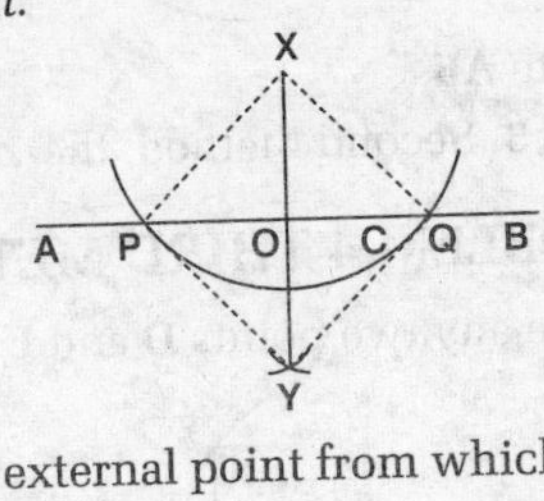

Let **X** be the given external point from which a perpendicular is to be drawn at **AB**.
Construction. Take any point **C** on the side of **AB** remote from **X**.
With centre **X**, and radius **XC**, draw an arc to cut **AB** at **P** and **Q**.

With centres **P** and **Q**, and radius **PX**, draw arcs cutting at **Y**, on the side of **AB** opposite to **X**. Join **XY** cutting **AB** at **O**. Then **XO** is perp. to **AB**.

Proof. Join **PX**, **QX**, **PY**, **QY**,

In the Δ^s **PXY, QXY**,

$$\text{because}\begin{cases}\mathbf{PX} = \mathbf{QX}\text{, being radii of a circle,}\\ \mathbf{PY} = \mathbf{QY}\text{, for the same reason,}\\ \text{and } \mathbf{XY} \text{ is common;}\end{cases}$$

∴ the ∠ **PXY** = the ∠ **QXY**. *Theor.* 7.

Again, in the Δ^s **PXO, QXO**.

$$\text{because}\begin{cases}\mathbf{PX} = \mathbf{QX},\\ \mathbf{XO} \text{ is common,}\\ \text{and the } \angle\, \mathbf{PXO} = \text{the } \angle \mathbf{QXO};\end{cases}$$

∴ the ∠ **XOP** the ∠ **XOQ**. *Theor.* 4.

And these being adjacent angles, each is a right angle, that is, **XO** is perp. to **AB**.

Obs. When the point **X** is nearly opposite one end of **AB**, one or other of the alternative constructions given below should be used.

PROBLEM 4. SECOND METHOD

Construction. Take any point **D** in **AB**. Join **DX**, and bisect it at **C**. With centre **C**, and radius **CX**, draw a circle cutting **AB** at **D** and **O**. Join **XO**.

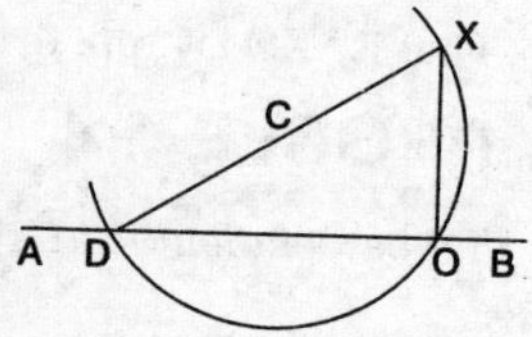

Then **XO** is perp. to **AB**.

For, as in Problem 3, Second Method, the ∠ **XOD** is a right angle.

PROBLEM 4 THIRD METHOD

Construction. Take any two points **D** and **E** in **AB**.

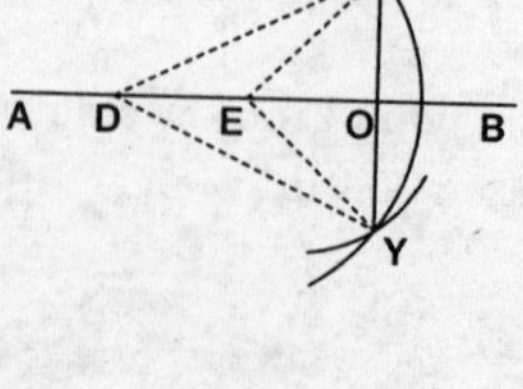

With centre **D**, and radius **DX**, draw an arc of a circle, on the side of **AB** opposite to **X**.

With centre **E**, and radius **EX**, draw another arc cutting the former at **Y**.

Join **XY**, cutting **AB** at **O**.

Then **XO** is perp. to **AB**.

(i) Prove the Δ^s **XDE, YDE** equal in all respects by Theorem 7, so that the $\angle$ **XDE** = the $\angle$**YDE**.

(ii) Hence prove the Δ^s **XDO, YDO** equal in respects by Theorem 4, so that the adjacent $\angle^s$ **DOX, DOY** are equal.

That is, **XO** is perp. to **AB**.

PROBLEM 5

At a given point in a given straight line to make an angle equal to a given angle.

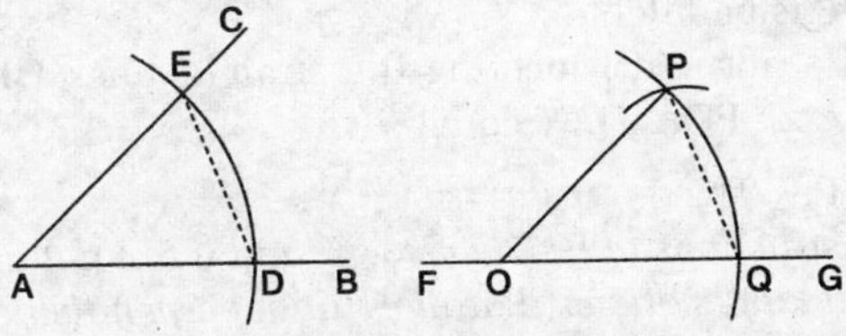

Let **BAC** be the given angle, and **FG** the given straight line; and let **O** be the point at which an angle is to be made equal to the $\angle$ **BAC**.

Construction With centre **A**, and with any radius, draw an arc cutting **AB** and **AC** at **D** and **E**.

With centre **O**, and with the same radius, draw an arc cutting **FG** at **Q**.

With centre **Q**, and with radius **DE**, draw an arc cutting the former arc at **P**.

Join **OP**.

Then **POQ** is the required angle.

Proof. Join **ED, PQ**.

In the Δ^s **POQ, EAD**,

because { **OP = AE**, being radii of equal circles,
OQ = AD, for the same reasons,
PQ = ED, by construction;

$\therefore$ the triangles are equal in all respects;

so that the $\angle$ **POQ** = the $\angle$ **EAD**. ***Theor.7.***

PROBLEM 6

Through a given point to draw a straight line parallel to a given straight line.

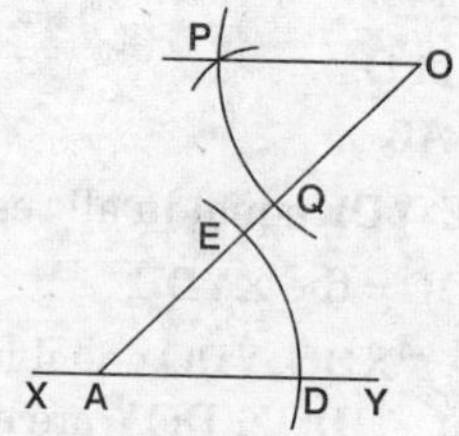

Let **XY** be the given straight line, and **O** the given point through which a straight line is to be drawn par[l] to **XY**.

Construction. In **XY** take any point **A**, and join **OA**.

Using the construction of Problem 5, at the point **O** in the line **AO** make the ∠ **AOP** equal to the ∠ **OAY** and alternate to it.

Then **OP** is parallel to **XY**.

Proof. Because **AO**, meeting the straight lines **OP**, **XY**, makes the alternate ∠[s] **POA, OAY** equal ;

∴ **OP** is par[l] to **XY**.

⁂ *The constructions of Problems* 3, 4, *and* 6 *are not usually followed in practical applications. Parallels and perpendiculars may be more quickly drawn by the aid of set squares.* (See LESSONS IN EXPERIMENTAL GEOMETRY).

PROBLEM 7

To divide a given straight line into any number of equal parts.

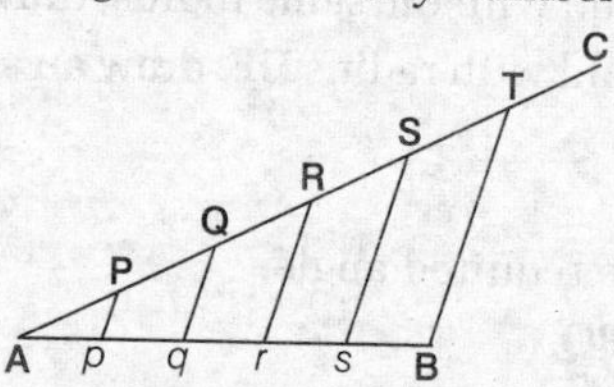

Let **AB** be the given straight line, and suppose it is required to divide it into *five* equal parts.

Construction. From **A** draw **AC**, a straight line of unlimited length, making any angle with **AB**.

From **AC** mark off *five* equal parts of *any* length, **AP, PQ, QR, RS, ST**.

Join **TB**; and through **P, Q, R, S** draw par[ls] to **TB**, meeting **AB** in *p, q, r, s*.

Then since the par[ls] **P***p*, **Q***q*, **R***r*, **S***s*, **TB** cut off five equal parts from **AT**, they also cut off five equal parts from **AB**. (Theorem 22.)

SECOND METHOD

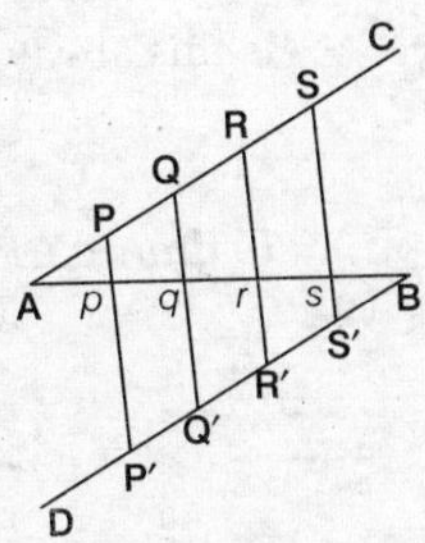

From **A** draw **AC** at any angle with **AB**, and on it mark off *four* equal parts **AP**, **PQ**, **QR**, **RS**, of any length.

From **B** draw **BD** par[l] to **AC**, and on it mark off **BS′**, **S′R′**, **R′Q′**, **Q′P′**, each equal to the parts marked on **AC**.

Join **PP′**, **QQ′**, **RR′**, **SS′** meeting **AB** in *p*, *q*, *r*, *s*. Then **AB** is divided intofive equal parts at these points.

[Prove by Theorems 20 and 22.]

EXERCISES ON LINES AND ANGLES

(Graphical Exercises)

1. Construct (with ruler and compasses only) an angle of 60°.
By repeated bisection divide this angle into *four* equal parts.

2. By means of Exercise 1, *trisect a right angle*; that is divide it into *three* equal parts.
Bisect each part, and hence show how to trisect an angle of 45°.
[No construction is known for exactly trisecting *any* angle.]

3. From a straight line 7.44 cm. long, cut off *one seventh*, and verify your work by calculation.

4. At a point **X** in a straight line **AB** draw **XP** perpendicular to **AB**, making **XP** 3.6 cm. in length. From **P** draw an oblique **PQ**, 6 cm. long, to meet **AB** in **Q**. Measure **XQ**.

(*Problems. State your construction, and give a theoretical proof.*)

5. In a straight line **XY** find a point which is equidistant from two given points **A** and **B**.
When is this impossible?

6. In a straight line **XY** find a point which is equidistant from two intersecting line **AB**, **AC**.
When is this impossible?

7. From a given point **P** draw a straight line **PQ**, making with a given straight line **AB** an angle of given magnitude.

8. From two given points **P** and **Q** on the same side of a straight line **AB**, draw two lines which meet in **AB** and make equal angles with it.
[**Construction.** From **P** draw **PH** perp. to **AB**, and produce **PH** to **P′** making **HP′** equal to **PH**. Join **P′Q** cutting **AB** at **K**. Join **PK**. Prove that **PK**, **QK** are the required lines.]

9. Through a given point **P** draw a straight line such that the perpendiculars drawn to it from two points **A** and **B** may be equal. Is this always possible?

PROBLEM 8

To draw a triangle having given the lengths of the three sides.

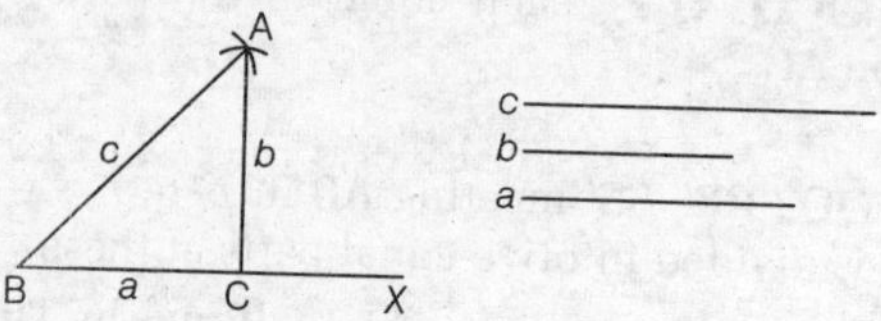

Let a, b, c be the lengths to which the sides of the required triangle are to be equal.

Construction. Draw any straight line **BX**, and cut off from it a part **BC** equal to a. With centre **B**, and radius c, draw an arc of a circle. With centre **C**, and radius b, draw a second arc cutting the first at **A**.

Join **AB**, **AC**.

Then **ABC** is the required triangle, for by construction the sides **BC**, **CA**, **AB** are equal to a, b, c respectively.

Obs. The three data a, b, c may be understood in two ways : either as three actual lines to which the sides of the triangle are to be equal, or as three *numbers* expressing the lengths of those lines in terms of centimetres, or some other linear unit.

NOTES. (i) In order that the construction may be possible it is necessary that any two of the given sides should be together greater than the third side (Theorem 11); for otherwise the arcs drawn from the centres **B** and **C** would not cut.

(ii) The arcs which cut at **A** would, if continued, cut again on the other side of **BC**. Thus the construction gives two triangles on opposite sides of a common base.

ON THE CONSTRUCTION OF TRIANGLES

It has been seen (page 44) that to prove two triangles identically equal *three* parts of one must be given equal to the corresponding parts of the other (though *any* three parts do not necessarily serve the purpose). This amounts to saying that *to determine the shape and size of a triangle we must know* **three** *of its parts*: or, in other words,

To construct a triangle three independent data are required.

For example, we may construct a triangle

(i) When *two sides* (b, c) and the *included angle* **(A)** are given.

The method of construction in this case is obvious.

(ii) When *two angles* **(A, B)** and one side (a) are given.

Here, since **A** and **B** are given, we at once know **C**;

for **A** + **B** + **C** = 180°

Hence we have only to draw the base equal to *a*, and at its ends make angles equal to **B** and **C**; for we know that the remaining angle must necessarily be equal to **A**.

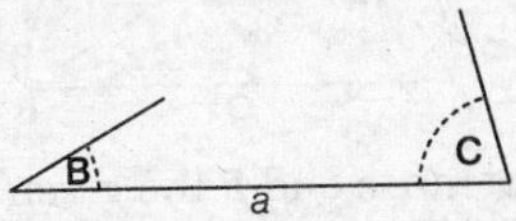

(iii) If the *three angles* **A, B, C** given (and no side), the problem is **indeterminate**, that is, the number of solutions is unlimited.

For if at the ends of *any* base we make angles equal to **B** and **C**, the third angle is equal to **A**.

This construction is indeterminate, because the three data are not *independent*, the third following necessarily from the other two.

PROBLEM 9

To construct a triangle having given two sides and an angle opposite to one of them.

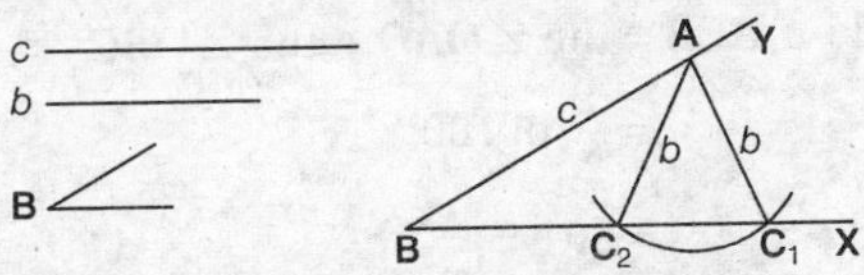

Let *b*, *c* be the given sides and **B** the given angle.

Construction. Take any straight line **BX**, and at **B** make the ∠ **XBY** equal to the given ∠ **B**.

From **BY** cut off **BA** equal to *c*.

With centre **A** and radius *b*, draw an arc of a circle.

If this arc cuts **BX** in two points C_1 and C_2, both on the same side of **B**, both Δ^s ABC_1, ABC_2 satisfy the given conditions.

This double solution is know as the **Ambiguous Case**, and will occur when *b* is less than *c* but greater than perp. from **A** on **BX**.

Draw figures to illustrate the nature and number of solutions in the following cases;

(i) When *b* is greater than *c*.

(ii) When *b* is equal to *c*.

(iii) When *b* is equal to the perpendicular from **A** on **BX**.

(iv) When *b* is less than this perpendicular.

PROBLEM 10

To construct a right-angled triangle having given the hypotenuse and one side.

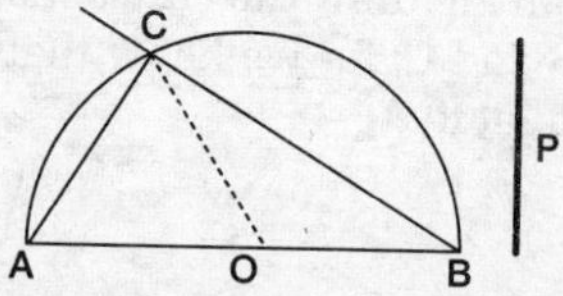

Let **AB** be the hypotenuse and **P** the given side.

Construction. Bisect **AB** at **O**; and with centre **O**, and radius **OA**, draw a semicircle.

With centre **A**, and radius **P**, draw an arc to cut the semicircle at **C**.

Join **AC**, **BC**.

Then **ABC** is the required triangle.

Proof. Join **OC**.

Because **OA** = **OC**;

∴ the ∠ **OCA** = the ∠**OAC**.

And because **OB** = **OC**;

∴ the ∠ **OCB** = the ∠ **OBC**.

∴ the whole ∠ **ACB** = the ∠ **OAC** + the ∠ **OBC**

$= \frac{1}{2}$ of 180° ***Theor.* 16.**

$= 90°$

ON THE CONSTRUCTION OF TRIANGLES
(*Graphical Exercises*)

1. Draw a triangle whose sides are 7.5 cm., 6.2 cm., and 5.3 cm. Draw and measure the perpendiculars dropped on these sides from the opposite vertices.

[N.B. The perpendiculars, if correctly drawn, will meet at a point, as will be seen later.

2. Draw a triangle **ABC**, having given $a = 7.62$ cm ‘ $b = 6.35$ cm’ $c = 6.98$ cm. Bisect the angle **A** by a line which meets the base at **X**. Measure **BX** and **XC** (to the nearest millimetre); and hence calculate the value of $\frac{\mathbf{BX}}{\mathbf{CX}}$ to two places of decimals. Compare your result with the value of $\frac{c}{b}$.

3. Two sides of a triangular field are 315 m., and 260 m., and the included angle is known to be 39°. Draw a plan (1 cm. to 50 m.) and find by measurement the length of the remaining side of the field.

4. **ABC** is a triangular plot of ground, of which the base **BC** is 75 metres, and the angles at **B** and **C** are 47° and 68° respectively. Draw a plan (scale 1 cm. to 10 metres). Write down without measurement the size of the angle **A**; and by measuring the plan, obtain the approximate lengths of the other sides of the field; also the perpendicular drawn from **A** to **BC**.

5. A yacht on leaving harbour steers **N.E.** sailing 9 knots an hour. After 20 minutes she goes about, steering **N.W.** for 35 minutes and making the same average speed as before. How far is she now from the harbour, and what course (approximately) must she set for the run home? Obtain your results from a chart of the whole course, scale 2 cm. to 1 knot.

6. Draw a right-angled triangle, given that the hypotenuse $c = 10.6$ cm. and one side $a = 5.6$ cm. Measure the third side b; and find the value of $\sqrt{c^2 - a^2}$. Compare the two results.

7. Construct a triangle, having given the following parts : $\mathbf{B} = 34°$, $b = 5.5$ cm., $c = 8.5$ cm. Show that there are two solutions. Measure the two values of a, and also of **C**, and show that the latter are supplementary.

8. In a triangle **ABC**, the angle $\mathbf{A} = 50°$ and $b = 6.5$ cm. Illustrate by figures the cases which arise in constructing the triangle, when

   (i) $a = 7$ cm. (ii) $a = 6$ cm.

   (iii) $a = 5$ cm. (iv) $a = 4$ cm.

9. Two straight roads, which cross at right angles at **A**, are carried over a straight canal by bridges at **B** and **C**. The distance between the bridges is 461 m., and the distance from the crossing **A** to the bridge **B** is 261 m. Draw a plan and by measurement of it ascertain the distance from **A** to **C**.

10. Draw an isosceles triangle on a base of 4 cm., and having an altitude of 6.2 cm. *Prove* the two sides equal, and measure them to the nearest millimetre.

11. Draw an isosceles triangle having its vertical angle equal to a given angle, and the perpendicular from the vertex on the base equal to a given straight line. Hence draw an equilateral triangle in which the perpendicular from one vertex on the opposite side is 6 cm. Measure the length of a side to the nearest millimetre.

12. Construct a triangle **ABC** in which the perpendicular from **A** on **BC** is 5.0 cm., and the sides **AB**, **AC** are, 5.8 cm. and 9.0 cm. respectively. Measure **BC**.

13. Construct a triangle **ABC** having the angle at **B** and **C** equal to two given angles **L** and **M**, and the perpendicular from **A** on **BC** equal to a given line **P**.

14. Construct a triangle **ABC** (without protractor) having given two angles **B** and **C** and the side b.

15. On a given base construct an isosceles triangle having its vertical angle equal to the given **L**.

16. Construct a right-angled triangle, having given the length of the hypotenuse c, and the sum of the remaining sides a and b.

If $c = 5.3$ cm., and $a + b = 7.3$ cm., find a and b graphically; and calculate the value of $\sqrt{a^2 + b^2}$.

17. Construct a triangle having given the perimeter and the angles at the base. For example, $a + b + c = 12$ cm, $\mathbf{B} = 70°$, $\mathbf{C} = 80°$.

18. Construct a triangle **ABC** from the following data :

$$a = 6.5 \text{ cm.}, b + c = 10 \text{ cm., and } \mathbf{B} = 60°.$$

Measure the lengths of b and c.

19. Construct a triangle **ABC** from the following data :

$$a = 7 \text{ cm.}, c - b = 1 \text{ cm., and } \mathbf{B} = 55°.$$

Measure the lengths of b and c.

THE CONSTRUCTION OF QUADRILATERALS

It has been shown that the shape and size of a triangle are completely determined when the lengths of its three sides are given. A quadrilateral, however, is not completely determined by the lengths of its four sides. From what follows it will appear that *five* independent data are required, in general, to construct a convex quadrilateral, *i.e.* a figure having no reflex angle. For a non-convex quadrilateral *six* independent data are generally required.

PROBLEM 11

To construct a convex quadrilateral, given the lengths of the four sides, and one angle.

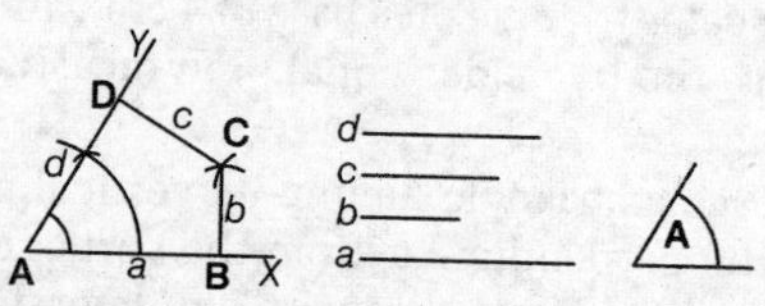

Let a, b, c, d be the given lengths of the sides, and **A** the angle between the sides equal to a and d.

Construction. Take any straight line **AX**, and cut off from it **AB** equal to a.

Make the ∠ **BAY** equal to the ∠ **A**.

From **AY** cut off **AD** equal to d.

With centre **D**, and radius c, draw an arc of a circle.

With centre **B** and radius b, draw another arc to cut the former at **C**.

Join **DC**, **BC**.

Then **ABCD** is the required quadrilateral; for by construction the sides are equal to a, b, c, d, and the ∠ **DAB** is equal to the given angle.

PROBLEM 12

To construct a parallelogram having given two adjacent sides and the included angle.

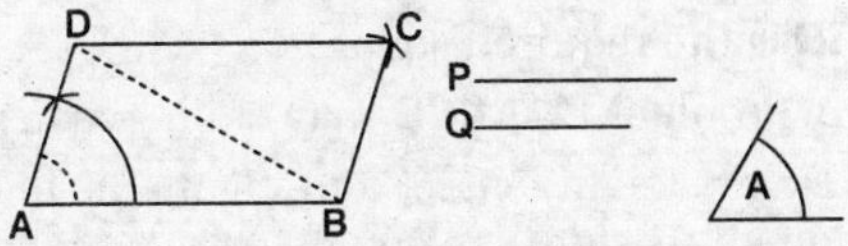

Let **P** and **Q** be the two given sides, and **A** the given angle.

Construction 1. (*With ruler and compasses*). Take a line **AB** equal to **P**, and at **A** make the ∠ **BAD** equal to the ∠ **A**, and make **AD** equal to **Q**.

With centre **D**, and radius **P**, draw an arc of a circle.

With centre **B**, and radius **Q**, draw another arc to cut the former at **C**.

Then **ABCD** is the required par^{m}. **Proof.** Join **DB**.

In the Δ^s **DCB, BAD,**

$$\text{because} \begin{cases} \mathbf{DC = BA}, \\ \mathbf{CB = AD}, \\ \text{and } \mathbf{DB} \text{ is common:} \end{cases}$$

∴ the ∠ **CDB** = the ∠ **ABD**; ***Theor.* 19.**

and these are alternate angles,

∴ **DC** is par^{l} to **AB**.

Also **DC** = **AB**

∴ **DA** and **BC** are also equal and parallel. ***Theor.* 20.**

∴ **ABCD** is a par^{m}.

Construction 2. (*With set squares.*) Draw **AB** and **AD** as before; then with set squares through **D** draw **DC** par^{l} to **AB**, and through **B** draw **BC** par^{l} to **AD**.

By construction, **ABCD** is a par^{m} having the required parts.

PROBLEM 13

To construct a square on a given side

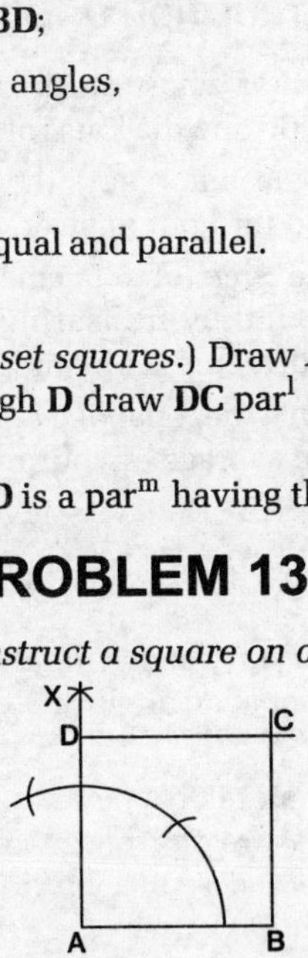

Let **AB** be the given side.

Construction 1. (*With ruler and compasses.*) At **A** draw **AX** perp. to **AB**, and cut off from it **AD** equal to **AB**.

With **B** and **D** as centres, and with radius **AB**, draw two arcs cutting at **C**.

Join **BC**, **DC**.

Then **ABCD** is the required square.

Proof. As in Problem 12, **ABCD** may be shown to be a par^{m}. And since the ∠ **BAD** is a right angle, the figure is a rectangle. Also, by construction all its sides are equal.

∴ **ABCD** is a square.

Construction 2. (*With set squares*) At **A** draw **AX** perp. to **AB**, and cut off from it **AD** equal to **AB**.

Through **D** draw **DC** par^{l} to **AB**, and through **B** draw **BC** par^{l} to **AD** meeting **DC** in **C**.

Then, by construction, **ABCD** is a rectangle. [Def. 3, page 50.]

Also it has the two adjacent sides **AB**, **AD** equal.

∴ it is a square.

EXERCISES

ON THE CONSTRUCTION OF QUADRILATERALS

1. Draw a rhombus each of whose sides is equal to a given straight line **PQ**, which is also to be one diagonal of the figure.

   Ascertain (without measurement) the number of degrees in each angle, giving a reason for your answer.
2. Draw a square on a side of 6.5 cm. Prove theoretically that its diagonals are equal; and by measuring the diagonals to the nearest millimetre test the correctness of your drawing.
3. Construct a square on a diagonal of 5 cm., and measure the lengths of each side. Obtain the average of your results.
4. Draw a parallelogram **ABCD**, having given that one side **AB** = 5.5 cm., and the diagonals **AC**, **BD** are 8 cm., and 6 cm. respectively. Measure **AD**.
5. The diagonals of a certain quadrilateral are equal, (each 6.0 cm.), and they bisect one another at an angle of 60°. Show that *five* independent data are here given.

   Construct the quadrilateral. Name its species; and give a *formal* proof of your answer. Measure the perimeter. If the angle between the diagonals were increased to 90°, by how much per cent would the perimeter be increased?

6. In a quadrilateral **ABCD**,

AB = 5.6 cm., **BC** = 2.5 cm., **CD** = 4.0 cm, and **DA** = 3.3 cm.

Show that the shape of the quadrilateral is settled by these data.

Draw the quadrilateral when (i) **A** = 30°, **A** = 60°. Why does the construction fail when **A** = 100°?

Determine graphically the least value of **A** for which the construction fails.

7. Show how to construct a quadrilateral, having the lengths of the four sides and of one diagonal. What conditions must hold among the data in order that the problem may be possible?

Illustrate your method by constructing a quadrilateral **ABCD**, when

(i) **AB** = 6 cm., **BC** = 3.7 cm., **CD** = 5.7 cm., **DA** = 5.5 cm., and the diagonal **BD** = 6.1 cm. Measure **AC**.

(ii) **AB** = 3.6 cm., **BC** = 7.7 cm., **CD** = 6.8 cm., **DA** = 5.1 cm., and the diagonal **AC** = 8.5 cm. Measure the angles at **B** and **D**.

LOCI

DEFINITION. The locus of a point is the path traced out by it when it moves in accordance with some given law.

***Example* 1.** Suppose the point **P** to move so that its distance from a fixed point **O** is constant (say 1 centimetre).

Then the locus of **P** is evidently the circumference of a circle whose centre is **O** and radius 1 cm.

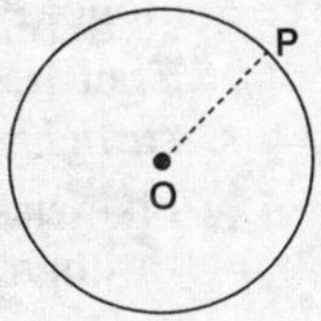

***Example* 2.** Suppose the point **P** moves at a constant distance (say 1 cm.) from a fixed straight line **AB**.

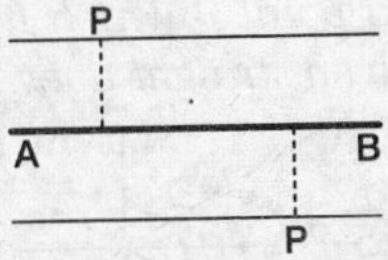

Then the locus of **P** is one or other of two straight lines parallel to **AB**, on either side, and at a distance of 1 cm. from it.

Thus the locus of a point, moving under some given condition, consists of the line or lines to which the point is thereby restricted; provided that the condition is satisfied by every point on such line or lines, and by no other.

When we find a series of points which satisfy the given law, and through which therefore the moving point must pass we are said to **plot the locus** of the point.

PROBLEM 14

To find the locus of a point **P** *which moves so that its distances from two fixed points* **A** *and* **B** *are always equal to one another.*

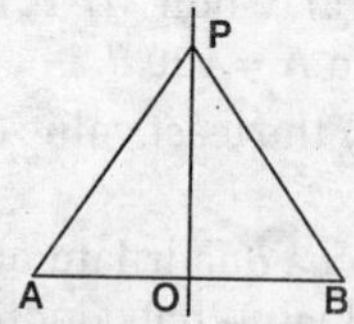

Here the point **P** moves through all positions in which **PA = PB** ;

∴ one position of the moving point is at **O** the middle point of **AB**.

Suppose **P** to be *any* other position of the moving point : that is, let **PA = PB**

Join **OP**.

Then in the Δ^s **POA, POB,**

because { **PO** is common, **OA = OB**, and **PA = PB**, by hypothesis;

∴ the ∠ **POA** = the ∠ **POB**.

Hence **PO** is perpendicular to **AB**. ***Theor.*** **7.**

That is, *every point* **P** *which is equidistant from* **A** *and* **B** *lies on the straight line bisecting* **AB** *at right angles.*

Likewise it may be proved that every point on the perpendicular through **O** is equidistant from **A** and **B**.

This line is therefore the required locus.

PROBLEM 15

To find the locus of a point **P** *which moves so that its perpendicular distances from two given straight lines* **AB**, **CD** *equal to one another.*

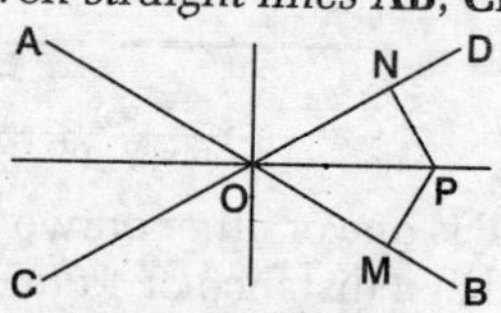

Let **P** be any point such that the perp. **PM** = the perp. **PN**.

Join **P** to **O**, the intersection of **AB, CD.**

Then in the Δ^s **PMO, PNO,**

because { the $\angle^s$ **PMO, PNO** are *right angles*, the hypotenuse **OP** is common, and one side **PM** = one side **PN**;

∴ the triangles are equal in all respects; *Theor.* 18.
so that the ∠ **POM** = the ∠ **PON**.
Hence, if **P** lies within the ∠ **BOD**, it must be on the bisector of that angle;
and, if **P** is within the ∠**AOD** it must be on the bisector of that angle.
It follows that *the required locus is the pair of lines which bisect the angles between* **AB** *and* **CD**.

INTERSECTION OF LOCI

The method of Loci may be used to find the position of a point which is subject to two conditions. For corresponding to each condition there will be a locus on which the required point must lie. Hence all points which are common to these two loci, that is, all the points of intersection of the loci, will satisfy *both* the given conditions.

***Example* 1.** *To find a point equidistant from three given points* **A, B, C,** *which are not in the same straight line.*

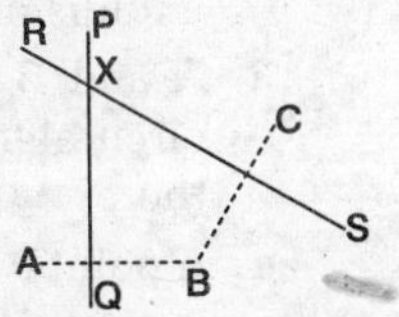

(i) The locus of points equidistant from **A** and **B** is the straight line **PQ**, which bisects **AB** at right angles.

(ii) Similarly, the locus of points equidistant from **B** and **C** is the straight line **RS** which bisects **BC** at right angles.

Hence the point common to **PQ** and **RS** must satisfy both conditions; that is to say, **X** the point of intersection of **PQ** and **RS** will be equidistant from **A, B,** and **C.**

***Example* 2.** *To construct a triangle, having given the base, the altitude and the length of the median which bisects the base.*

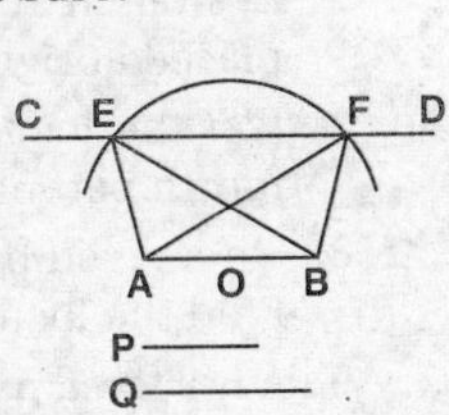

Let **AB** be the given base, and **P** and **Q** the lengths of the altitude and median respectively.
Then the triangle is known if its *vertex* is known.

(i) Draw a straight line **CD** parallel to **AB**, and at a distance from it equal to **P** : *then the required vertex must lie on* **CD**.

(ii) Again, from **O** the middle point of **AB** as centre, with radius equal to **Q**, describe a circle.
then the required vertex must lie on this circle.

Hence any points which are common to **CD** and the circle, satisfy both the given conditions : that is to say, if **CD** intersect the circle in **E, F,** each of the points of intersection might be the vertex of the required triangle. This supposes the length of the median **Q** to be greater than the altitude.

It may happen that the data of the problem are so related to one another that the resulting loci do not intersect. In this case the problem is impossible.

Obs. In examples on the Intersection of Loci the student should make a point of investigating the relations which must exist among the data, in order that the problem may be possible; and he must observe that if under ceriain relations *two* solutions are possible, and under other relations no solution exists, there will always be some *intermediate* relation under which the two solutions combine in a single solution.

EXAMPLES ON LOCI

1. Find the locus of a point which moves so that its distance (measured radially) from the circumference of a given circle is constant.
2. A point **P** moves along a straight line **RQ**; find position in which it is equidistant from two given points **A** and **B**.
3. **A** and **B** are two fixed points within a circle: find points on the circumference equidistant from **A** and **B**. How many such points are there?
4. A point **P** moves along a straight line **RQ**; find the position in which it is equidistant from two given straight lines **AB** and **CD**.
5. **A** and **B** are two fixed points 6 cm. apart. Find by the method of loci two points which are 4 cm. distant from **A**, and 5 cm. from **B**.
6. **AB** and **CD** are two given straight lines. Find points 3 cm. distance from **AB**, and 4 cm. from **CD**. How many solutions are there?
7. A straight rod of given lengths slides between two straight rulers placed at right angles to one another.

   Plot the locus of its middle point; and show that this locus is the fourth part of the circumference of a circle. [See Problem 10.]
8. On a given base as hypotenuse right-angled triangles are described. Find the locus of their vertices.
9. **A is a fixed point, and the point X moves on a fixed** straight line **BC.**

   Plot the locus of **P**, the middle point of **AX**; and *prove* the locus to be a straight line parallel to **BC**.
10. **A** is a fixed point, and the point **X** moves on the circumference of a given circle.

    Plot the locus of **P**, the middle point of **AX**; and *prove* that this locus is a circle. [See Ex. 3, p. 57.]

11. **AB** is a given straight line, and **AX** is the perpendicular drawn from **A** to any straight line passing through **B**. If **BX** revolve about **B**, find the locus of the middle point of **AX**.

12. Two straight lines **OX**, **OY** cut at right angles, and from **P**, a point within the angle **XOY**, perpendiculars **PM**, **PN** are drawn to **OX**, **OY** respectively. Plot the locus of **P** when.

    (i) **PM** + **PN** is constant (= 6 cm., say) :

    (ii) **PM** – **PN** is constant (= 3 cm., say).

    And in each case give a theoretical proof of the result you arrive at experimentally.

13. Two straight lines **OX**, **OY** intersects at right angles at **O**; and from a movable point **P** perpendiculars **PM**, **PN** are drawn to **OX**, **OY**.

    Plot (without proof) the locus of **P**, when.

    (i) **PM** = 2**PN**;

    (ii) **PM** = 3**PN**.

14. Find a point which is at a given distance from a given point and is equidistant from two given parallel straight lines.

    When does this problem admit of two solutions, when of one only, and when is it impossible?

15. **S** is a fixed point 5.1 cm. distant from a given straight line **MX**. Find two points which are 7 cm. distant from **S**, and also 5.5 cm. distant from **MX**.

16. Find a series of point equidistant from a given point **S** and a given straight line **MX**. Draw a curve freehand passing through all the points so found.

17. On a given base construct a triangle of given altitude, having its vertex on a given straight line.

18. Find a point equidistant from the three sides of a triangle.

19. Two straight lines **OX**, **OY** cut at right angles; and **Q** and **R** are points in **OX** and **OY** respectively. Plot the locus of the middle point of **QR**, when.

    (i) **OQ** + **OR** = constant.

    (ii) **OQ** – **OR** = constant.

20. **S** and **S′** are two fixed points. Find a series of points **P** such that

    (i) **SP** + **S′ P** = constant (say 8.9 cm).

    (ii) **SP** – **S′ P** = constant (say 3.8 cm).

    In each case draw a curve freehand passing through all the points so found.

ON THE CONCURRENCE OF STRAIGHT LINES IN A TRIANGLE

I. *The perpendiculars drawn to the sides of a triangle from their middle points are concurrent.*

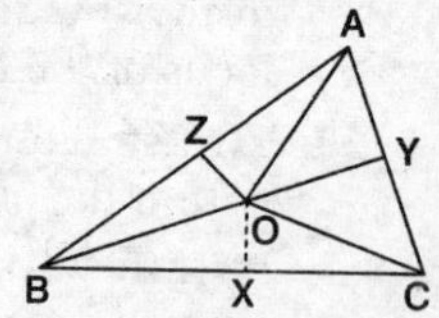

Let **ABC** be a Δ, and **X, Y, Z** the middle points of its sides.

From **Z** and **Y** draw perps. to **AB, AC,** meeting at **O.** *Join* **OX.**

It is required to prove that **OX** *is prep. to* **BC.**

Join **OA, OB, OC.**

Proof. Because **YO** bisects **AC** at right angles,

∴it is the locus of points equidistant from **A** and **C**;

∴ **OA = OC.**

Again, because **ZO** bisects **AB** at right angles,

∴It is the locus of points equidistant from **A** and **B**;

∴ **OA = OB.**

Hence **OB = OC.**

∴**O** is on the locus of points equidistant from **B** and **C**;

that is, **OX** is perp. to **BC.**

Hence the perpendiculars from the mid-points of the sides meet at **O.**

Q.E.D.

II. *The bisectors of the angles are concurrent.*

Let **ABC** be a Δ. Bisect the $\angle^s$ **ABC, BCA** by straight lines which meet at **O.**

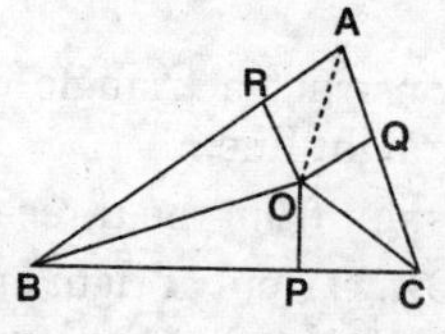

Join **AO**

It is required to prove that **AO** *bisects the* ∠ **BAC.**

From **O** draw **OP, OQ, OR** prep. to the sides of the Δ.

Proof. Because **BO** bisects the ∠**ABC.**

∴it is the locus of points equidistant from **BA** and **BC**;

∴ **OP = OR.**

Similarly **CO** is the locus of points equidistant from **BC** and **CA**;

∴ **OP = OQ.**

Hence **OR = OQ.**

∴ **O** is on the locus of points equidistant from **AB** and **AC**;

that is, **OA** is the bisector of the∠ **BAC**

Hence the bisectors of the angles meet at **O.** **Q.E.D.**

III. *The medians of a triangle concurrent.*

Let **ABC** be a Δ.

Let **BY** and **CZ** be two of its medians, and let them intersect at **O**.

Join **AO**,

and produce it to meet **BC** in **X**.

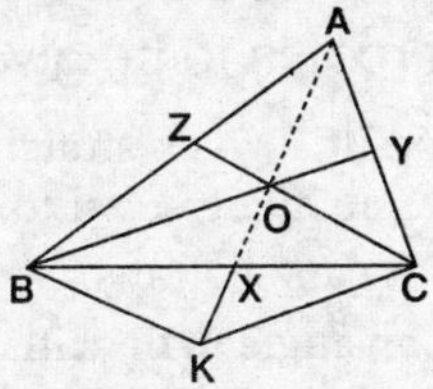

It is required to show that **AX** *is the remaining median of the* Δ.

Through **C** draw **CK** parallel to **BY**;

produce **AX** to meet **CK** at **K**.

Join **BK**.

Proof. In the Δ **AKC**.

because **Y** is the middle point of **AC**, and **YO** is parallel to **CK**,

∴**O** is the middle point of **AK**. ***Theor.* 22.**

Again in the Δ **ABK**,

Since **Z** and **O** are the middle points of **AB**, **AK**,

∴**ZO** is parallel to **BK**,

that is, **OC** is parallel to **BK**,

∴the figure **BKCO** is a par^{m}.

But the diagonals of a par^{m} bisect one another;

∴**X** is the middle point of **BC**.

That is, **AX** is a median of the Δ.

Hence the three medians meet at the point **O** **Q.E.D.**

DEFINITION. The point of intersection of the medians is called the centroid of the triangle.

COROLLARY. *The three medians of a triangle cut one another at a point of trisection, the greater segment in each being towards the angular point.*

For in the above figure it has been proved that **AO** = **OK**,

also that **OX** is half of **OK**;

∴**OX** is half of **OA**:

that is, **OX** is one third of **AX**.

Similarly **OY** is one third of **BY**

and **OZ** is one third of **CZ**. **Q.E.D.**

By means of this Corollary it may be shown that in any triangle the shorter median bisects the greater side.

NOTE. It will be proved hereafter that *the perpendiculars drawn from the vertices of a triangle to the opposite sides are concurrent.*

MISCELLANEOUS PROBLEMS

(A theoretical proof is to be given in each case)

1. **A** is a given point, and **BC** a given straight line. From **A** draw a straight line to make with **BC** an angle equal to a given angle **X**.

   How many such lines can be drawn?
2. Draw the bisector of an angle **AOB**, without using the vertex **O** in your construction.
3. **P** is a given point within the angle **AOB**. Draw through **P** a straight line terminated by **OA** and **OB**, and bisected at **P**.
4. **OA**, **OB**, **OC** are three straight lines meeting at **O**. Draw a transversal terminated by **OA** and **OC**, and bisected by **OB**.
5. Through a given point **A** draw a straight line so that the part intercepted between two given parallels may be of given length.

   When does this problem admit of two solutions? When of only one? And when is it impossible?
6. In a triangle **ABC** inscribe a rhombus having one of its angles coinciding with the angle **A**.
7. Use the properties of an equilateral triangle to trisect a given straight line.

(*Construction of Triangles*)

8. Construct a triangle, having given
   (i) The middle points of the three sides.
   (ii) The lengths of two sides and of the median which bisects the third side.
   (iii) The lengths of one side and the medians which bisect the other two sides.
   (iv) The lengths of the three medians.

PART II

ON AREAS

DEFINITIONS

1. The **altitude** (or **height**) of a parallelogram with reference to a given side as base, is the perpendicular distance between the base and the opposite side.
2. The **altitude** (or **height**) of a triangle with reference to a given side as base, is the perpendicular distance of the opposite vertex from the base.

NOTE. It is clear that *parallelograms or triangles which are between the same parallels have the same altitude.*

For let **AP** and **DQ** be the altitudes of the Δ^s **ABC, DEF**, which are between the same parallels **BF, GH**.

Then the fig. **APQD** is evidently a rectangle;

$\therefore$ **AP = DQ**.

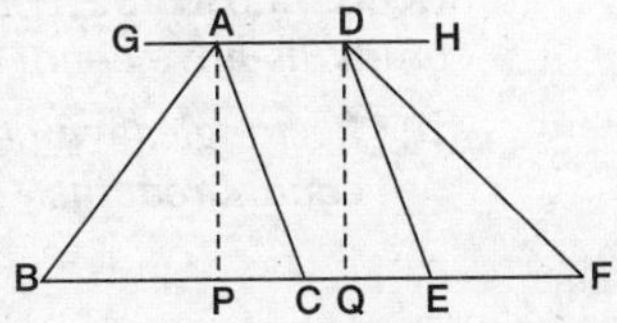

3. The **area** of a figure is the amount of surface contained within its bounding lines.
4. Hence a **square centimetre** is the area of a square drawn on a side one centimetre in length.
   The terms *square metre, square millimetre* are to be understood in the same sense.

5. Thus the **unit of area** is the area of a square on a side of unit length.

THEOREM 23

Area of a rectangle. *If the number of units in the length of a rectangle is multiplied by the number of units in its breadth, the product gives the number of square units in the area.*

Let **ABCD** represent a rectangle whose length **AB** is 5 cm., and whose breadth **AD** is 4 cm.

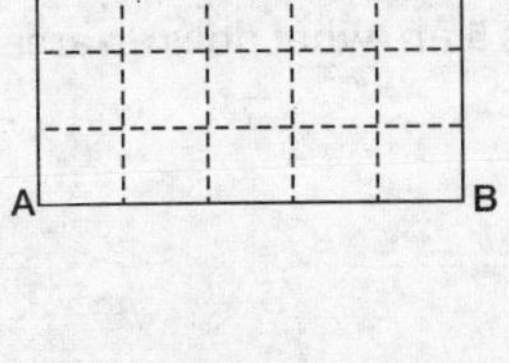

Divide **AB** into 5 equal parts, and **BC** into 4 equal parts, and through the points of division of each line draw parallels to the other.

The rectangle **ABCD** is now divided into compartments, each of which represents one square centimetre.

Now there are 4 rows, each containing 5 squares,

∴ the rectangle contains 5×4 square centimetres.

Similarly, if the length $= a$ linear units, and the breadth $= b$ linear units.

the rectangle contains **ab** *units of* **area.**

And if each side of a square $= a$ linear units,

the square contains $\mathbf{a}^2$ *units of* **area.**

These statements may be thus abridged:

the area of a rectangle = length × breadth ...(i),

the area of a square = $(side)^2$ ...(ii). **Q.E.D.**

COROLLARIES. (i) *Rectangles which have equal lengths and equal breadths have equal areas.*

(ii) *Rectangles which have equal areas and equal lengths have also equal breadths.*

NOTATION

The rectangle **ABCD** is said to be **contained** by **AB, AD**; for these adjacent sides fix its size and shape.

A rectangle whose adjacent sides are **AB, AD** is denoted by *rect.* **AB, AD**, or simply **AB × AD**.

A square drawn on the side **AB** is denoted by *sq. on* **AB**, or $\mathbf{AB}^2$.

EXERCISES

(*On Tables of Length and Area*)

1. Draw a figure to show *why*

(i) 1 sq. cm. $= 10^2$ sq. mm.

(ii) 1 sq. m. $= 100^2$ sq. cm.

2. Draw a figure to show that the square on a straight line is four times the square on half the line.

3. Use squared paper to show that the square on 1 cm. $= 10^2$ times the square on 0.1 cm.

4. If 1 cm. represents 5 m., what does an area of 6 square cm. represent?

EXTENSION OF THEOREM 23

The proof of Theorem 23 here given supposes that the length and breadth of the given rectangle are expressed by *whole numbers*, but the formula holds good when the length and breadth are fractional. This may be illustrated thus :

Suppose the length and breadth are 3.2 cm. and 2.4; we shall show that the area is (3.2×2.4) sq. cm.

For length $= 3.2$ cm. $= 32$ mm.

breadth $= 2.4$ cm. $= 24$ cm.

$\therefore$ area $= (32 \times 24)$ sq. mm. $= \dfrac{32 \times 24}{10^2}$ sq. cm.

$= (3.2 \times 2.4)$ sq. cm.

EXERCISES

(*On the Area of a Rectangle*)

Draw on squared paper the rectangles of which the length (a) and breadth (b) are given below. Calculate the areas, and verify by the actual counting of squares.

1. $a = 5$ cm., $b = 7.5$ cm.

2. $a = 3$ cm., $b = 8$ cm.

3. $a = 1.5$ cm., $b = 7$ cm.

4. $a = 5$ cm., $b = 3$ cm.

5. $a = 4.5$ cm., $b = 3$ cm.

6. $a = 3.2$ cm., $b = 5.5$ cm.

Calculate the areas of the rectangles in which

7. $a = 18$ metres, $b = 11$ metres.

8. $a = 7$ m., $b = 7$ cm.

9. $a = 2.5$ km., $b = 4$ metres.

10. $a = \frac{1}{4}$ km., $b = 1$ m.

11. The area of rectangle is 30 sq. cm., and its length is 6 cm. Find the breadth. Draw the rectangle on squared paper; and verify your work by counting the squares.

12. Find the length of a rectangle whose area is 3.9 sq. cm., and breadth 1.5 cm. Draw the rectangle on squared paper; and verify your work by counting the squares.

13. (i) When you treble the length of a rectangle without altering its breadth, how many times do you multiply the area?

(ii) When you treble both length and breadth, how many times do you multiply the area?

Draw a figure to illustrate your answers; and state a general rule.

14. In a plan of a rectangular garden the length and breadth are 3.6 cm. and 2.5 cm., one cm. standing for 10 metres. Find the area of the garden.

If the area is increased by 300 sq. m., the breadth remaining the same, what will the new length be? And how many centimetres will represent it on your plan?

15. Find the area of a rectangular enclosure of which a plan (scale 1 cm. to 20 metres) measures 6.5 cm. by 4.5 cm.

16. The area of a rectangle is 1440 sq. m. If in a plan the sides of the rectangle are 3.2 cm. and 4.5 cm., on what scale is the plan drawn?

17. The area of a rectangular field is 52000 sq. m. On a plan of this, drawn to the scale of 1 cm. 100 m., the length is 3.25 cm. What is the breadth?

Calculate the areas of the enclosures of which plans are given below. All the angles are right angles, and the dimensions are marked in metres.

Calculate the areas represented by the shaded parts of the following plans. The dimensions are marked in metres.

18.

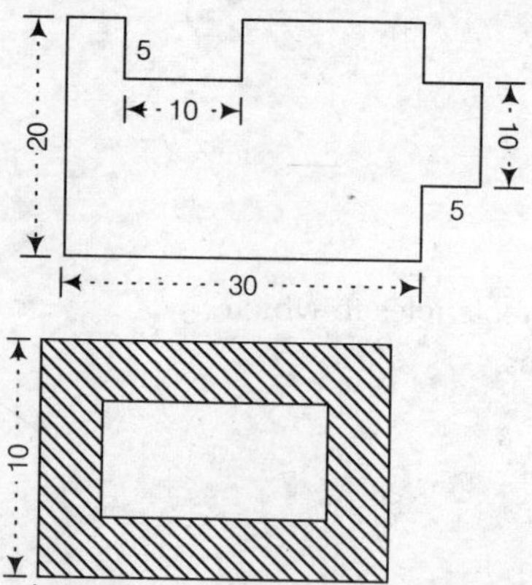

19.

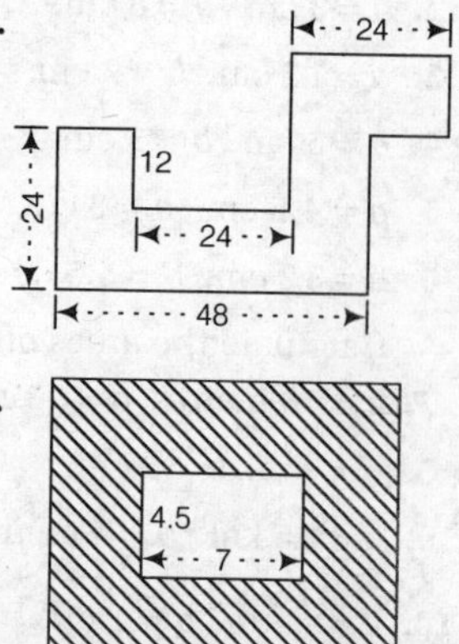

20.

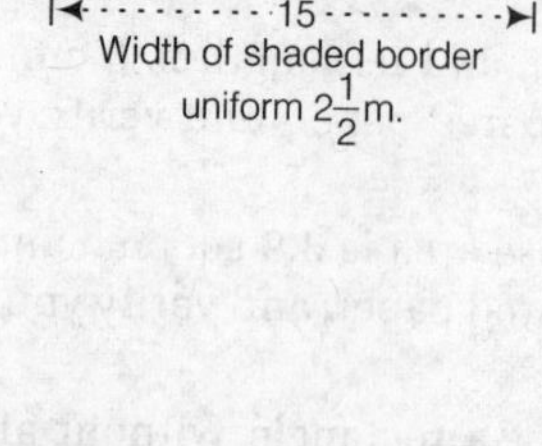

Width of shaded border uniform $2\frac{1}{2}$m.

21.

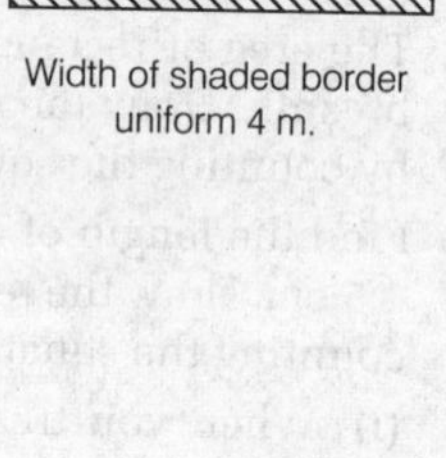

Width of shaded border uniform 4 m.

22.

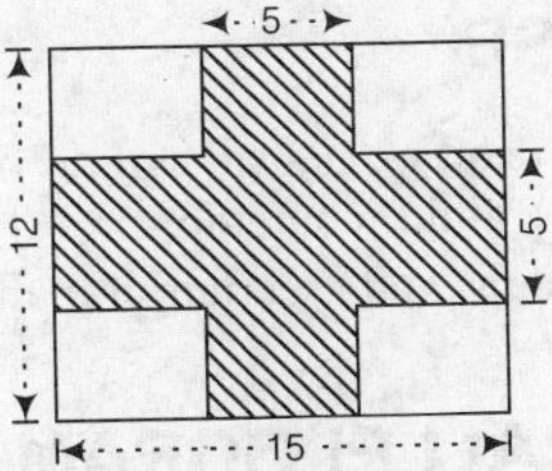

23.

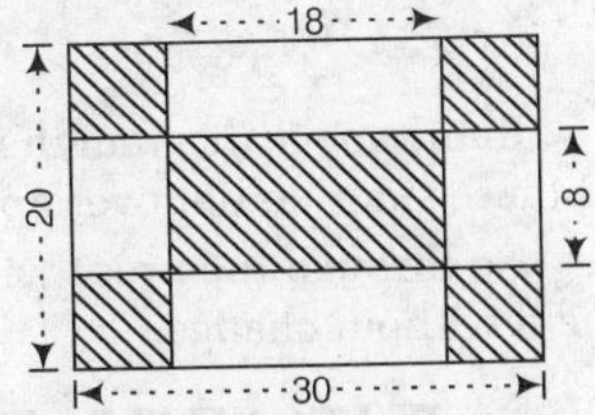

24.

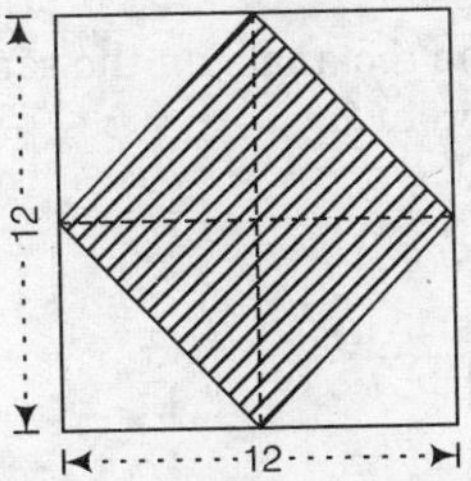

25.

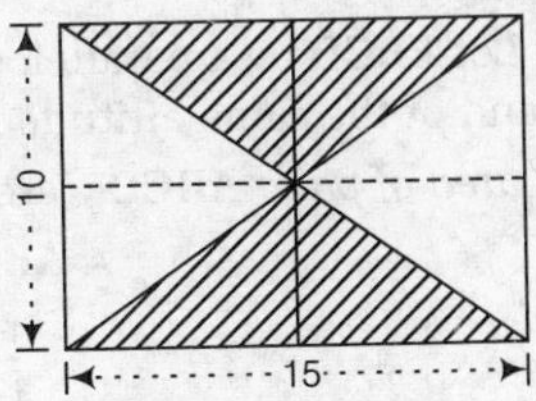

THEOREM 24. [Euclid I. 35]

Parallelograms on the same base and between the same parallels are equal in area.

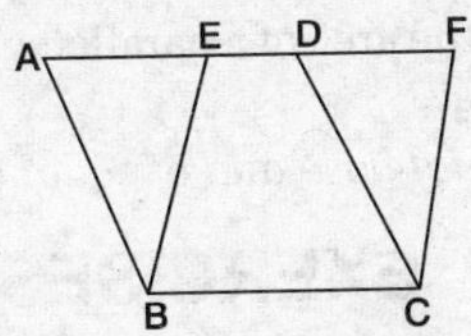

Let the par^{ms} **ABCD, EBCF** be on the same base **BC**, and between the same par^{ls} **BC, AF**.

It is required to prove that

the par^{m} **ABCD** = *the par*^{m} **EBCF** *in area.*

Proof. In the Δ^s **FDC, EAB**,

because { **DC** = the opp. side **AB**; *Theor.* **21.**
the ext. ∠**FDC** = the int. opp. ∠**EAB**; *Theor.* **14.**
the int. ∠**DFC** = ext. ∠**AEB**. }

∴ the Δ **FDC** = the Δ **EAB**. *Theor.* **17.**

Now, if from the whole fig. **ABCF** the Δ**FDC** is taken, the remainder is the par^{m} **ABCD**.

And if from the whole fig. **ABCF** the Δ**EAB** is taken, the remainder is the par^{m} **EBCF**.

∴ these remainders are equal;

that is, the par^{m} **ABCD** = the par^{m} **EBCF**. **Q.E.D.**

EXERCISE

In the above diagram the sides **AD**, **EF** overlap. Draw diagrams in which (i) these sides do not overlap; (ii) the ends **E** and **D** coincide.

Go through the proof with these diagrams, and ascertain if it applies to them without change.

THE AREA OF A PARALLELOGRAM

Let **ABCD** be a parallelogram, and **ABEF** the rectangle on the same base **AB** and of the same altitude **BE** . Then by Theorem 24,

area of par^{m} **ABCD** = area of rect. **ABEF**

= **AB** × **BE** = *base* × *altitude.*

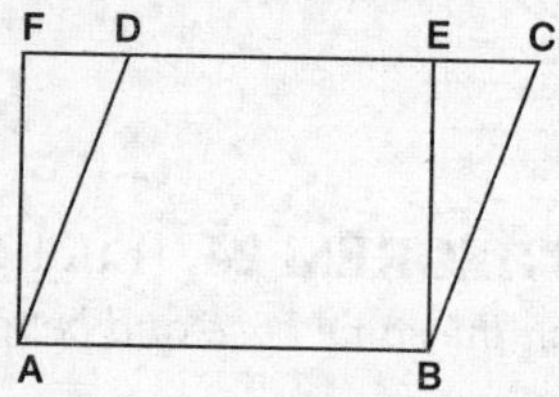

COROLLARY. Since the area of a parallelogram depends only on its base and altitude, it follows that

Parallelograms on equal base and of equal altitudes are equal in area.

EXERCISES

(*Numerical and Graphical*)

1. Find the area of parallelograms in which
   (i) the base = 5.5 cm., and the height = 4 cm.
   (ii) the base = 6.1 cm., and the height = 3.8 cm.
2. Draw a parallelogram **ABCD** having given **AB** = 6.4 cm, **AD** = 3.8 cm., and the ∠ **A** = 65°. Draw and measure the perpendicular from **D** on **AB**, and hence calculate the approximate area. Why *approximate*? Again calculate the area from the length of **AD** and the perpendicular on it from **B**. Obtain the average of the two results.
3. Two adjacent sides of a parallelogram are 30 metres and 25 metres; and the included angle is 50°. Draw a plan 1 cm representing 5 metres; and by measuring each altitude make two independent calculations of the area. Give the average result.
4. The area of a parallelogram **ABCD** is 27.3 sq. cm., and the base **AB** is 7 cm. Find the height. If **AD** = 5 cm., draw the parallelogram.

5. Each side of a rhombus is 5.1 cm., and its area is 25 sq. cm. Calculate an altitude. Hence draw the rhombus, and measure one of its acute angles.

THEOREM 25

The Area of a Triangle. *The area of a triangle is half the area of the rectangle on the same base and having the same altitude.*

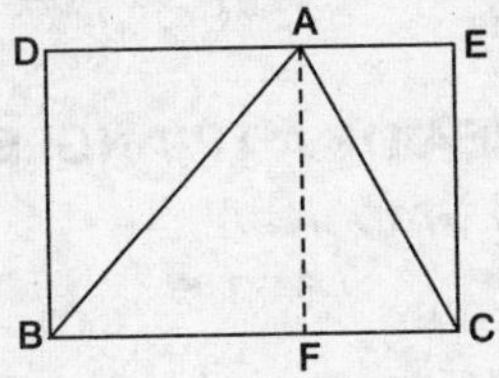

Fig. 1.

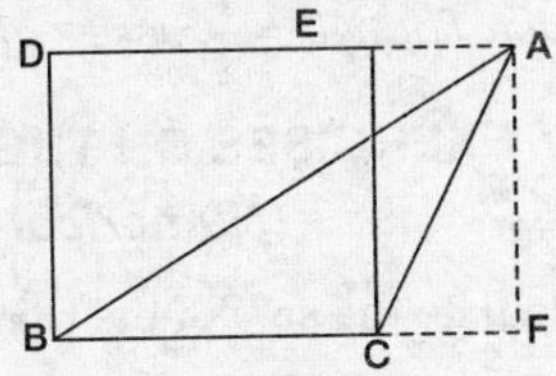

Fig. 2.

Let **ABC** be a triangle, and **BDEC** a rectangle on the same base **BC** and with the same altitude **AF**.

It is required to prove that the Δ **ABC** *is half the rectangle* **BDEC.**

Proof. Since **AF** is perp. to **BC**, each of the figures **DF**, **EF** is a rectangle.

Because the diagonal **AB** bisects the rectangle **DF**,

∴ the Δ **ABF** is half the rectangle **DF**.

Similarly, the Δ **AFC** is half the rectangle **FE**.

∴ adding these results Fig. 1, and taking the difference in Fig. 2,

the Δ **ABC** is half rectangle **BDEC**. **Q.E.D.**

COROLLARY. *A triangle is half any parallelogram on the same base and between the same parallels.*

For the Δ **ABC** is half the rect. **BCED.**

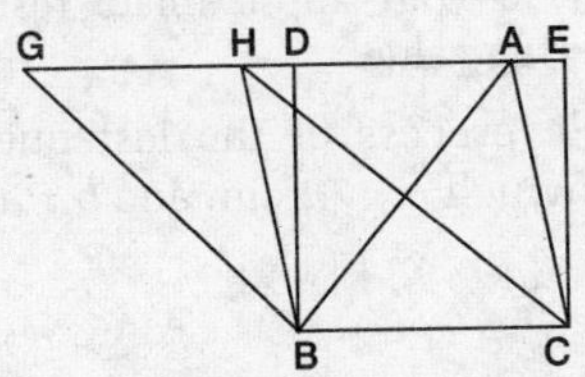

And the rect. **BCED** = any par^{m} **BCHG** on the same base and between the same par^{ls}

∴ the Δ **ABC** is half the par^{m} **BCHG**.

THE AREA OF A TRIANGLE

If **BC** and **AF** respectively contain a units and p units of length, the rectangle **BDEC** contains ap units of area.

$\therefore$ the area of the Δ**ABC** $= \frac{1}{2}\, ap$ units of area.

This result may be stated thus :

Area of a Triangle $= \frac{1}{2}$. *base* $\times$ *altitude.*

EXERCISES ON THE AREA OF A TRIANGLE

(*Numerical and Graphical*)

1. Calculate the area of the triangles in which

(i) the base = 24 m., the height = 15 m.

(ii) the base = 4.8 cm., the height = 3.5 cm.,

(iii) the base = 160 m., the height = 125 m.

2. Draw triangles from the following data. In each case draw and measure the altitude with reference to a given side as base : hence calculate the approximate area.

(i) $a = 8.4$ cm., $b = 6.8$ cm., $c = 4.0$ cm,

(ii) $b = 5.0$ cm., $c = 6.8$ cm., **A** $= 65°$.

(iii) $a = 6.5$ cm., **B** $= 52°$, **C** $= 76°$.

3. **ABC** is a triangle *right-angled* at **C**; show that its area $= \frac{1}{2}$ **BC** $\times$ **CA**.

Given $a = 6$ cm., $b = 5$ cm., calculate the area.

Draw the triangle and measure the hypotenuse c; draw and measure the perpendicular from **C** on the hypotenuse; hence calculate the approximate area.

NOTE. The error in your approximate result, and express it has a percentage of the true value.

4. Repeat the whole process of the last question for a right-angled triangle **ABC**, in which $a = 7.1$ cm. and $b = 11.4$ cm; **C** being the right angle as before.

5. In a triangle, given

(i) Area = 800 sq. cm., base = 1 m. 60 cm.; calculate the altitude.

(ii) Area = 10.4 sq. cm., altitude = 1.6 cm.; calculate the base.

6. Construct a triangle **ABC**, having given $a = 3$ cm., $b = 2.8$ cm., $c = 2.6$ cm. Draw and measure the perpendicular from **A** on **BC**; hence calculate the approximate area.

THEOREM 26. [Euclid I. 37]

Triangles on the same base and between the same parallels (hence, of the same altitude) are equal in area.

Let the Δ^s **ABC, GBC** be on the same base **BC** and between the same par[ls] **BC, AG.**

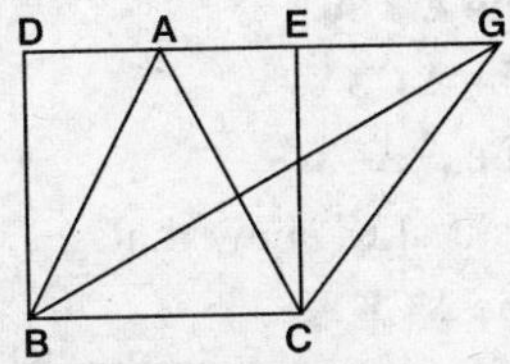

It is required to prove that the Δ **ABC** = the Δ **GBC** *in area.*

Proof. If **BCED** is the rectangle on the base **BC**, and between the same parallels as the given triangles,

the Δ **ABC** is half the rect. **BCED**; *Theor.* **25.**

also the Δ **GBC** is half the rect. **BCED**;

∴ the Δ **ABC** = the Δ **GBC**.

Similarly, *triangles on equal bases and of equal altitudes are equal in area.* **Q.E.D.**

THEOREM 27. [Euclid I. 39]

If two triangles are equal in area, and stand on the same base and on the same side of it, they are between the same parallels.

Let the Δ^s **ABC, GBC**, standing on the same base **BC**, be equal in area; and let **AF** and **GH** be their altitudes.

It is required to prove that **AG** *and* **BC** ***are*** par[l].

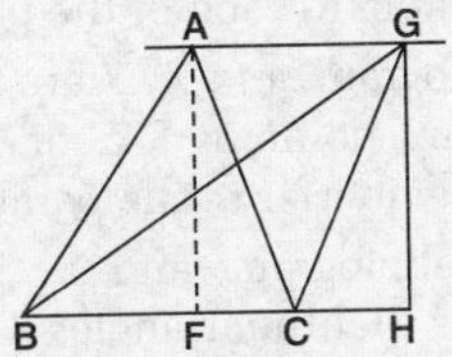

Proof. The Δ **ABC** is half the rectangle contained by **BC** and **AF**; and the Δ **GBC** is half the rectangle contained by **BC** and **GH**;

∴ the rect. **BC, AF** = the rect. **BC, GH**;

∴ **AF** = **GH** ***Theor.*** 23, ***Cor.*** 2.

Also **AF** and **GH** are par[l];

hence **AG** and **FH**, that is **BC**, are par[l]. **Q.E.D.**

EXERCISES ON THE AREA OF A TRIANGLE

(*Theoretical*)

1. **ABC** is a triangle and **XY** is drawn parallel to the base **BC**, cutting the other sides at **X** and **Y**. Join **BY** and **CX**; and show that

   (i) the Δ **XBC** = the Δ **YBC**;

   (ii) the Δ **BXY** = the Δ **CXY**;

   (iii) the Δ **ABY** = the Δ **ACX**.

   If **BY** and **CX** cut at **K**, shew that

   (iv) the Δ **BKX** = the Δ **CKY**.

2. Show that a median of a triangle divides it into two parts of equal area.

   How would you divide a triangle into *three* equal parts by straight lines drawn from its vertex?

3. Prove that a parallelogram is divided by its diagonals into four triangles of equal area.

4. **ABC** is a triangle whose base **BC** is bisected at **X**. If **Y** is any point in the median **AX**, show that the Δ **ABY** = the Δ **ACY** in area.

5. **ABCD** is a parallelogram, and **BP**, **DQ** are the perpendiculars from **B** and **D** on the diagonal **AC**. Show that **BP** = **DQ**.

   Hence if **X** is any point in **AC**, or **AC** produced,

   prove (i) the Δ **ADX** = the Δ **ABX**;

   (ii) the Δ **CDX** = the Δ **CBX**.

6. Prove by means of Theorems 26 and 27 that *the straight line joining the middle points of two sides of a triangle is parallel to the third side.*

7. The straight line which joins the middle points of the oblique sides of a trapezium is parallel to each of the parallel sides.

8. **ABCD** is a parallelogram, and **X**, **Y** are the middle points of the sides **AD**, **BC**; if **Z** is any point in **XY**, or **XY** produced, show that the triangle **AZB** is one quarter of the parallelogram **ABCD**.

9. If **ABCD** is a parallelogram, and **X**, **Y** any points in **DC** and **AD** respectively : show that the triangles **AXB**, **BYC** are equal in area.

10. **ABCD** is a parallelogram, and **P** is any point within it; show that the sum of the triangles **PAB**, **PCD** is equal to half the parallelogram.

EXERCISES ON THE AREA OF A TRIANGLE

(*Numerical and Graphical*)

1. The sides of a triangular field are 370 m. 200 m., and 190 m. Draw a plan (scale 1 cm. to 50 m.). Draw and measure an altitude; hence calculate the approximate area of the field in square metres.

2. Two sides of a triangular enclosure are 124 metres and 144 metres respectively, and the included angle is observed to be 45°. Draw a plan (scale 1 cm. to 20 metres). Make any necessary measurement, and calculate the approximate area.
3. In a triangle **ABC**, given that the area $= 6.6$ sq. cm., and the base **BC** $= 5.5$ cm., find the altitude. Hence determine the locus of the vertex **A**.

   If in addition to the above data, **BA** $= 2.6$ cm., construct the triangle; and measure **CA**.
4. In a triangle **ABC**, given *area* $= 19.9$ sq. cm., and $a = 7.7$ cm. Find the altitude, and the locus of **A**. Given **C** $= 68°$, construct the triangle and measure b.
5. **ABC** is a triangle in which **BC**, **BA** have constant lengths 6 cm. and 5 cm. If **BC** is fixed, and **BA** revolves about **B**, trace the changes in the area of the triangle as the angle **B** increases from 0° to 180°.

   Answer this question by drawing a series of triangles, increasing **B** by increments of 30°. Find the area in each case and tabulate the results.

(*Theoretical*)

6. If two triangles have two sides of one respectively equal to two sides of the other, and the angles contained by those sides *supplementary*, show that the triangles are equal in *area*. Can such triangles ever be *identically* equal.
7. Show how to draw on the base of a given triangle an isosceles triangle of equal area.
8. If the middle points of the sides of a quadrilateral are joined in order, prove that the *parallelogram* so formed [see Ex. 7, P.57.] is half the quadrilateral.
9. **ABC** is a triangle, and **R, Q** the middle points of the sides **AB**, **AC**; show that if **BQ** and **CR** intersect in **X**, the triangle **BXC** is equal to the quadrilateral **AQXR**.
10. Two triangles of equal area stand on the same base but on opposite sides of it : show that the straight line joining their vertices is bisected by the base, or by the base produced.

    [The method given below may be omitted from a first course. In any case it must be postponed till Theorem 29 has been read.]

The Area of a Triangle. *Given the three sides of a triangle, to calculate the area.*

EXAMPLE. *Find the area of a triangle whose sides measure* 21 m., 17 m., *and* 10 m.

Let **ABC** represent the given triangle.

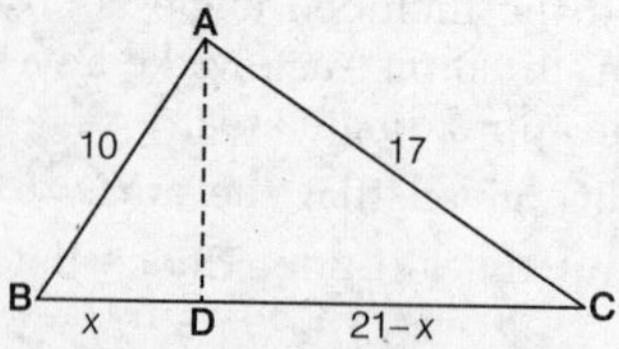

Draw **AD** perp. to **BC**, and denote **AD** by *p*.

We shall first find the length of **BD**

Let **BD** = x metres; then **DC** = $21 - x$ metres.

From the right-angled Δ **ADB**, we have by Theorem 29

$$AD^2 = AB^2 - BD^2 = 10^2 - x^2.$$

And from the right-angled Δ **ADC**,

$$AD^2 = AC^2 - DC^2 = 17^2 - (21 - x)^2;$$

$$\therefore\ 10^2 - x^2 = 17^2 - (21 - x)^2$$

or $$100 - x^2 = 289 - 441 + 42x - x^2;$$

whence $x = 6$.

Again, $$AD^2 = AB^2 - BD^2;$$

or $$p^2 = 10^2 - 6^2 = 64;$$

∴ $$p = 8.$$

Now *Area of triangle* $= \frac{1}{2} \cdot$ *base* × *altitude*

$$= \left(\frac{1}{2} \times 21 \times 8\right) \text{ sq. m.} = 84 \text{ sq. m.}$$

EXERCISES

Find by the above method the areas of the triangles, whose sides are as follows :

1. 20 m., 13 m., 11 m.

2. 15 cm., 14 cm., 13 cm.

3. 21 m., 20 m., 13 m.

4. 30 cm., 25 cm., 11 cm.

5. 37 m., 30 m., 13 m.

6. 51 m., 37 m., 20 m.

7. If the given sides are a, b and c units in length, prove

(i) $x = \dfrac{a^2 + c^2 - b^2}{2a}$;

(ii) $p^2 = c^2 - \left\{\dfrac{a^2 + c^2 - b^2}{2a}\right\}^2$;

(iii) $\Delta = \frac{1}{4}\sqrt{(a + b + c)(-a + b + c)(a - b + c)(a + b - c)}$.

THE AREA OF QUADRILATERALS

THEOREM 28

To find the area of (i) *a trapezium.*

(ii) *any quadrilateral.*

(i) Let **ABCD** be a trapezium, having the sides **AB**, **CD** parallel. Join **BD**, and from **C** and **D** draw perpendiculars **CF**, **DE** to **AB**.

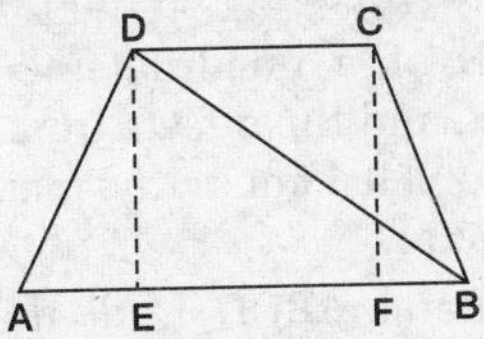

Let the parallel sides **AB**, **CD** measure a and b units of length, and let the height **CF** contain h units.

Then the area of **ABCD** = Δ**ABD** + Δ**DBC**

$$= \frac{1}{2}\,\mathbf{AB}\cdot\mathbf{DE} + \frac{1}{2}\,\mathbf{DC}\cdot\mathbf{CF}$$

$$= \frac{1}{2}ah + \frac{1}{2}bh = \frac{h}{2}(a+b).$$

That is *the area of a trapezium* $= \frac{1}{2}$ *height* × (*the sum of the parallel sides*).

(ii) Let **ABCD** be any quadrilateral. Draw a diagonal **AC**; and from **B** and **D** draw perpendiculars **BX**, **DY** to **AC**. These perpendiculars are called **offsets.**

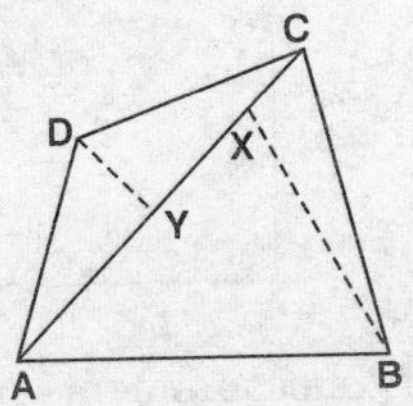

If **AC** contains d units of length, and **BX**, **DY** p and q units respectively,

the area of the quad[1] **ABCD** = Δ**ABC** + Δ**ADC**

$$= \frac{1}{2}\,\mathbf{AC}\cdot\mathbf{BX} + \frac{1}{2}\,\mathbf{AC}\cdot\mathbf{DY} = \frac{1}{2}dp + \frac{1}{2}dq = \frac{1}{2}d(p+q).$$

That is to say,

the area of a quadrilateral $= \frac{1}{2}$ *diagonal* × (*sum of offsets*).

EXERCISES

(*Numerical and Graphical*)

1. Find the area of the trapezium in which the two parallel sides are 4.7 cm. and 3.3 cm., and the height 1.5 cm.
2. In a quadrilateral **ABCD**, the diagonal **AC** = 17 m., and the offsets from it to **B** and **D** are 11 m. and 9 m. Find the area.
3. In a plan **ABCD** of a quadrilateral enclosure, the diagonal **AC** measures 8.2 cm., and the offsets from it to **B** and **D** are 3.4 cm. and 2.6 cm. respectively. If 1 cm. in the plan represents 5 metres, find the area of the enclosure.
4. Draw a quadrilateral **ABCD** from the adjoining rough plan, the dimensions being given in centimetres.

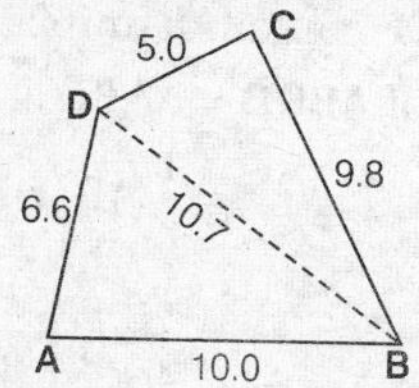

Draw and measure the offsets to **A** and **C** from the diagonal **BD** ; and hence calculate the area of the quadrilateral.

5. Draw a quadrilateral **ABCD** from the details given in the adjoining plan. The dimensions are to be in centimetres.

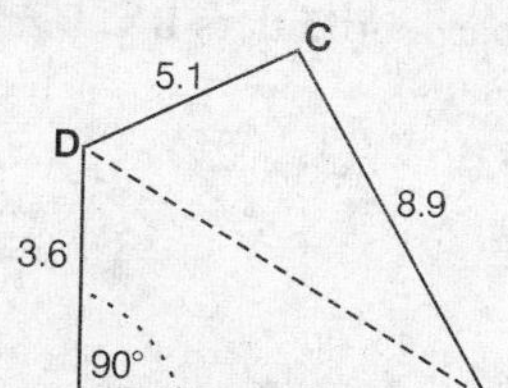

Make any necessary measurements of your figure, and calculate its area.

6. Draw a trapezium **ABCD** from the following data : **AB** and **CD** are the parallel sides. **AB** = 10.2 cm.; **AD** = **BC** = 5.1 cm; the $\angle$**A** = the $\angle$**B** = 60°. Make any necessary measurements, and calculate the area.
7. Draw a trapezium **ABCD** in which **AB** and **CD** are the parallel sides ; and **AB** = 9 cm., **CD** = 3 cm., and **AD** = **BC** = 5 cm . Make any necessary measurement, and calculate the area.

8. From the formula area *af quad*[1] $= \frac{1}{2}$ diag. × (*sum of offsets*) show that, if the diagonals are at *right angles, area* $= \frac{1}{2}$ (*product of diagonals*).

9. Given the lengths of the diagonals of a quadrilateral, and the angle between them, prove that the area is the same wherever they intersect.

THE AREA OF ANY RECTILINEAL FIGURE

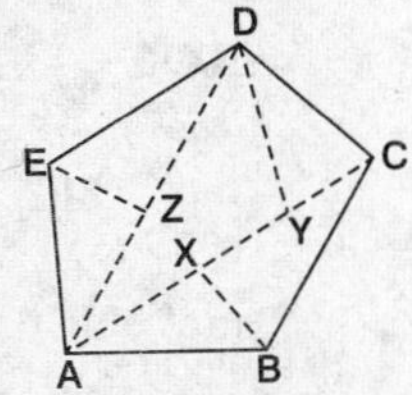

1st **METHOD.** A rectilineal figure may be divided into triangles whose areas can be separately calculated from suitable measurements. The sum of these areas will be the area of the given figure.

Example. The measurements required to find the area of the figure **ABCDE** are **AC**, **AD** and the offsets **BX**, **DY**, **EZ**.

2nd **METHOD.** The area of a rectilineal figure is also found by taking a base-line (**AD** in the diagram below) and offsets from it. These divide the figure into *right-angled* triangles and *right-angled* trapeziums, whose areas may be found after measuring the offsets and the various sections of the base-line.

Example. Find the area of the enclosure **ABCDEF** from the plan and measurements tabulated below.

	Metres	
	AD = 56	
VC = 12	AV = 50	
	AZ = 40	ZE = 18
YB = 20	AY = 18	
	AX = 10	XF = 15

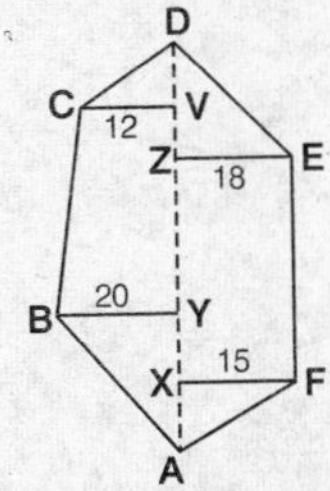

The measurements are made from **A** along the base line to the points from which the offsets spring.

Here

	Sq. m.	Sq. m.
$\Delta AXF = \frac{1}{2} . AX \times XF$	$= \frac{1}{2} \times 10 \times 15$	$= 75$
$\Delta AYB = \frac{1}{2} . AY \times YB$	$= \frac{1}{2} \times 18 \times 20$	$= 180$
$\Delta DZE = \frac{1}{2} . DZ \times ZE$	$= \frac{1}{2} \times 16 \times 28$	$= 144$
$\Delta DVC = \frac{1}{2} . DV \times VC$	$= \frac{1}{2} \times 6 \times 12$	$= 36$
trap^m $XFEZ = \frac{1}{2} . XZ \times (XF + ZE)$	$= \frac{1}{2} \times 30 \times 33$	$= 495$
trap^m $YBCV = \frac{1}{2} . YV \times (YB + VC)$	$= \frac{1}{2} \times 32 \times 32$	$= 512$

∴ by addition, the fig. **ABCDEF** = 1442sq. m.

EXERCISES

1. Calculate the areas of the figures (i) and (ii) from the plans and dimensions (in cms.) given below.

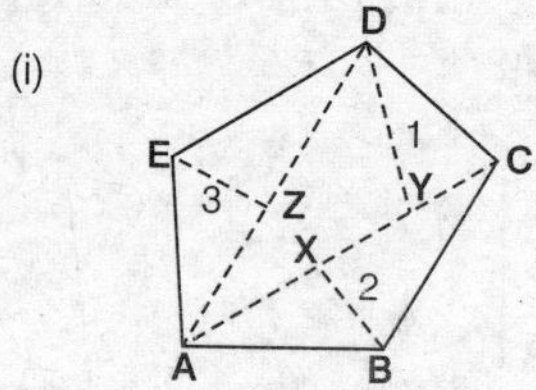

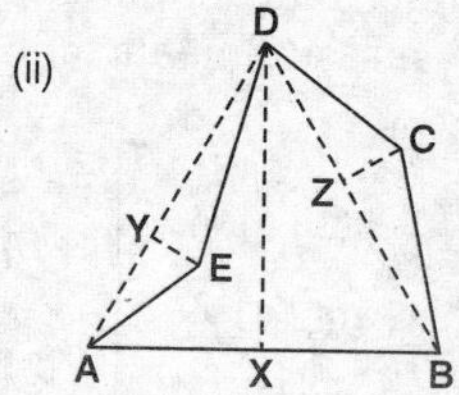

AC = 6 cm., **AD** = 5 cm.
AB = **BD** = **DA** = 6 cm.

Lengths of offsets figured **EY** = **CZ** = 1 cm. in diagram. **DX** = 5.2 cm.

2. Draw full size the figures whose plans and dimensions are given below; and calculate the area in each case

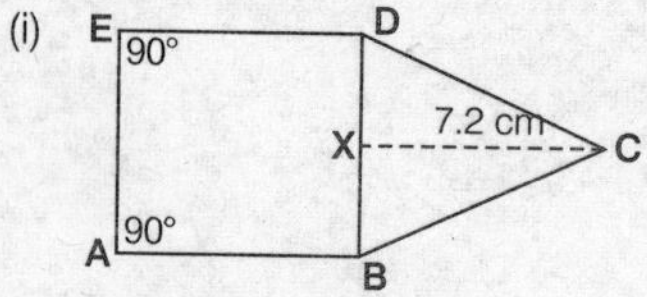

The fig. is equilateral: each side is 8.3 cm.

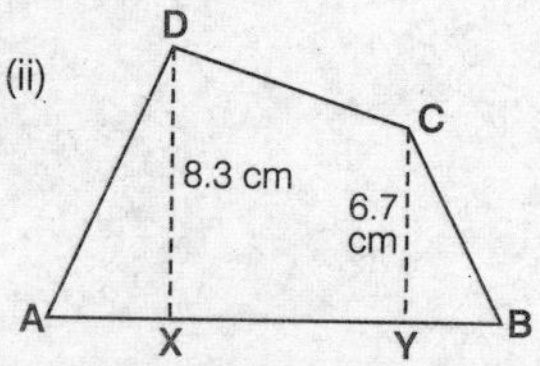

AX = 4.2 cm., **XY** = 9.2 cm., **YB** = 5.8 cm.

3. Find the area of the figure **ABCDEF** from the following measurements and draw a plan in which 1 cm. represents 20 metres.

	METRES.	
	to **C**	
	180	
80 to **D**	150	
40 to **E**	120	50 to **B**
60 to **F**	50	
	From **A**	

THE PLAN.

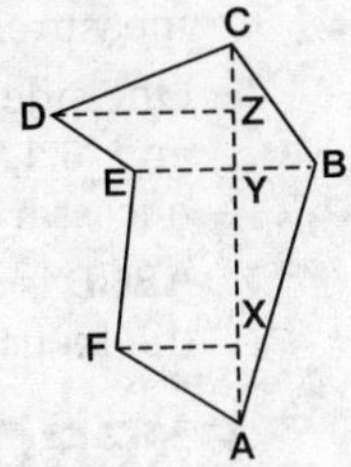

EXERCISES ON QUADRILATERALS

(*Thoeretical*)

1. **ABCD** is a rectangle, and **PQRS** the figure formed by joining in order the middle points of the sides.

   Prove (i) that **PQRS** is a rhombus ;

   (ii) that the area of **PQRS** is half that of **ABCD**.

   Hence show that *the area of a rhombus is half the product of its diagonals.*

   Is this true of any quadrilateral whose diagonals cut at right angles ? Illustrate your answer by a diagram.

2. Prove that a parallelogram is bisected by any straight line which passes through the middle point of one of ite diagonals.

   Hence show how a parallelogram **ABCD** may be bisected by a straight line drawn

   (i) through a given point **P** ;

   (ii) perpendicular to the side **AB** ;

   (iii) parallel to a given **QR**.

3. In the trapezium **ABCD**, **AB** is parallel to **DC**; and **X** is the middle point of **BC**, Though **X** draw **PQ** parallel to **AD** to meet **AB** and **DC** produced at **P** and **Q**. Then prove

   (i) trapezium **ABCD** = par^{m} **APQD**.

   (ii) trapezium **ABCD** = twice the Δ**AXD**.

(*Graphical*)

4. The diagonals of a quadrilateral **ABCD** cut at right angles, and measure 7.6 cm. and 5.6 cm. respectively. Find the area.

   Show by a figure that the area is the same wherever the diagonals cut, so long as they are at right angles.

5. In the parallelogram **ABCD**, **AB** = 8.0 cm., **AD** = 3.2 cm ., and the perpendicular between **AB** and **DC** = 3.0 cm. Draw the parallelogram. Calculate the distance between **AD** and **BC**; and check your result by measurement.
6. One sides of a parallelogram is 6.4 cm., and its diagonals are 8.7 cm., and 6.1 cm. Construct the parallelogram; and, after making any necessary measurement, calculate the area.
7. **ABCD** is a parallelogram on a fixed base **AB** and of constant area. Find the locus of the intersection of its diagonals.

EXERCISES LEADING TO THEOREM 29

In the adjoining diagram, **ABC** is a triangle *right-angled* at **C**; and squares are drawn on the three sides. Let us compare the area of the square on the hypotenuse **AB** with the *sum* of the squares on the sides **AC**, **CB** which contain the right angle.

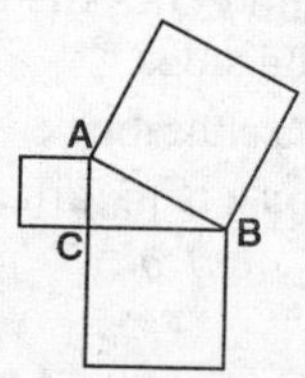

1. Draw the above diagram, making **AC** = 3 cm., and **BC** = 4 cm .;

   Then the area of the square on **AC** $= 3^2$, or 9 sq. cm.
   and .... the square on **BC** $= 4^2$, or 16 sq. cm.

   ∴ the sum of the squares on **AC**, **BC** = 25 sq. cm.

   Now *measure* **AB**; hence calculate the area of the square on **AB**, and compare the result with the *sum* already obtained.
2. Repeat the process of the last exercise, making **AC** = 2.5 cm. and **BC** = 6 cm.
3. If $a = 15, b = 8, c = 17$, show arithmetically that $c^2 = a^2 + b^2$.

   Now draw on squared paper a triangle **ABC**, whose sides a, b, and c are 15, 8, and 17 units of length; and *measure the angle* **ACB**.
4. Take any triangle **ABC**, right-angled at **C** ; and draw squares on **AC**, **CB**, and on the hypotenuse **AB**.

   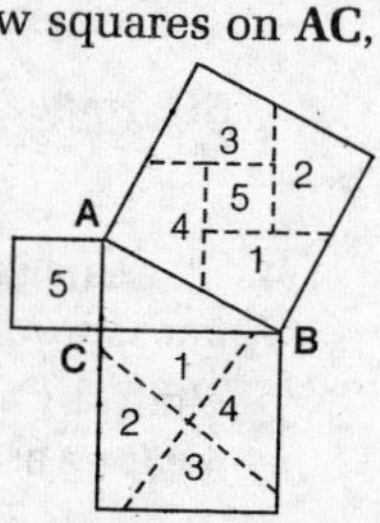

   Through the mid-point of the square on **CB** (*i.e.* the intersection of the diagonals) draw lines parallel and perpendicular to the hypotenuse, thus dividing the square into four *congruent* quadrilaterals. These, together with the square on **AC** will be found exactly to fit into the square on **AB**, in the way indicated by corresponding numbers.

These experiments point to the conclusion that:

In any right-angled triangle the square on the hypotenuse is equal to the sum of the squares on the other two sides.

A formal proof of this theorem is given below.

THEOREM 29. [Euclid I. 47]

In a right-angled triangle the square described on the hypotenuse is equal to the sum of the squares described on the other two sides.

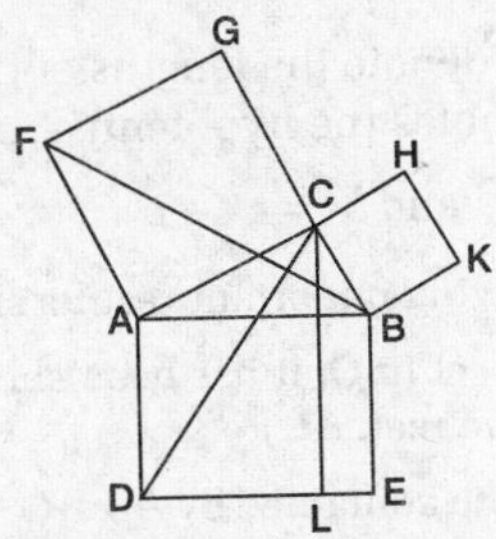

Let **ABC** be a right-angled Δ, having the angle **ACB** a rt. ∠ .

It is required to prove that the square on the hypotenuse **AB** = *the sum of the squares on* **AC, CB**.

On **AB** describe the sq. **ADEB**; and on **AC**, **CB** describe the sqq. **ACGF**, **CBKH**.

Through **C** draw **CL** par[1] to **AD** or **BE**.

Join **CD**, **FB**.

Proof. Because each of the ∠[s] **ACB, ACG** is a rt. ∠,

∴ **BC** and **CG** are in the same st. line.

Now the rt. ∠**BAD** = the rt. ∠**FAC**;

add to each the ∠**CAB** :

then the whole ∠**CAD** = the whole ∠**FAB**.

Then in the Δ[s] **CAD, FAB**,

because { **CA** = **FA**, **AD** = **AB**, and the included ∠**CAD** = the included ∠**FAB**;

∴ the Δ**CAD** = the Δ**FAB**. ***Theor.* 4.**

Now the rect. **AL** is double of the Δ**CAD**, being on the same base **AD**, and between the same par[ls] **AD, CL**.

And the sq. **GA** is double of the Δ**FAB**, being on the same base **FA**, and between the same part[ls] **FA, GB**.

∴ the rect. **AL** = the sq. **GA**.

Similarly by joining **CE, AK**, it can be shown that
the rect. **BL** = the sq. **HB**.

∴ the whole sq. **AE** = the sum of the sqq. **GA, HB** :
that is, the square on the hypotenuse **AB** = the sum of the squares on the two sides **AC, CB**. **Q.E.D.**

Obs. This is know as the Theorem of Pythagoras. The result established may be stated as follows :

$$AB^2 = BC^2 + CA^2.$$

That is, if a and b denote the lengths of the sides containing the right angle; and if c denotes the hypotenuse, $c^2 = a^2 + b^2$.

Hence $a^2 = c^2 - b^2$; and $b^2 = c^2 - a^2$.

NOTE 1. The following important results should be noticed.

If **CL** and **AB** intersect in **O**, it has been shown in the course of the proof that the sq. **GA** = the rect. **AL** ;

that is, AC^2 = the rect. contained by **AB, AO**. ... (i)

Also the sq. **HB** = the rect. **BL**;

that is, BC^2 = the rect. contained by **BA, BO** ...(ii)

NOTE 2. It can be proved by superposition that *squares standing on equal sides are equal in area*. Hence we conclude, conversely,

If two squares are equal in area they stand on equal sides.

EXPERIMENTAL PROOFS OF PYTHAGORAS'S THEOREM

I. Here **ABC** is the given rt.-angled Δ; and **ABED** is the square on the hypotenuse **AB**.

By drawing lines par[1] to the sides **BC, CA**, it is easily seen that the sq. **BD** is divided into 4rt.-angled Δ[s], each identically equal to **ABC**, together with a central square. Hence

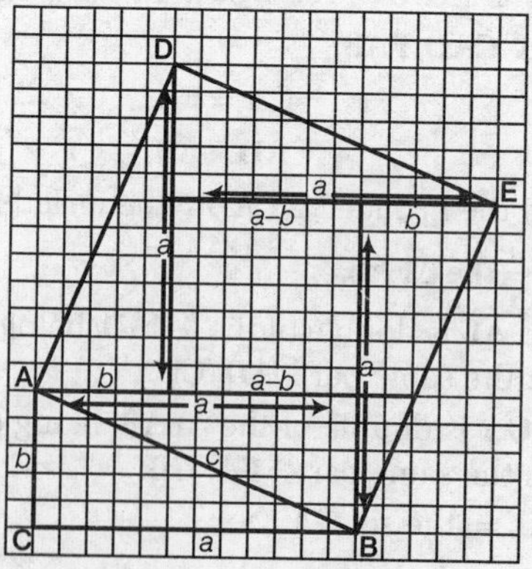

sq. on hypotenuse $c = 4$ rt.$\angle^{d}\,\Delta^{s}$ + the central square

$$= 4.\frac{1}{2}ab + (a-b)^2$$

$$= 2ab + a^2 - 2ab + b^2 = a^2 + b^2 \quad .$$

II. Here **ABC** is the given rt.-angled Δ, and the figs. **CF, HK** are the sqq. on **CB, CA** placed side by side.

FE is made equal to **DH** or **CA**; and the two sqq. **CF, HK** are cut along the lines **BE, ED**.

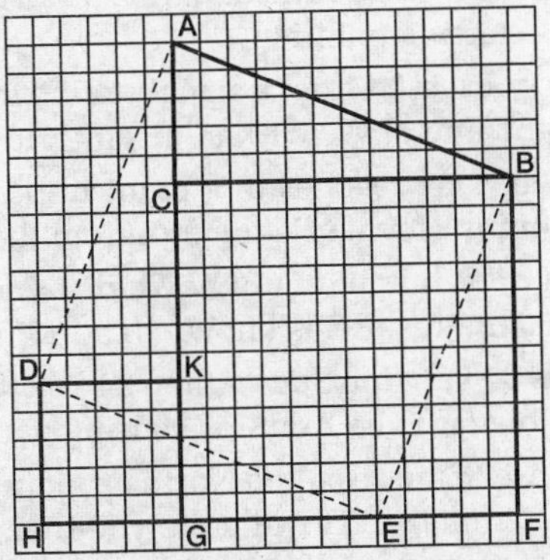

Then it will be found that the Δ**DHE** may be placed so as to fill up the space **ACB**; and the Δ**BFE** may be made to fill the space **AKD**.

Hence the two sqq. **CF, HK** may be fitted together so as to form the single fig. **ABED**, which will be found to be a perfect square, namely the square on the hypotenuse **AB**.

EXERCISES

(*Numerical* and *Graphical*)

1. Draw a triangle **ABC**, right-angled at **C**, having given:

(i) $a = 3$ cm.,
$b = 4$ cm.;

(ii) $a = 2.5$ cm.,
$b = 6.0$ cm.;

(iii) $a = 3$ cm.,
$b = 8.9$ cm.

In each case calculate the length of the hypotenuse c, and verify your result by measurement.

2. Draw a triangle **ABC**; right-angled at **C**, having given:

(i) $c = 8.7$ cm., $a = 7.7$ cm.; [See Problem 10]

(ii) $c = 5.3$ cm., $b = 4.5$ cm.

In each case calculate the remaining side, and verify your result by measurement.

(The following examples are to be solved by calculation; but in each case a plan should be drawn on some suitable scale, and the calculated result verified by measurement.)

3. A ladder whose foot is 9 m. from the front of a house reached to a window—sill 40 m. above the ground. What is the length of the ladder?

4. A ship sails 33 km. due South, and then 56 km. due West: How far is it then from its starting point?

5. Two ships are observed from a signal station to bear respectively N.E. 6.0 km. distant, and N.W. 1.1 km. distant. How far are they apart?

6. A ladder 41 m. long reaches to a point in the fact of a house 40 m. above the ground. How far is the foot from the house?

7. **B** is due East of **A**, but at an unknown distance. **C** is due South of **B**, and distant 55 metres. **AC** is known to be 73 metres. Find **AB**.

8. A man travels 27 km. due South; then 24 km. due West; finally 20km. due North. How far is he from his starting point?

9. From **A** go West 25 metres, then North 60 metres, then East 80 metres, finally South 12 metres. How far are you then from **A**?

10. A ladder 25 m. long is placed so as to reach a window 24 m. high; and on turning the ladder over to the other side of the street, it reaches a point 7 m. high. Find the breadth of the street.

THEOREM 30. [Euclid I. 48]

If the square described on one side of a triangle is equal to the sum of the squares described on the other two sides, then the angle contained by these two sides is a right angle.

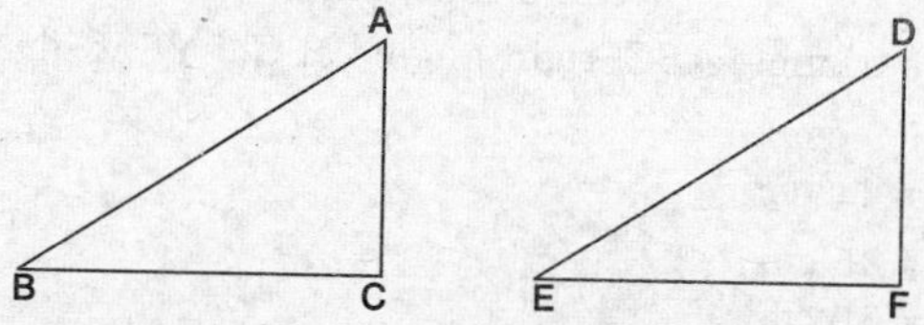

Let **ABC** be a triangle in which

the sq. on **AB** = the sum of the sqq. on **BC, CA**.

It is required to prove that **ACB** is a right angle.

Make **EF** equal to **BC**.

Draw **FD** perp[r] to **EF**, and make **FD** equal to **CA**.

Join **ED**.

Proof. Because **EF** = **BC**,

$\therefore$ the sq. on **EF** = the sq. on **BC**.

And because **FD** = **CA**,

$\therefore$ the sq. on **FD** = the sq. on **CA**,

Hence the sum of the sqq. on **EF**, **FD** = the sum of the sqq. on **BC**,**CA**.

But since **EFD** is a rt. $\angle$,

$\therefore$ the sum of the sqq. on **EF**, **FD** = the sq. on **DE** : *Theor*. 29.

And, by hypothesis, the sqq. on **BC**, **CA** = the sq. on **AB**.

$\therefore$ the sq. on **DE** = the sq. on **AB**.

$\therefore$ **DE** = **AB** .

Then in the $\triangle^s$ **ACB**, **DFE**,

because { **AC** = **DF**, **CB** = **FE**, and **AB** = **DE**;

$\therefore$ the $\angle$**ACB** = the $\angle$**DFE** *Theor*. 7.

But, by construction, **DFE** is a right angle;

$\therefore$ the $\angle$**ACB** is a right angle. **Q.E.D.**

EXERCISES ON THEOREMS 29, 30

(Theoretical)

1. Show that the square on the diagonal of a given square is double of the given square.
2. In the $\triangle$**ABC**, **AD** is drawn perpendicular to the base **BC**. If the side c is greater than b, show that $c^2 - b^2 = BD^2 - DC^2$.
3. If from any point **O** within a triangle **ABC**, perpendiculars **OX**, **OY**, **OZ** are drawn to **BC**, **CA**, **AB** respectively; show that $AZ^2 + BX^2 + CY^2 = AY^2 + CX^2 + BZ^2$.
4. **ABC** is a triangle right-angled at **A**; and the sides **AB**, **AC** are intersected by a straight line **PQ**, and **BQ**, **PC** are joined. Prove that $BQ^2 + PC^2 = BC^2 + PQ^2$.
5. In a right-angled triangle four times the sum of the squares on the medians drawn from the acute angles is equal to five times the square on the hypotenuse.
6. Describe a square equal to the sum of two given squares.
7. Describe a square equal to the difference between two given squares.
8. Divide a straight line into two parts so that the square on one part may be twice the square on the other.
9. Divide a straight line into two parts such that the sum of their squares shall be equal to a given square.

(*Numerical and Graphical*)

10. Determine which of the following triangles are right-angled:

(i) $a = 14$ cm., $b = 48$ cm., $c = 50$ cm.;

(ii) $a = 40$ cm., $b = 10$ cm., $c = 41$ cm.;

(iii) $a = 20$ cm., $b = 99$ cm., $c = 101$ cm.

11. **ABC** is an isosceles triangle right-angled at **C**; deduce from Theorem 29 that $\mathbf{AB}^2 = 2\mathbf{AC}^2$.

Illustrate this result graphically by drawing both diagonals of the square on **AB**, and one diagonal of the square on **AC**.

If **AC** = **BC** = 5.1 cm., find **AB** to the nearest millimetre, and verify your calculation by actual construction and measurement.

12. Draw a square on a diagonal of 6 cm. Calculate, and also measure, the length of a side. Find the area.

PROBLEM 16

To draw squares whose areas shall be respectively twice, three-times, four-times, ... , that of a given square.

Hence find graphically approximate values of $\sqrt{2}, \sqrt{3}, \sqrt{4}, \sqrt{5}, \ldots$

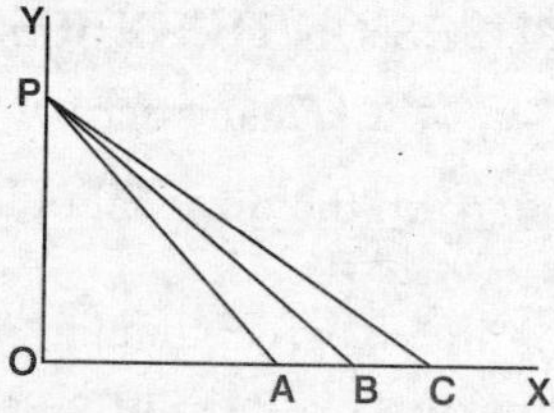

Take **OX**, **OY** at right angles to one another, and from them mark off **OA**, **OP**, each *one* unit. of length. Join **PA**.

Then $\mathbf{PA}^2 = \mathbf{OP}^2 + \mathbf{OA}^2 = 1 + 1 = 2.$

$\therefore \mathbf{PA} = \sqrt{2}$

From **OX** mark off **OB** equal to **PA**, and join **PB**; then

$$\mathbf{PB}^2 = \mathbf{OP}^2 + \mathbf{OB}^2 = 1 + 2 = 3.$$

$$\mathbf{PB} = \sqrt{3}$$

From **OX** mark off **OC** equal to **PB**, and join **PC**; then

$$\mathbf{PC}^2 = \mathbf{OP}^2 + \mathbf{OC}^2 = 1 + 3 = 4.$$

$$\therefore \quad \mathbf{PC} = \sqrt{4}.$$

The lengths of **PA, PB, PC** may now be found by *measurement*; and by continuing the process we may find $\sqrt{5}, \sqrt{6}, \sqrt{7}, \ldots$.

EXERCISES ON THEOREMS 29, 30 (*Continued*)

13. Prove the following formula:

Diagonal of square = side $\times\sqrt{2}$.

Hence find to the nearest centimetre the diagonal of a square on a side of 50 metres.

Draw a plan (scale 1 cm. to 10 metres) and obtain the result as nearly as you can by measurement.

14. **ABC** is an equilateral triangle of which each side $= 2m$ units, and the perpendicular from any vertex to the opposite side $= p$.

Prove that $p = m\sqrt{3}$.

Test this result graphically, when each side = 8 cm .

15. If in a triangle $a = m^2 - n^2$, $b = 2mn$, $c = m^2 + n^2$; prove algebraically that $c^2 = a^2 + b^2$.

Hence by giving various numerical values to m and n, find sets of numbers representing the sides of right-angled triangles.

16. In a triangle **ABC**, **AD** is drawn perpendicular to **BC**. Let p denote the length of **AD**.

(i) If $a = 25$ cm ., $p = 12$ cm., **BD** = 9 cm .; find b and c.

(ii) If $b = 82$ cm ., $c = 1$ m., **BD** = 60 cm .; find p and a.

And prove that $\sqrt{b^2 - p^2} + \sqrt{c^2 - p^2} = a$.

17. In the triangle **ABC**, **AD** is drawn perpendicular to **BC**. Prove that

$$c^2 - \mathbf{BD}^2 = b^2 - \mathbf{CD}^2.$$

If $a = 51$ cm ., $b = 20$ cm ., $c = 37$ cm .; find **BD**.

Thence find p, the length of **AD**, and the area of the triangle **ABC**.

18. Find by the method of the last example the areas of the triangles whose sides are as follows:

(i) $a = 17$ cm ., $b = 10$ cm ., $c = 9$ cm .

(ii) $a = 25$ m ., $b = 17$ m ., $c = 12$ m .

(iii) $a = 41$ cm ., $b = 28$ cm ., $c = 15$ cm .

(iv) $a = 40$ km ., $b = 37$ km ., $c = 13$ km .

19. A straight rod **PQ** slides between two straight rulers **OX**, **OY** placed at right angles to one another. In one position of the rod **OP** = 5.6 cm., and **OQ** = 3.3 cm. If in another position **OP** = 4.0 cm., find **OQ** graphically; and test the accuracy of your drawing by calculation.

20. **ABC** is a triangle right-angled at **C**, and p is the length of the perpendicular from **C** on **AB**. By expressing the area of the triangle in two ways, show that $pc = ab$.

Hence deduce $$\frac{1}{p^2} = \frac{1}{a^2} + \frac{1}{b^2}.$$

PROBLEMS ON AREA

PROBLEM 17

To describe a parallelogram equal to a given triangle, and having one of its angles equal to a given angle.

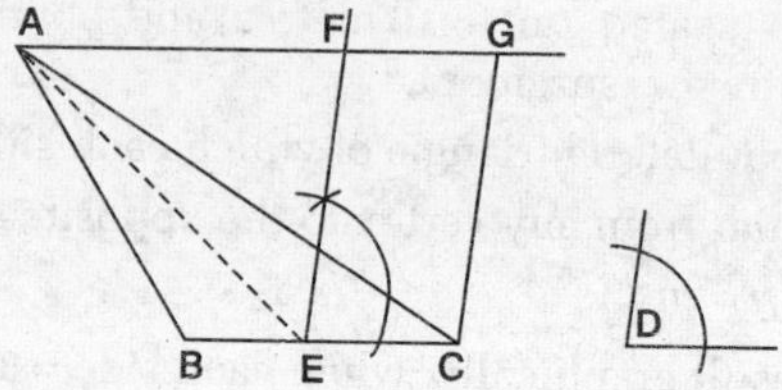

Let **ABC** be the given triangle, and **D** the given angle.

It is required to describe a parallelogram equal to **ABC**, *and having one of its angles equal to* **D**.

Construction. Bisect **BC** at **E**.

At **E** in **CE**, make the ∠**CEF** equal to **D**;

through **A** draw **AFG** part[l] to **BC**;

and through **C** draw **CG** par[l] to **EF**.

Then **FECG** is the required par[l].

Proof. Join **AE**.

Now the Δ[s] **ABE, AEC** are on equal bases **BE, EC**, and of the same altitude;

∴ the Δ**ABE** = the Δ**AEC**.

∴ the Δ**ABC** is double of the Δ**AEC** .

But **FECG** is a par[m] by construction;

and it is double of the Δ**AEC**,

being on the same base **EC**, and between the same part[l] **EC** and **AG**.

∴the par[m] **FECG** = Δ**ABC**;

and one of its angles, namely **CEF** = the given ∠**D**.

EXERCISES

(*Graphical*)

1. Draw a square on a side of 5 cm., and make a parallelogram of equal area on the same base, and having an angle of 45°.

Find (i) by calculation, (ii) by measurement the length of an oblique side of the parallelogram.

2. Draw any parallelogram **ABCD** in which **AB** = 5 cm. and **AD** = 4 cm. and on the base **AB** draw a rhombus of equal area.

DEFINITION. In a parallelogram **ABCD**, if through any point **K** in the diagonal **AC** parallels **EF**, **HG** are drawn to the sides, then the figures **EH**, **GF** are called **parallelograms** about **AC**, and the figures **EF**, **HF** are said to be their **complements**.

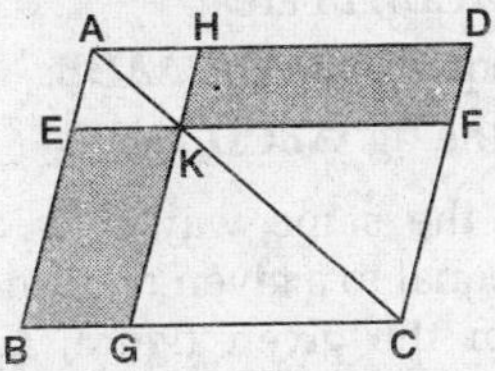

3. *In the diagram of the preceding definition show by Theorem 21 that the complements* **EF**, **HF** *are equal in area.*

Hence, given a parallelogram **EG**, and a straight line **HK**, deduce a construction for drawing on **HK** as one side a parallelogram equal and equiangular to the parallelogram **EG**.

4. Construct a rectangle equal in area to a given rectangle **CDEF**, and having one side equal to a given line **AB**.

If **AB** = 6 cm., **CD** = 8 cm., **CF** = 3 cm., find by measurement the remaining side of the constructed rectangle.

5. Given a parallelogram **ABCD**, in which **AB** = 4.8 cm., **AD** = 3.6 cm., and the $\angle A = 55°$. Construct an equiangular parallelogram of equal area, the greater side measuring 5.4 cm. Measure the shorter side.

Repeat the process giving to **A** any other value; and compare your results. What conclusion do you draw? ,

6. Draw a rectangle on a side of 5 cm. equal in area to an equilateral triangle on a side of 6 cm.

Measure the remaining side of the rectangle, and calculate its approximate area.

PROBLEM 18

To draw a triangle equal in area to a given quadrilateral.

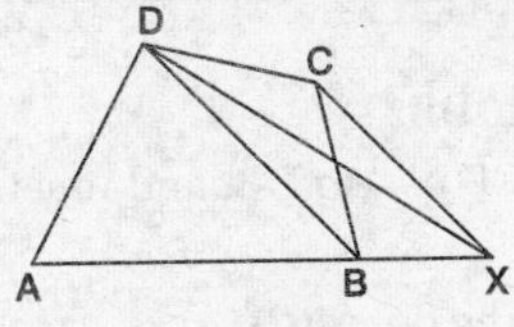

Let **ABCD** be the given quadrilateral.

It is required to describe a triangle equal to **ABCD** *in area.*

Construction. Join **DB**.

Through **C** draw **CX** par[l] to **DB**, meeting **AB** produced in **X.**

Join **DX**.

Then **DAX** is the required triangle.

Proof. Now the Δ^s **XDB, CDB** are on the same base **DB** and between the same par[ls] **DB, CX;**

∴ the Δ**XDB** = the Δ**CDB** in area.

To each of these equals add the Δ**ADB**;

then the Δ**DAX** = the fig. **ABCD**.

COROLLARY. In the same way it is always possible to draw a rectilineal figure equal to a given rectilineal figure, and having fewer sides by one than the given figure; and thus step by step, any rectilineal figure may be reduced to a triangle of equal area.

For example, in the adjoining diagram the five-sided fig. **EDCBA** is equal in area to the four-sided fig. **EDXA**.

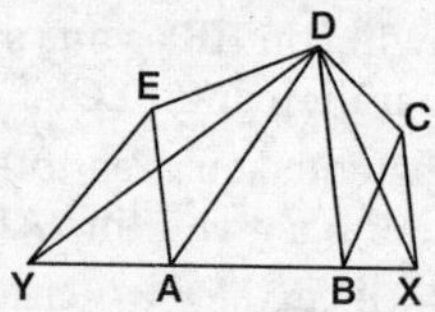

The fig. **EDXA** may now be reduced to an equal Δ**DXY**.

PROBLEM 19

To draw a parallelogram equal in area to a given rectilineal figure, and having an angle equal to a given angle.

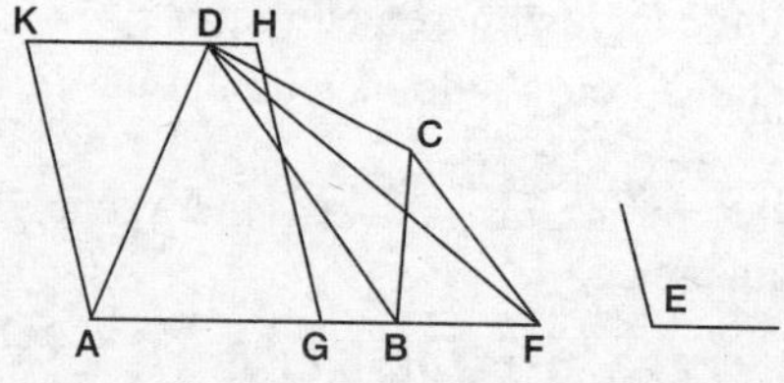

Let **ABCD** be the given rectil. fig. and **E** the given angle.

It is required to draw a par[m] equal to **ABCD** *and having an angle equal to* **E**.

Construction. Join **DB**.

Through **C** draw **CF** par[l] to **DB**, and meeting **AB** produced in **F**.

Join **DF**.

Then the Δ**DAF** = the fig. **ABCD**. ***Prob.* 18.**

Draw the par[m] **AGHK** equal to the Δ**ADF** ; and having the ∠**KAG** equal to the ∠**E** . ***Prob.* 17.**

Then the par^m **KG** = the Δ**ADF**

= the fig. **ABCD**;

and it has the $\angle$**KAG** equal to the $\angle$**E**.

NOTE. If the given rectilineal figure has more than four sides, it must first be reduced, step by step, until it is replaced by an equivalent triangle.

EXERCISES

(*Reduction of a Rectilineal Figure to an equivalent Triangle*)

1. Draw a quardrilateral **ABCD** from the following data:

   AB = **BC** = 5.5 cm.; **CD** = **DA** = 4.5 cm.; the $\angle$**A** = 75°.

   Reduce the quadrilateral to a triangle of equal area. Measure the base and altitude of the triangle; and hence calculate the approximate area of the given figure.

2. Draw a quadrilateral **ABCD** having given:

   AB = 5.6 cm., **BC** = 6.4 cm., **CD** = 6.6 cm., **DA** = 7.2 cm., and the diagonal **BD** = 6 cm.

   Construct an equivalent triangle; and hence find the approximate area of the quadrilateral.

3. On a base **AB**, 4 cm. in length, describe an equilateral pentagon (5 sides), having each of the angles at **A** and **B** 108°.

   Reduce the figure to a triangle of equal area; and by measuring its base and altitude, calculate the approximate area of the pentagon.

4. A quadrilateral field **ABCD** has the following measurements:

   AB = 450 metres, **BC** = 380 m., **CD** = 330 m., **AD** = 390 m., and the diagonal **AC** = 660 m.

   Draw a plan (scale 1 cm. to 50 metres). Reduce your plan to an equivalent triangle, and measure its base and altitude. Hence estimate the area of the field.

   (*Problems. State your construction, and give a theoretical proof*)

5. Reduce a triangle **ABC** to a triangle of equal area having its base **BD** of given length. (**D** lies in **BC**, or **BC** produced.)

6. Construct a triangle equal in area to a given triangle, and having a given altitude.

7. **ABC** is a given triangle, and **X** a given point. Draw a triangle equal in area to **ABC**, having its vertex at **X**, and its base in the same straight line as **BC**.

8. Construct a triangle equal in area to the quadrilateral **ABCD**, having its vertex at a given point **X** in **DC**, and its base in the same straight line as **AB**.

9. Show how a triangle may be divided into n equal parts by straight lines drawn through one of its angular points.

10. *Bisect a triangle by a straight line drawn through a given point in one of its sides.*

[Let **ABC** be the given Δ, and **P** the given point in the side **AB**.

Bisect **AB** at **Z**; and join **CZ, CP**.

Through **Z** draw **ZQ** parallel to **CP**.

Join **PQ**.

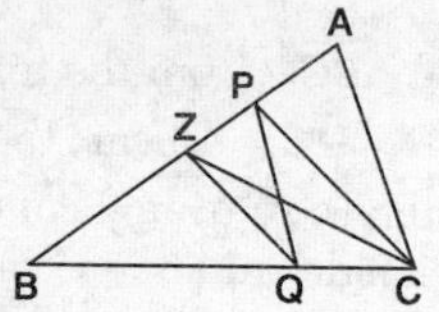

Then **PQ** bisects the Δ.]

11. *Trisect triangle by straight lines drawn from a given point in one of its sides.*

[Let **ABC** be the given Δ, and **X** the given point in the side **BC**.

Trisect **BC** at the points **P, Q**. ***Prob.* 7.**

Join **AX**, and through **P** and **Q** draw **PH** and **QK** parallel to **AX**.

Join **XH, XK**.

These straight lines trisect the Δ; as may be shown by joining **AP, AQ**.]

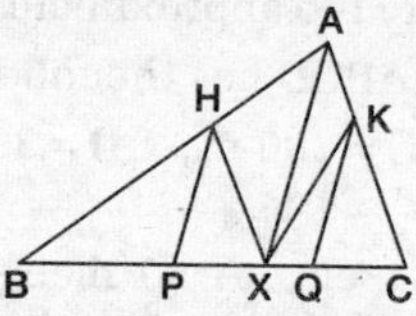

12. Cut off from a given triangle a fourth, fifth, sixth, or any part required by a straight line drawn from a given point in one of its sides.

13. *Bisect a quadrilateral by a straight line drawn through an angular point.*

[Reduce the quadrilateral to a triangle of equal area, and join the vertex to the middle point of the base.]

14. Cut off from a given quadrilateral a third, a fourth, a fifth, or any part required, by a straight line drawn through a given angular point.

AXES OF REFERENCE, COORDINATES EXERCISES FOR SQUARED PAPER

If we take two fixed straight lines **XOX′, YOY′** cutting one another at right angles at **O**, the position of any point **P** with reference to these lines is known when we know its distances from each of them. Such lines are called **axes of reference**, **XOX′** being known as the **axis of *x***, and **YOY′** as the **axis of *y***. Their point of intersection **O** is called the **origin.**

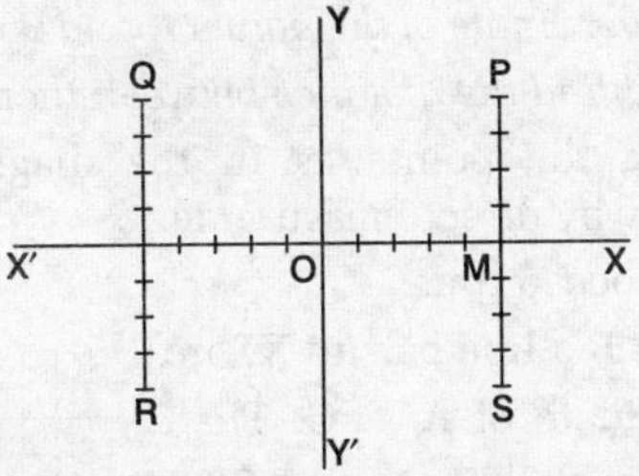

The lines **XOX′, YOY′** are usually drawn horizontally and vertically. In practice the distances of **P** from the axes are estimated thus:

From **P, PM** is drawn perpendicular to **X′ X**; and **OM** and **PM** are measured.

OM is called the **abscissa** of the point P, and is denoted by x.

PM is ,, **ordinate** ,, P ,, y.

The abscissa and ordinate taken together are called the **coordinates** of the point **P**, and are denoted by (x, y).

We may thus find the position of a point if its coordinates are known.

EXAMPLE. *Plot the point whose coordinates are* (5, 4).

Along **OX** mark off **OM**, 5 units in length.

At **M** draw **MP** perp. to **OX**, making **MP** 4 units in length.

Then **P** is the point whose coordinates are (5, 4).

The axes of reference divide the plane into four regions **XOY, YOX, X′OY′, Y′OX**, known respectively as the first, second, third, and fourth **quadrants.**

It is clear that in each quadrant there is a point whose distances from the axes are equal to those of **P** in the above diagram, namely, 5 units and 4 units.

The coordinates of these points are distinguished by the use of the *positive* and *negative* signs, according to the following system:

Abscissae measured along the x-axis to the right of the origin are positive, those measured to the left of the origin are negative. Ordinates which lie above the x-axis (that is, in the first and second quadrants) are positive; those which lie below the x-axis (that is, in the third and fourth quadrants) are negative.

Thus the coordinates of the points **Q**, **R**, **S** are

$$(-5, 4), (-5-4), \text{ and } (5, -4) \text{ respectively.}$$

NOTE. The coordinates of the origin are (0, 0). In practice it is convenient to use squared paper. Two intersecting lines should be chosen as axes, and slightly thickened to aid the eye, then one or more of the length-divisions may be taken as the linear unit. The paper used in the following examples is ruled to tenths of an inch.

Example 1. *The coordinate of the points* **A** *and* **B** *are* (7, 8) *and* (– 5, 3): *plot the points and find the distance between them.*

After plotting the points as in the diagram, we may find **AB** approximately by direct measurement.

Or we may proceed thus:

Draw through **B** a line par[l] to **XX′** to meet the ordinate of **A** at **C**. Then **ACB** is a rt.- angled Δ in which **BC** = 12, and **AC** = 5.

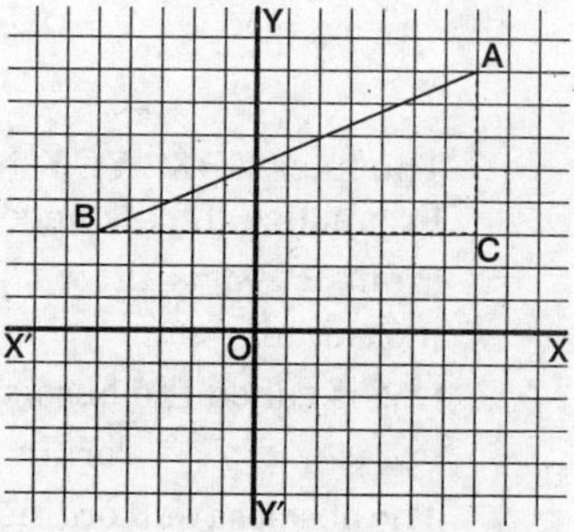

Now $AB^2 = BC^2 + AC^2$

$$= 12^2 + 5^2$$

$$= 144 + 25$$

$$= 169.$$

$\therefore$ **AB** = 13.

Example 2. *The coordinates of* **A**, **B**, *and* **C** *are* (5, 7), (– 8, 2), *and* (3, – 5); *plot these point and find the area of the triangle of which these are the vertices.*

Having plotted the points as in the diagram, we may measure **AB**, and draw and measure the perp. from **C** on **AB**. Hence the approximate area may be calculated.

Or we may proved thus:

Through **A** and **B** draw **AP**, **BQ** par[l] to **YY′**.

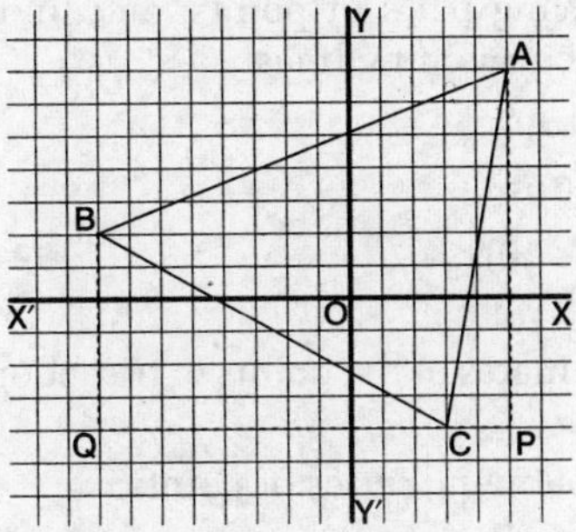

Through **C** draw **PQ** par[l] to **XX′**.

Then the Δ**ABC** = the trap[m] **APQB** – the two rt.-angled Δ^s **APC, BQC**

$$= \frac{1}{2}\,\mathbf{PQ(AP + BQ)}$$

$$- \frac{1}{2}\cdot\mathbf{AP\cdot PC} - \frac{1}{2}\cdot\mathbf{BQ\cdot QC}$$

$$= \frac{1}{2}\times 13\times 19$$

$$- \frac{1}{2}\times 12\times 2 - \frac{1}{2}\times 7\times 11$$

$= 73$ units of area.

EXERCISES

1. Plot the following sets of points:

(i) $(6, 4), (-6, 4), (-6, -4), (6, -4)$;

(ii) $(8, 0), (0, 8), (-8, 0), (0, -8)$;

(iii) $(12, 5), (5, 12), (-12, 5), (-5, 12)$.

2. Plot the following points, and show experimentally that each set lies in one straight line.

(i) $(9, 7), (0, 0), (-9, -7)$;

(ii) $(-9, 7), (0, 0), (9, -7)$.

Explain these results theoretically.

3. Plot the following pairs of points; join the points in each case, and measure the coordinates of the mid-point of the joining line.

(i) $(4, 3), (12, 7)$;

(ii) $(5, 4), (15, 16)$.

Show *why* in each case the coordinates of the mid-point are respectively *half the sum of the abscissae* and *half the sum of the ordinates* of the given points.

4. Plot the following pairs of points; and find the coordinates of the mid-point of their joining lines.

(i) (0, 0), (8, 10);

(ii) (8,0), (0, 10);

(iii) (0,0), (– 8, – 10);

(iv) (– 8, 0), (0, – 10).

5. Find the coordinates of the points of trisection of the line joining (0,0) to (18, 15).

6. Plot the two following series of points:

(i) (5, 0), (5, 2), (5, 5), (5, – 1), (5, – 4);

(ii) (– 4, 8), (– 1, 8), (0, 8), (3, 8), (6, 8).

Show that they lie on two lines respectively parallel to the axis of y, and the axis of x. Find the coordinates of the point in which they intersect.

7. Plot the following points, and calculate their distances from the origin.

(i) (15, 8);

(ii) (– 15, – 8);

(iii) (2.4″, .7″),

(iv) (– .7″, 2.4″).

Check your results by measurement.

8. Plot the following pairs of points, and in each case calculate the distance between them.

(i) (4, 0), (0, 3);

(ii) (9, 8), (5, 5);

(iii) (15, 0), (0, 8);

(iv) (10, 4), (– 5, 12);

(v) (20, 12), (– 15, 10);

(vi) (20, 9), (– 15, – 3).

Verify your calculation by measurement.

9. Show that the points (– 3, 2), (3, 10), (7, 2) are the angular points of an isosceles triangle. Calculate and measure the lengths of the equal sides.

10. Plot the eight points (0, 5), (3,4), (5,0), (4, – 3), (– 5, 0), (0, – 5), (– 4, 3), (– 4, – 3), and show that they all lie on a circle whose centre is the origin.

11. Explain by a diagram why the distances between the following pairs of points are all equal;

(i) $(a, 0)$, $(0, b)$;

(ii) $(b, 0)$, $(0, a)$;

(iii) $(0, 0)$, (a, b).

12. Draw the straight lines joining

(i) $(a, 0)$ and $(0, a)$;

(ii) $(0, 0)$ and (a, a);

and prove that these lines bisect each other at right angles.

13. Show that $(0, 4)$, $(12, 9)$, $(12, -4)$ are the vertices of an isosceles triangle whose base is bisected by the axis of x.

14. Three vertices of a rectangle as $(14, 0)$, $(14, 10)$, and $(0, 10)$; find the coordinates of the fourth vertex, and of the intersection of the diagonals.

15. Prove that the four points $(0, 0)$, $(13, 0)$, $(18, 12)$, $(5, 12)$ are the angular points of a rhombus. Find the length of each side, and the coordinates of the intersection of the diagonals.

16. Plot the locus of a point which moves so that its distances from the points $(0, 0)$ and $(4, -4)$ are always equal to one another. Where does the locus cut the axes?

17. Show that the following groups of points are the vertices of rectangles. Draw the figures, and calculate their areas.

(i) $(4, 3)$, $(17, 3)$, $(17, 12)$, $(4, 12)$;

(ii) $(3, 2)$, $(3, 15)$, $(-6, 15)$, $(-6, 2)$;

(iii) $(5, 1)$, $(-8, 1)$, $(-8, -8)$, $(5, -8)$.

18. Join in order the points $(1'', 0)$, $(0, 1'')$, $(-1'', 0)$, $(0, -1'')$. Of what kind is the quadrilateral so formed? Find its area.

If a second figure is formed by joining the middle points of the first, find its area.

19. Plot the triangles given by the following sets of points; and find their areas.

(i) $(10, 10)$, $(4, 0)$, $(18, 0)$;

(ii) $(10, -10)$, $(4, 0)$, $(18, 0)$;

(iii) $(-10, 10)$, $(-4, 0)$, $(-18, 0)$;

(iv) $(-10, -10)$, $(-4, 0)$, $(-18, 0)$.

20. Draw the triangles given by the points

(i) $(0, 0)$, $(5, 3)$, $(6, 0)$;

(ii) $(0, 0)$, $(3, 0)$, $(0, 6)$.

Find their areas; and measure the angles of the first triangle.

21. Plot the triangles given by the following sets of points. Show that in each case one side is parallel to one of the axes. Hence find the area.

(i) (0, 0), (12, 10), (12 – 6);

(ii) (0, 0), (5, 8), (– 15, 8);

(iii) (0, 0), (– 12, 12), (– 12, – 8);

(iv) (0, 0), (– 6, – 8), (20, – 8).

22. In the following triangles show that two sides of each are parallel to the axes. Find their areas.

(i) (5, 5), (15, 5), (15, 15);

(ii) (8, 3), (8,18), (0, 18);

(iii) (4, 8), (– 16, – 4), (4, – 4);

(iv) (1, 15), (– 11, 15), (1, – 7).

23. Show that (– 5, 5), (7, 10), (10, 6), (– 2, 1) are the angular points of a parallelogram. Find its sides and area.

24. Show that each of the following sets of points gives a trapezium. Find the area of each.

(i) (3, 0), (3, 3), (9, 0),(9, 6);

(ii) (0, 3), (– 5, 3), (– 2, – 3), (0, – 3);

(iii) (8, 4), (4, 4), (11, – 1), (3, – 1);

(iv) (0, 0), (– 1, 5), (– 4, 5), (– 8, 0).

25. Find the area of the triangles by the following points;

(i) (5, 5), (20, 10), (12, 14);

(ii) (7, 6), (– 10, 4), (– 4, – 3);

(iii) (0, – 6), (0, – 3), (14, 5);

(iv) (6, 4), (– 7, – 6), (– 2, – 15).

26. Show that (– 5, 0), (7, 5), (19, 0), (7, – 5) are the angular points of a rhombus. Find its sides and its area.

27. Join the points (0, – 5), (12, 0), (4, 6), (– 8, – 3), in the order given. Calculate the lengths of the first three sides and measure the fourth. Find the areas of the portions of the figure lying in the first and fourth quadrants.

28. The coordinates of four points **A**, **B**, **C**, **D** are respectively (– 4, – 4), (– 10, 4), (– 10, 13), (5, 5).

Calculate the lengths of **AB**, **BC**, **CD**, and measure **AD**. Also calculate the area of **ABCD** by considering it as the difference of two triangles.

29. Draw the figure whose angular points are given by

(0, – 3), (8, 3), (– 4, 8), (– 4, 3), (0, 0).

Find the lengths of its sides, taking the points in the above order. Also divide it into three right-angled triangles, and hence find its area.

30. A plan of a triangular field **ABC** is drawn on squared paper (scale 1 cm. = 100 m.). On the plan the coordinates of **A, B, C** are (– 2 cm., – 6 cm.), (6 cm., 8 cm.), (– 10 cm., – 2 cm.) respectively. Find the area of the field, the length of the side represented by **BC**, and the distance from this side of the opposite corner of the field.

31. Show that the points (6, 0), (20, 6), (14, 20), (0, 14) are the vertices of a square. Measure a side and hence find the approximate area, Calculate the area exactly (i) by drawing a circumscribing square through its vertices; (ii) by subdividing the given square as in the first figure on page 106.

MISCELLANEOUS EXERCISES

1. **AB** and **AC** are unequal sides of a triangle **ABC**; **AX** is the median through **A**, **AP** bisects the angle **BAC**, and **AD** is the perpendicular from **A** to **BC**. Prove that **AP** is intermediate in position and magnitude to **AX** and **AD**.
2. In a triangle if a perpendicular is drawn from one extremity of the base to the bisector of the vertical angle, (i) it will make with either of the sides containing the vertical angle an angle equal to half the sum of the angles at the base; (ii) it will make with the base an angle equal to half the difference of the angles at the base.
3. In any triangle the angle contained by the bisector of the vertical angle and the perpendicular from the vertex to the base is equal to half the difference of the angles at the base.
4. Construct a right-angled triangle having given the hypotenuse and the difference of the sides.
5. Construct a triangle, having given the base, the difference of the angles at the base, and (i) the difference, (ii) the sum of the remaining sides.
6. Construct an isosceles triangle, having given the base and the sum of one of the equal sides and the perpendicular from the vertex to the base.
7. Show how to divide a given straight line so that the square on one part may be double of the square on the other.
8. **ABCD** is a parallelogram, and **O** is any point without the angle **BAD** or its opposite vertical angle; show that the triangle **OAC** is equal to the sum of the triangles **OAD**, **OAB**.

   If **O** is within the angle **BAD** or its opposite vertical angle, show that the triangle **OAC** is equale to the difference of the triangles **OAD**, **OAB**.
9. The area of a quadrilateral is equal to the area of a triangle having two of its sides equal to the diagonals of the given figure, and the included angle equal to either of the angles between the diagonals.

10. Find the locus of the intersection of the medians of triangles described on a given base and of given area.

11. On the base of a given triangle construct a second triangle equal in area to the first, and having its vertex in a given straight line.

12. **ABCD** is a parallelogram made of rods connected by hinges. If **AB** is fixed, find the locus of the middle point of **CD**.

ANSWERS TO NUMERICAL EXERCISES

Since the utmost care cannot ensure absolute accuracy in graphical work, results so obtained are likely to be only approximate. The answers here given are those found by calculation, and being true so far as they go, furnish a standard by which the student may test the correctness of his drawing and measurement. Results within one per cent of those given in the Answers may usually be considered satistactory.

Exercises. Page 10.

1. 30°; 126°; 261°; 85° . 11 min.; 37 min.

2. $112\frac{1}{2}$°; 155°; 5 hrs. 45 mm. **3.** 50°; 8 hrs. 40 min.

4. (i) 145°, 35°, 145°. (ii) 55°, 55°, 86°, 94°.

Exercises. Page 20.

1. 68°, 37°, 75° v. nearly. **2.** 6.0 cm.

4. 5.6 cm., 50°, 73° nearly. **5.** 11.1 m.

6. 101 metres. **7.** 8 m.

8. 424 m., nearly; N. W.

Exercises. Page 30.

1. 125°, 55°, 125°. **12.** 15 secs., 30 secs.

Exercises. Page 32.

3. 21°. **4.** 27°.

5. 92°, 46°. **6.** 67°, 62°.

Exercises. Page 33.

1. 30°, 60°, 90°.

2. (i) 36°, 72°, 72°; (ii) 20°, 80°, 80°.

3. 40°. **4.** 51°, 111°, 18°.

5. (i) 34°; (ii) 107°. **6.** 68°.

7. 120°. **8.** 36°, 72°, 108°, 144°.

9. 165°. **11.** 5, 15.

Exercises. Page 34.

2. (i) 45°; (ii) 36°.

3. (i) 12; (ii) 15.

Exercises. Page 41.

4. (i) 81°; *c* (ii) 55°.

10.

Degrees	15°	30°	45°	60°	75°
Cm.	4.1	4.6	5.7	8.0	15.6

11.

Degrees	0°	30°	60°	90°	120°	150°	180°
Cm.	1.0	2.0	3.6	5.0	6.1	6.8	7.0

12. 12.2 m.

13. 34 m.

14. 316 m., 634 m.

Exercises. Page 47.

14. 54°, 72°, 54°.

15. 36°.

16. 4.

18. (i) 16; (ii) 45°; (iii) $11\frac{1}{4}$ ° per sec.

Exercises. Page 53.

2. 0.39.

5. 9.174 cm.

6. 8.5 cm.

7. 17.6 km.

8. 235.2 km.

9. 33 : 25.

Exercises. Page 61.

4. 4.8 cm.

Exercises. Page 64.

1. 4.3 cm., 5.2 cm., 6.1 cm.

2. 1.10.

3. 200 m.

4. 65°, 77 m., 61., 56 m.

5. 6.04 knots. S, 15° E, nearly.

6. Results equal. 9 cm.

7. 4.3 cm.; 9.8 cm., 60°; 120°.

8. (i) One solution; (ii) two; (iii) one, right-angled; (iv) impossible.

9. 380 m.

10. 6.5 cm.

11. 6.9 cm.

12. Two solutions; 10.4 cm. or 4.5 cm.

16. 2.8 cm., 4.5 cm., 5.3 cm.

18. 5.8 cm., 4.2 cm.

19. 7 cm., 8 cm.

Exercises. Page 68.

1. 60°, 120°.
2. 9.2 cm.
3. 3.55 cm.
4. 4.4 cm.
5. 16.4 cm., 3.4%.
6. 90°.
7. (i) 8.5 cm.; (ii) $B = D = 90°$.

Exercises. Page 79.

1. 37.5 sq. cm.
2. 24 sq. cm.
3. 10.5 sq. cm.
4. 15 sq. cm.
5. 13.5 sq. cm.
6. 17.6 sq. cm.
7. 198 sq. cm.
8. 4900 sq. cm.
9. 10,000 sq. cm.
10. 250 sq. m.
11. 5 cm.
12. 2.6 cm.
13.
14. 900 sq. m.; 48 m.; 4.8 cm.
15. 11,700 sq. m.
16. 1 cm. = 10 m.
17. 1.6 cm.
18. 600 sq. m.
19. 1152 sq. cm.
20. 100 sq. m.
21. 156 sq. m.
22. 110 sq. m.
23. 288 sq. m.
24. 72 sq. m.
25. 75 sq. m.

Exercises. Page 82.

1. (i) 22 sq. cm.; (ii) 23.18 sq. cm.
2. 22.1 sq. cm.
3. 574.5 sq. m.
4. 3.9 cm.
5. 4.9 cm., 75°.

Exercises. Page 84.

1. (i) 180 sq. m.; (ii) 8.4 sq. cm.; (iii) 1 hectare.
2. (i) 13.44 sq. cm.; (ii) 15.40 sq. cm.; (iii) 20.50 sq. cm.
3. 15 sq. cm.
4. 40.5 sq. cm.; 13 cm.
5. (i) 10 cm.; (ii) 13 cm.
6. 3.36 sq. cm.

Exercises. Page 86.

1. 11,400 sq. m.

2. 6312 sq. m.

3. 2.4 cm.; 5.1 cm.

4. 5.2 cm.; 5.6 cm.

5.

Angle	0°	30°	60°	90°	120°	150°	180°
Area in sq. cm.	0	7.5	13.0	15.0	13.0	7.5	0

Exercises. Page 88.

1. 66 sq. m.

2. 84 sq. cm.

3. 126 sq. m.

4. 132 sq. cm.

5. 180 sq. m.

6. 306 sq. m.

Exercises. Page 90.

1. 6 sq. cm.

2. 170 sq. m.

3. 615 sq. m.

4. 53.5 sq. cm.

5. 31.2 sq. cm.

6. 33.8 sq. cm.

7. 24 sq. cm.

Exercises. Page 92.

1. (i) 25.5 sq. cm.; (ii) 15.6 sq. cm.

2. (i) 8.95 sq. in.; (ii) 9.5 sq. in.

3. 12,500 sq. m.

Exercises. Page 93.

4. 21.28 sq. cm.

5. 7.5 cm.

6. 23.4 sq. cm.

Exercises. Page 97.

1. (i) 5 cm.; (ii) 6.5 cm.; (iii) 9.4 cm.

2. (i) 4.41 cm.; (ii) 2.8 m.

3. 41 m.

4. 65 km.

5. 6.1 km.

6. 9 m.

7. 48 m.

8. 25 km.

9. 73 m.

10. 31 m.

Exercises. Page 99.

10. (i) and (iii).

11. 7.2 mm.

12. 4.24 cm.; 18 sq. cm.

13. 70.71 sq. m.

14. $p = 6.93$ cm.

16. (i) 20 cm.; 15 cm. (ii) 40 cm.; 39 cm.

17. 35 cm.; 12 cm.; 306 sq. cm.

18. (i) 36 sq. cm.; (ii) 90 sq. m.; (iii) 126 sq. cm.; (iv) 240 sq. km.

19. 5.1 cm nearly.

Exercises. Page 102.

1. 7.1 cm.

4. 40 cm.

5. 3.2 cm.

6. 3.1 cm.; 15.6 sq. cm.

Exercises. Page 105.

1. 23.90 sq. cm.

2. 33.6 sq. cm.

3. 27.52 sq. cm.

4. 129,800 sq. cm.

Exercises. Page 109.

3. (i) (8, 5); (ii) (10, 10).

4. (i) (4, 5); (ii) (4, 5); (iii) (– 4, – 5); (iv) (– 4, – 5).

5. (6, 5), (12, 10).

6. (5, 8).

7. (i) 17; (ii) 17; (iii) 2.5″; 2.5″.

8. (i) and (ii) 5;
(iii) and (iv) 17;
(v) and (vi) 37.

9.

10.

14. (0, 0). (7, 5).

15. 13; (9, 6).

16. A straight line passing through the points (4, 0), (0, – 4).

17. 117 units of area in each case.

18. A square. 2 sq. in. 1 sq. in.

19. Each = 70 units of area.

20. 9 units of area. 31°, 71°, 78°.

21. (i) 96; (ii) 80; (iii) 120; (iv) 104.

22. (i) 50; (ii) 60; (iii) 120; (iv) 132.

23. Sides 5, 13; area 63.

24. (i) 27; (ii) 21; (iii) 30; (iv) 27.5.

25. (i) 50; (ii) 65.5; (iii) 21; (iv) 83.5.

26. Each side 13; area 120.

27. 13, 10, 15, 8.24, 42, 30.

28. **AB** = 10, **BC** = 9, **CD** = 17, **DA** = 12.7. Area = 130.5.

29. 10, 13, 5, 5, 3. Area = 60.

30. 640,000 sq. m., 2000 m., 640 m.

31. Side = 15.23; area = 232 units of area.

PART III

THE CIRCLE

DEFINITIONS AND FIRST PRINCIPLES

1. A **circle** is a plane figure contained by a line traced out by a point which moves so that its distance from a certain fixed point is always the same.

   The fixed point is called the **centre**, and the bounding line is called the **circumference**.

   NOTE. According to the definition the term circle strictly applies to the *figure* contained by the circumference; it is often used however for the circumference itself when no confusion is likely to arise.

2. A **radius** of a circle is a straight line drawn from the centre to the circumference. It follows that all radii of a circle are equal.
3. A **diameter** of a circle is a straight line drawn through the centre and terminated both ways by the circumference.
4. A **semi-circle** is the figure bounded by a diameter of a circle and the part of the circumference cut off by the diameter.

   It will be proved on page 131 that a diameter divides a circle into two identically equal parts.

5. Circles that have the same centre are said to be **Concentric**.

From these definitions we draw the following inferences:

(i) A circle is a *closed* curve; so that if the circumference is crossed by a straight line, this line if produced will cross the circumference at a second point.

(ii) The distance of a point from the centre of a circle is greater or less than the radius according as the point is without or within the circumference.

(iii) A point is outside or inside a circle according as its distance from the centre is greater or less than the radius.

(iv) Circles of equal radii are identically equal. For by superposition of one centre on the other the circumferences most coincide at every point.

(v) Concentric circles of unequal radii cannot intersect, for the distance from the centre of every point on the smaller circle is less than the radius of the larger.

(vi) If the circumferences of two circles have a common point they cannot have the same centre, unless they coincide altogether.

6. An arc of a circle is any part of the circumference.
7. **A chord** of a circle is a straight line joining any two points or the circumference.

NOTE. From these definitions it may be seen that a chord of a circle, which does not pass through the centre, divides the circumference into two unequal arcs; of these, the greater is called the **major arc**, and the less the **minor arc**,. Thus the major arc is *greater*, and the minor arc *less* than the semi-circumference. The major and minor arcs, into which a circumference is divided by a chord, are said to be **conjugate** to one another.

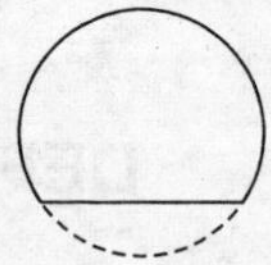

SYMMETRY

Some elementary properties of circles are easily proved by considerations of symmetry. For convenience the definition given on page 18 is here repeated.

DEFINITION 1. A figure is said to be **symmetrical about** a line when, on being folded about that line, the parts of the figure on each side of it can be brought into coincidence. The straight line is called an **axis of symmetry.**

That this may be possible, it is clear that the two parts of the figure must have the same size and shape, and must be similarly placed with regard to the axis.

DEFINITION 2. Let **AB** be a straight line and **P** a point outside it.

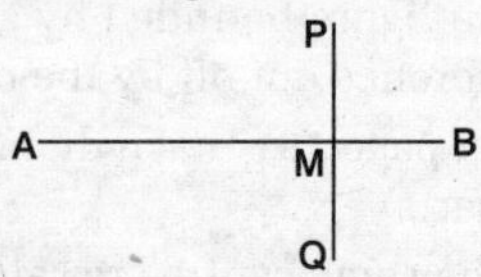

From **P** draw **PM** perp. to **AB**, and produce it to **Q**, making **MQ** equal to **PM**.

Then if the figure is folded about **AB**, the point **P** may be made to coincide with **Q**, for the ∠**AMP** = the ∠**AMQ**, and **MP** = **MQ**.

The points **P** and **Q** are said to be **symmetrically opposite** with regard to the axis **AB**, and each point is said to be the **image** of the other in the axis.

NOTE. A point and its image are equidistant from every point on the axis. See Prob. 14, page, 79.

SOME SYMMETRICAL PROPERTIES OF CIRCLES

I. *A circle is symmetrical about any diameter.*

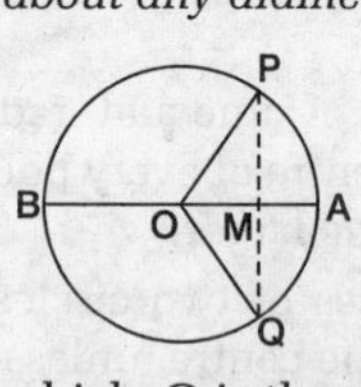

Let **APBQ** be a circle of which **O** is the centre, and **AB** any diameter.

It is required to prove that the circle is symmetrical about **AB**.

Proof. Let **OP** and **OQ** be two radii making any equal $\angle^s$ **AOP**, **AOQ** on opposite sides of **OA**.

Then if the figure is folded about **AB**, **OP**, may be made to fall along **OQ**, since the $\angle$**AOP** = the $\angle$**AOQ**.

And thus **P** will coincide with **Q**, since **OP** = **OQ**.

Thus every point in the arc **APB** must coincide with some point in the arc **AQB** ; that is, the two parts of the circumference on each side of **AB** can be made to coincide.

∴ the circle is symmetrical about the diameter **AB**.

COROLLARY. If **PQ** is drawn cutting **AB** at **M**, then on folding the figure about **AB**, since **P** falls on **Q**. **MP** will coincide with **MQ**.

∴ **MP** = **MQ** ;

and the $\angle$**OMP** will coincide with the $\angle$**OMQ**,

∴ these angles, being adjacent, are rt. $\angle^s$;

∴ the points **P** and **Q** are symmetrically opposite with regard to **AB**.

Hence, conversely, *if a circle passes through a given point* **P** *it also passes through the symmetrically opposite point with regard to any diameter.*

DEFINITION.

I. The straight line passing through the centres of two circles is called the **line of centres.**

II. *Two circles are divided symmetrically by their line of centres.*

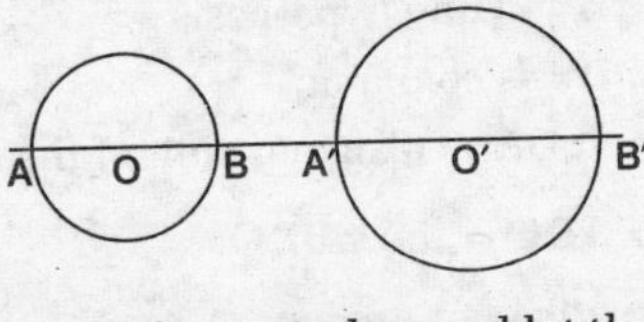

Let **O, O′** be the centres of two circles, and let the st. line through **O, O′** cut the **O**^{ces} at **A, B** and **A′, B′**. Then **AB** and **A′ B′** are diameters and therefore axes of symmetry of their respective circles. That is, the line of centres divides each circle symmetrically.

III. *If two circles cut at one point, they must also cut at a second point; and the common chord is bisected at right angles by the line of centres.*

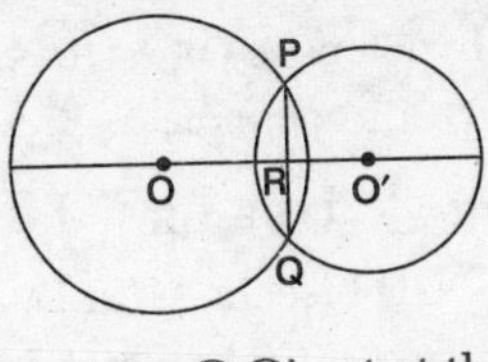

Let the circles whose centres are **O, O′** cut at ths point **P**.

Draw **PR** perp. to **OO′**, and produce it to **Q**, so that **RQ** = **RP**.

Then **P** and **Q** are symmetrically opposite points with regard to the line of centres **OO′**;

∴since **P** is on the **O**^{ce} of both circles, it follows that **Q** is also on the **O**^{ce} of both. [I. Cor.]

And, by construction, the common chord **PQ** is bisected at right angles by **OO′**.

ON CHORDS

THEOREM 31. [Euclid III. 3]

If a straight line drawn from the centre of a circle bisects a chord which does not pass through the centre, it cuts the chord at right angles.

Conversely, if it cuts the chord at right angles, it bisects it.

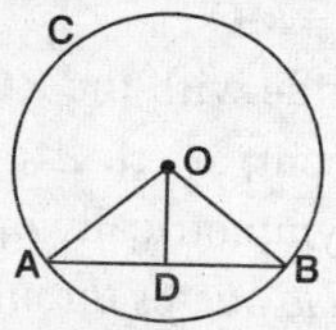

Let **ABC** be a circle whose centre is **O**; and let **OD** bisect a chord **AB** which does not pass through the centre.

It is required to prove that **OD** *is perp. to* **AB**.

Join **OA, OB**.

Proof. Then in the △^{s} **ADO, BDO**

because { **AD** = **BD**, by hypothesis; **OD** = is common; and **OA** = **OB**, being radii of the circle;

∴ the ∠**ADO** = the ∠**BDO**; *Theor.* 7.

and these are adjacent angles,

∴ **OD** is perp. to **AB**. **Q.E.D.**

Conversely. Let **OD** be perp. to the chord **AB** .

It is required to prove that **OD** *bisects* **AB**.

Proof. In the △^{s} **ODA, ODB,**

because { the ∠^{s}**ODA, ODB** are *right angles*, the hypotenuse **OA** = the hypotenuse **OB**, and **OD** is common;

∴ **DA** = **DB**; *Theor.* 18.

that is, **OD** bisects **AB** at **D**.

COROLLARY 1. *The straight line which bisects a chord at right angles passes through the centre.*

COROLLARY 2. *A straight line cannot meet a circle at more than two points.*

For suppose a st. line meets a circle whose centre is **O** at the points **A** and **B**.

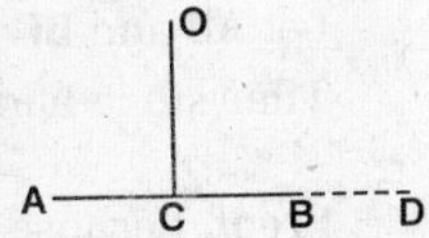

Draw **OC** perp. to **AB**.

Then **AC** = **CB**.

Now if the circle were to cut **AB** in a third point **D**, **AC** would also be equal to **CD**, which is impossible.

COROLLARY 3. *A chord of a circle ties wholly within it.*

EXERCISES
(Numerical and Graphical)

1. In the figure of Theorem 31, if **AB** = 8 cm., and **OD** = 3 cm, find **OB**. Draw the figure, and verify your result by measurement.
2. Calculate the length of a chord which stands at a distance 5 cm. from the centre of a circle whose radius is 13 cm.
3. In a circle of 5 cm. radius draw two chords 8 cm. and 6 cm. in length. Calculate and measure the distance of each from the centre.
4. Draw a circle whose diameter is 8.0 cm. and place in it a chord 6.0 cm. in length. Calculate to the nearest millimetre the distance of the chord from the centre; and verify your result by measurement.
5. Find the distance from the centre of a chord 70 cm. in length in a circle whose diameter is 74 cm. Verify the result graphically by drawing a figure in which 1 cm. represents 10 cm.
6. AB is a chord 4.8 cm. long in a circle whose centre is **O** and whose radius is 2.6 cm; find the area of the triangle **OAB** in square centimetres.
7. Two points **P** and **Q** are 9 cm. apart. Draw a circle with radius 5.1 cm. to pass through **P** and **Q**. Calculate the distance of its centre from the chord **PQ** and verify by measurement.

THEOREM 32

One circle, and only one, can pass through any three points not in the same straight line.

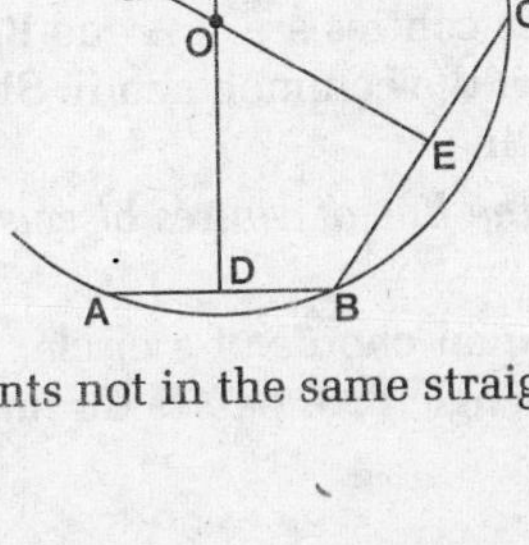

Let **A, B, C** be three points not in the same straight line.

It is required to prove that one circle, and only one, can pass through **A**, **B**, *and* **C**.

Join **AB**, **BC**,

Let **AB** and **BC** be bisected at right angles by the lines **DF**, **EG**.

Then since and **BC** are not in the same st. line, **DF** and **EG** are not par[1].

Let **DF** and **EG** meet in **O**.

Proof. Because **DF** bisects **AB** at right angles,

∴every point on **DF** is equidistant from **A** and **B**. ***Prop.*** 14.

Similarly every point on **EG** is equidistant from **B** and **C**

∴ **O**, the only point common to **DF** and **EG**, is equidistant from **A**, **B** and **C**;
and there is no other point equidistant from **A**, **B**, and **C**.

∴ a circle having its centre at **O** and radius **OA** will pass through **B** and **C**; and this is the only circle which will pass through the three given points.

Q.E.D.

COROLLARY 1. *The size and position of a circle are fully determined if it is known to pass through three given points;* for then the position of the centre and length of the radius can be found.

COROLLARY 2. *Two circles cannot cut one another in more than two points without coinciding entirely;* for if they cut at three points they would have the same centre and radius.

HYPOTHETICAL CONSTRUCTION. *From Theorem 32 it appears that we may suppose a circle to be drawn through any three points not in the same straight line.*

For example, a circle can be assumed to pass through the vertices of any triangle.

DEFINITION. The circle which passes through the vertices of a triangle is called its **circum-circle,** and is said to be **circumscribed** about the triangle. The centre of the circle is called the **circum-centre** of the triangle, and the radius is called the **circum-radius.**

EXERCISES ON THEOREM 31 AND 32

(*Theoretical*)

1. The parts of a straight line intercepted between the circumferences of two concentric circles are equal.
2. Two circles, whose centres are at **A** and **B**, intersect at **C**, **D**; and **M** is the middle point of the common chord. Show that **AM** and **BM** are in the same straight line.

   Hence prove that the line of centres bisects the common chord at right angles.
3. **AB**, **AC** are two equal chords of a circle; show that the straight line which bisects the angle **BAC** passes through the centre.

4. *Find the locus of the centres of all circles which pass through two given points.*
5. *Describe a circle that shall pass through two given points and have its centre in a given straight line.*

   When is this impossible?
6. *Describe a circle of given radius to pass through two given points. When is this impossible?*

*THEOREM 33. [Euclid III. 9]

If from a point within a circle more than two equal straight lines can be drawn to the circumference, that point is the centre of the circle.

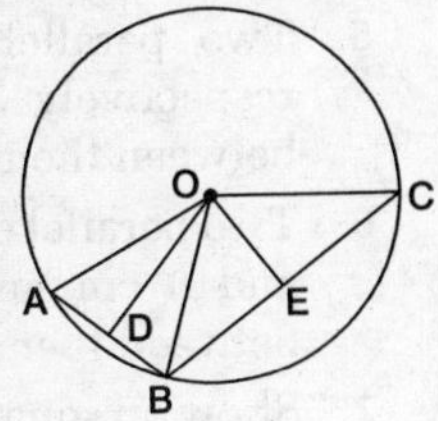

Let **ABC** be a circle, and **O** a point within it from which more than two equal st. lines are drawn to the **O**ce, namely **OA, OB, OC.**

It is required to prove that **O** *is the centre of the circle* **ABC**.

Join **AB, BC** .

Let **D** and **E** be the middle points of **AB** and **BC** respectively

Join **OD, OE**

Proof. In the Δ^s**ODA, ODB,**

because $\begin{cases} \mathbf{DA = DB}, \\ \mathbf{DO} \text{ is common}, \\ \text{and } \mathbf{OA = OB}, \text{ by hypothesis;} \end{cases}$

∴ the ∠**ODA** = the ∠**ODB**; ***Theor*** . 7.

∴ these angles, being adjacent, are rt. $\angle^s$.

Hence **DO** bisects the chord **AB** at right angles, and therefore passes through the centre. ***Theor.*** 31, ***Cor.*** 1.

Similarly it may be shown that **EO** passes through the centre.

∴ **O**, which is the only point common to **DO** and **EO**, must be the centre.

Q.E.D.

EXERCISES ON CHORDS

(*Numerical and Graphical*)

1. **AB** and **BC** are lines at right angles, and their lengths are 3.2 cm. and 6 cm. respectively. Draw the circle through the points **A, B,** and **C**; find the length of its radius, and verify your result by measurement.
2. Draw a circle in which a chord 6 cm. in length stands at a distance of 3 cm, from the centre.

   Calculate (to the nearest millimetre) the length of the radius and verify your result by measurement.

3. Draw a circle on a diameter of 8 cm., and place in it a chord equal to the radius.

   Calculate (to the nearest millimetre) the distance of the chord from the centre, and verify by measurement.

4. Two circles, whose radii are respectively 26 m. and 25 m. intersect at two points which are 48 m. apart. Find the distances between their centres.

   Draw the figure (scale 1 cm. to 10 cm.), and verify your result by measurement.

5. Two parallel chords of a circle whose diameter is 13 cm: are respectively 5 cm. and 12 cm. in length: show that the distance between them is 8.5 cm. or 3.5 cm.

6. Two parallel chords of a circle on the same side of the centre are 6 cm. and 8 cm. in length respectively, and the perpendicular distance between them is 1 cm. Calculate and measure the radius.

7. Show on squared paper that if a circle has its centre at *any* point on the z-axis and passes through the point (6, 5), it also passes through the point (6, – 5). [See page 117.]

(*Theoretical*)

8. The line joining the middle points of two parallel chords of a circle passes through the centre.

9. *Find the locus of the middle points of parallel chords in a circle.*

10. Two intersecting chords of a circle cannot bisect each other unless each is a diameter.

11. If a parallelogram can be inscribed in a circle, the point of intersection of its diagonals must be at the centre of the circle.

12. Show that rectangles are the only parallelograms that can be inscribed in a circle.

THEOREM 34. [Euclid III. 14]

Equal chords of a circle are equidistant from the centre.

Conversely, chords which are equidistant from the centre are equal.

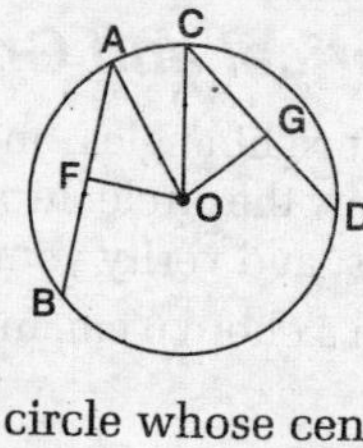

Let **AB**, **CD** be chords of a circle whose centre is **O**, and let **OF**, **OG**, be perpendiculars on them from **O**.

First, Let **AB** = **CD**.

It is required to prove that **AB** *and* **CD** *are equidistant from* **O**.

Join **OA**, **OC**.

Proof. Because **OF** is perp. to the chord **AB**,

∴ **OF** bisects **AB**; ***Theor.* 31.**

∴ **AF** is half of **AB**.

Similarly **CG** is half of **CD**.

But, the hypothesis, **AB** = **CD**,

∴ **AF** = **CG**.

Now in the Δ^s**OFA**, **OGC**,

because { the $\angle^s$**OFA**, **OGC** are *right angles*, the hypotenuse **OA** = the hypotenuse **OC**, and **AF** = **CG**;

∴ the triangles are equal in all respects; ***Theor.* 18.**

so that **OF** = **OG**;

that is, **AB** and **CD** are equidistant from **O**. **Q.E.D.**

Conversely. Let **OF** = **OG**.

It is required to prove th at **AB** = **CD**.

Proof. As before it may be shown that **AF** is half of **AB**, and **CG** half of **CD**.

Then in the Δ^s**OFA**, **OGC**,

because { the Δ^s**OFA**, **OGC** are *right angles*, the hypotenuse **OA** = the hypotenuse **OC**, and **OF** = **OG**;

∴ **AF** = **CG**; ***Theor.*** 18.

∴ the doubles of these are equal;

that is, **AB** = **CD**. **Q.E.D.**

Exercises

(*Theoretical*)

1. *Find the locus of the middle points of equal chords of a circle.*
2. If two chords of a circle cut one another, and make equal angles with the straight line which joins their point of intersection to the centre, they are equal.
3. If two equal chords of a circle intersect, show that the segments of the one are equal respectively to the segments of the other.
4. In a given circle draw a chord which shall be equal to one given straight line (not greater than the diameter) and parallel to another.

5. **PQ** is a fixed chord in a circle, and **AB** is any diameter: show that the sum or difference of the perpendiculars let fall from **A** and **B** on **PQ** is constant, that is, the same for all positions of **AB**. [**See Ex.** 9, p. 57.]

(Graphical)

4. In a circle of radius 4.1 cm. any number of chords are drawn each 1.8 cm. in length. Show that the middle points of these chords all lie on a circle. Calculate and measure the length of its radius, and draw the circle.

7. The centres of two circles are 4 cm. apart, their common chord is 2.4 cm in length, and the radius of the larger circle is 3.7 cm. Give a construction for finding the points of intersection of the two circles, and find the radius of the smaller circle.

THEOREM 35. [Euclid III. 15]

Of any two chords of a circle, that which is nearer to the centre is greater than one more remote.

Conversely, the greater of two chords is nearer to the centre than the less.

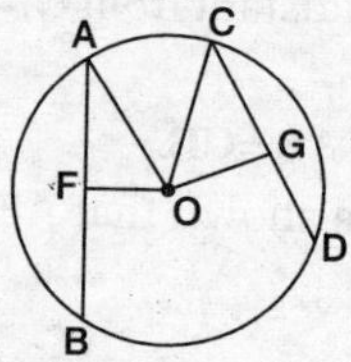

Let **AB, CD** be chords of a circle whose centre is **O**, and let **OF, OG** be perpendiculars on them from **O**.

It is required to prove that

(i) *if* **OF** *is less than* **OG**, *then* **AB** *is greater than* **CD**;

(ii) *If* **AB** *is greater than* **CD**, *then* **OF** *is less than* **OG**.

Join **OA, OC**

Proof. Because **OF** is perp. to the chord **AB**

∴ **OF** bisects **AB**;

∴ **AF** is half of **AB**.

Similarly **CG** is half of **CD**.

Now **OA** = **OC**,

∴ the sq. on **OA** = the sq. on **OC**.

But since ∠**OFA** is a rt. angle,

∴ the sq. on **OA** = the sqq. on **OF, FA**.

Similarly the s.q. on **OC** = the sqq. on **OG, GC**.

∴ the sqq. on **OF, FA** = the sqq. on **OG, GC**.

(i) Hence if **OF** is given less than **OG**;

the sq. on **OF** is less than the sq. on **OG**;

∴ the sq. on **FA** is greater than the sq. on **GC**;

∴ **FA** is greater than **GC**.

∴ **AB** is greater than **CD**.

(ii) But if **AB** is given greater than **CD**,

that is, if **FA** is greater than **GC**;

then the sq. on **FA** is greater than the sq. on **GC**.

∴ the sq. on **OF** is less than the sq. on **OG**;

∴ **OF** is less than **OG**. **Q.E.D.**

COROLLARY. *The greatest chord in a circle is a diameter.*

EXERCISES
(Miscellaneous)

1. Through a given point within a circle draw the least possible chord.
2. Draw a triangle **ABC** in which $a = 7$ cm., $b = 2.4$ cm. $c = 7.4$ cm. Through the ends of the side a draw a circle with its centre on the side c. Calculate and measure the radius.
3. Draw the circumcircle of a triangle whose sides are 5.2 cm, 5.6 cm. and 6 cm. Measure its radius.
4. **AB** is fixed chord of a circle, and **XY** any other chord having its middle point **Z** on **AB**; what is the greatest, and what the least length that **XY** may have?

   Show that **XY** increases, as **Z** approaches the middle point of **AB**.
5. Show on squared paper that a circle whose centre is at the origin, and whose radius in 6 cm., passes through the points (4.8 cm. 3.6cm.), (3.6 cm., 4.8. cm.).

   Find (i) the length of the chord joining these points, (ii) the coordinates of its middle point, (iii) its perpendicular distance from the origin.

*THEOREM 36. [Euclid III. 7]

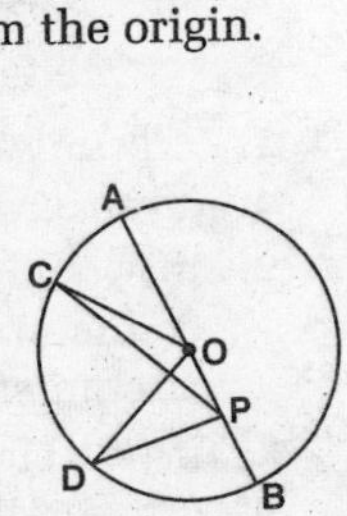

If from any internal point, not the centre, straight lines are drawn to the circumference of a circle, then the greatest is that which passes through the centre, and the least is the remaining part of that diameter.

And of any other two such lines the greater is that which subtends the greater angle at the centre.

Let **ABCD** be a circle, and from **P** any internal point, which is not the centre, let **PA, PB, PC, PD** be drawn to the O^{ce}, so that **PA** passes through the centre **O**, and **PB** is the remaining part of that diameter.

Also let the ∠**POC** at the centre subtended by **PC** be greater than the ∠**POD** subtended by **PD**.

It is required to prove that of these st. lines

(i) **PA** *is the greatest,* (ii) **PB** *is the least,*

(iii) **PC** *is greater than* **PD**.

Join **OC, OD**.

Proof. (i) In the **ΔPOC**, the sides **PO, OC** are together greater than **PC**. *Theor.* **11.**

But **OC = OA**, being radii;

∴ **PO, OA** are together greater than **PC**;

that is **PA** is greater than **PC**.

Similarly **PA** may be shown to be greater than any other st. line drawn from P to the **O**ce;

∴ **PA** is the greatest of all such lines.

(ii) In the **ΔOPD**, the sides **OP, PD** are together greater than **OD**.

But **OD = OB**, being radii;

∴ **OP, PD** are together greater than **OB**.

Take away the common part **OP**;

then **PD** is greater than **PB**.

Similarly any other st. line drawn from **P** to the **O**ce may be shown to be greater than **PB**;

∴ **PB** is the least of all such lines.

(iii) In the Δs **POC, POD**,

because { **PO** is common, **OC = OD**, being radii but the ∠**POC** is greater than the ∠**POD**,

∴ **PC** is greater than **PD**. *Theor.* **19. Q.E.D.**

EXERCISES
(*Miscellaneous*)

1. *All circles which pass through a fixed point, and have their centres on a given straight line, pass also through a second fixed point.*
2. If two circles which intersect are cut by a straight line parallel to the common chord, show that the parts of it intercepted between the circumferences are equal.
3. If two circles cut one another, any two parallel straight lines drawn through the points of intersection to cut the circles are equal.
4. If two circles cut one another, any two straight lines drawn through a point of section, making equal angles with the common chord, and terminated by the circumferences, are equal.
5. Two circles of diameters 74 and 40 cm. respectively have a common chord 24 cm. in length; find the distance between their centres. Draw the figure (1 cm. to represent 10 cm.) and verify your result by measurement.

6. Draw two circles of radii 2 cm. and 3.4 cm., and with their centres 4.2 cm. apart. Find by calculation, and by measurement, the length of the common chord and its distance from the two centres.

*THEOREM 37. [Euclid III. 8]

If from any external point straight lines are drawn to the circumference of a circle, the greatest is that which passes through the centre, and the least is that which when produced passes through the centre.

And of any other two such lines, the greater is that which subtends the greater angle at the centre.

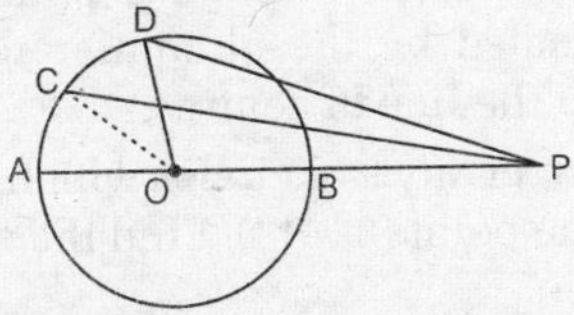

Let **AODB** be a circle, and from any external point **P** let the lines **PBA**, **PC**, **PD** be drawn to the **O**ce, so that PBA passes through the centre **O**, and so that the ∠**POC** subtended by **PO** at the centre is greater than the ∠**POD** subtended by **PD**.

It is required to prove that of these st. lines

(i) **PA** *is the greatest,* (ii) **PB** *is the least,*

(iii) **PC** *is greater than* **PD**.

Join **OC**, **OD**.

Proof.

(i) In the Δ**POC**, the sides **PO**, **OC** are together greater than **PC**.

But **OO** = **OA**, being radii;

∴ **PO**, **OA** are together greater than **PC**;

that is, **PA** is greater than **PC**.

Similarly **PA** may be shown to be greater than any other st. line drawn **P** to the **O**ce;

that is, **PA** is the greatest of all such lines.

(ii) In the Δ**POD**, the sides **PD**, **DO** are together greater than **PO**,

But **OD** = **OB**, being radii;

∴ the remainder **PD** is greater than the remainder **PB**.

Similarly any other st. line drawn from **P** to the **O**ce may be shown to be greater than **PB** ; that is, **PB** is the least of all such lines.

(iii) In the Δs **POC**, **POD**,

because { **PO** is common,
OC = **OD**, being radii;
but the ∠**POC** is greater than the ∠**POD**;

∴ **PC** is greater than **PD**. ***Theor.*** 19. **Q.E.D.**

EXERCISES
(*Miscellaneous*)

1. Find the greatest and least straight lines which have one extremity on each of two given circles which do not intersect.
2. If from any point on the circumference of a circle straight lines are drawn to the circumference, the greatest is that which passes through the centre; and of any two such lines the greater is that which subtends the greater angle at the centre.
3. Of all straight lines drawn through a point of intersection of two circles, and terminated by the circumferences, the greatest is that which is parallel to the line of centres.
4. Draw on squared paper any two circles which have their centres on the x-axis, and cut at the point (8, –11). Find the coordinates of their other point of intersection.
5. Draw on squared paper two circles with centres at the points (15, 0) and (– 6, 0) respectively, and cutting at the point (0, 8). Find the lengths of their radii, and the coordinates of their other point of intersection.
6. Draw an isosceles triangle **OAB** with an angle of 80° at its vertex **O**. With centre **O** and radius **OA** draw a circle, and on its circumference take any number of points **P**, **Q**, **R**. ... on the same side of **AB** as the centre. Measure the angles subtended by the chord **AB** at the points **P**, **Q**, **R**, ... Repeat the same exercise with any other given angle at **O**. What inference do you draw?

ON ANGLES IN SEGMENTS, AND ANGLES AT THE CENTRES AND CIRCUMFERENCES OF CIRCLES

THEOREM 38. [Euclid III. 20]

The angle at the centre of a circle is double of an angle at the circumference standing on the same arc.

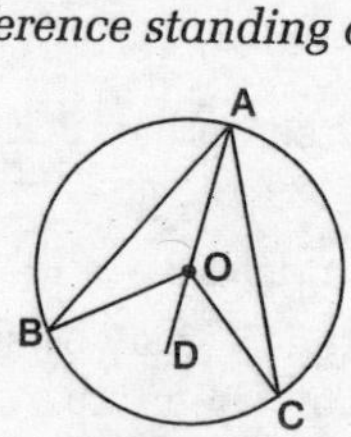

Fig.1.

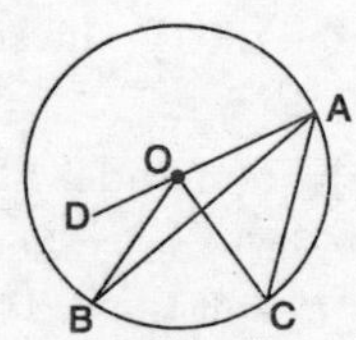

Fig. 2.

Let **ABC** be a circle, of which **O** is the centre; and let **BOC** be the angle at the centre, and **BAC** an angle at the **O**^{ce}, standing on the same arc **BC**.

It is required to prove that the ∠**BOC** *is twice the* ∠**BAC**.

Join **AO**, and produce it to **D**.

Proof. In the Δ**OAB**, because **OB** = **OA**,

$\therefore$ the $\angle$**OAB** = the $\angle$**OBA**.

$\therefore$ the sum of the $\angle^s$**OAB, OBA** = twice the $\angle$**OAB**.

But the ext. $\angle$**BOD** = the sum of the $\angle^s$**OAB, OBA**;

$\therefore$ the $\angle$**BOD** = twice the $\angle$**OAB**.

Similarly the $\angle$**DOC** = twice the $\angle$**OAC**.

$\therefore$ adding these results in Fig. 1, and taking the difference in Fig. 2, it follows in each case that

the $\angle$**BOC** = twice the $\angle$**BAC**. **Q.E.D.**

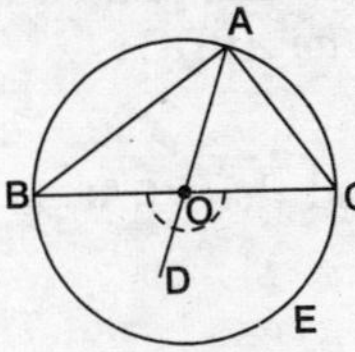

Fig. 3.

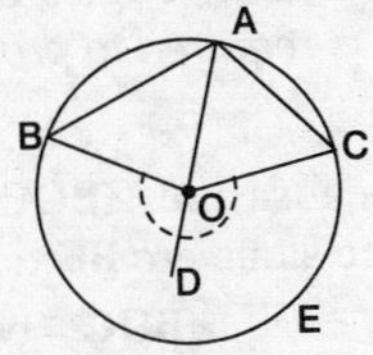

Fig. 4.

Obs. If the arc **BEC**, on which the angles stand, is a semi-circumference, as in Fig. 3, the $\angle$**BOC** at the centre is a *straight angle*; and if the arc **BEC** is greater than a semi-circumference, as in Fig. 4, the $\angle$**BOC** at the centre is *reflex*. But the proof for Fig. 1 applies without change to both these cases, showing that whether the given arc is greater than, equal to, or less than a semi-circumference,

the $\angle$**BOC** = *twice the* $\angle$**BAC**, *on the same arc* **BEC**.

DEFINITIONS

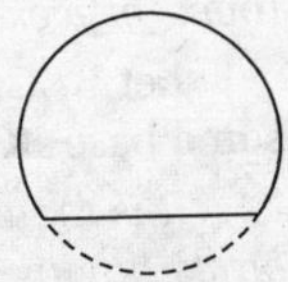

A **segment** of a circle is the figure bounded by a chord and one of the two arcs into which the chord divides the circumference.

NOTE. The chord of a segment is sometimes called its base.

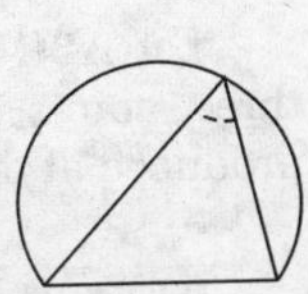

An **angle in a segment** is one formed by two straight lines drawn from any points in the arc of the segment to the extremities of its chord.

We have *seen* in Theorem 32 that a circle may be drawn through *any three* points not in a straight line. But it is only under certain conditions that a circle can be drawn through more than three points.

DEFINITION. If four or more points are so placed that a circle may be drawn through them, they are said to be **concyclic.**

THEOREM 39. [Euclid III. 21]

Angles in the same segment of a circle are equal.

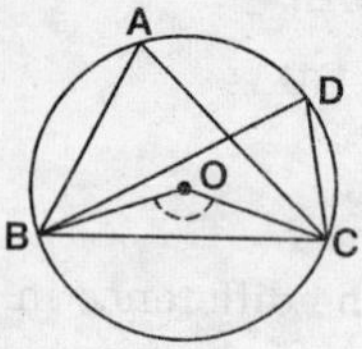

Fig. 1.

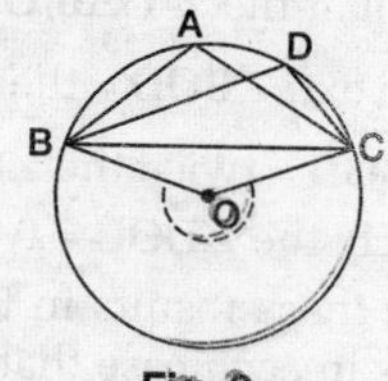

Fig. 2.

Let **BAC**, **BDC** be angles in the same segment **BADC** of a circle whose centre is **O**. *It is required to prove that the* ∠**BAC** = *the* ∠**BDC**.

Join **BO, OC**.

Proof. Because the ∠**BOC** is at the centre, and the ∠**BAC** at the **O**ce, standing on the same arc **BC**,

∴ the ∠**BOC** = twice the ∠**BAC**. *Theor.* 38.

Similarly the ∠**BOC** = twice the ∠**BDC**.

∴ the ∠**BAC** = the ∠**BDC**. Q.E.D.

NOTE. The given segment may be greater than a semicircle as in Fig. 1, or less than a semicircle as in Fig. 2 ; in the latter case the angle **BOC** will be reflex. But by virtue of the extension of Theorem 38, given on the preceding page, the above proof applies equally to both figures,

CONVERSE OF THEOREM 39

Equal angles standing on the same base, and on the same side of it have their vertices on an arc of a circle, of which the given base is the chord.

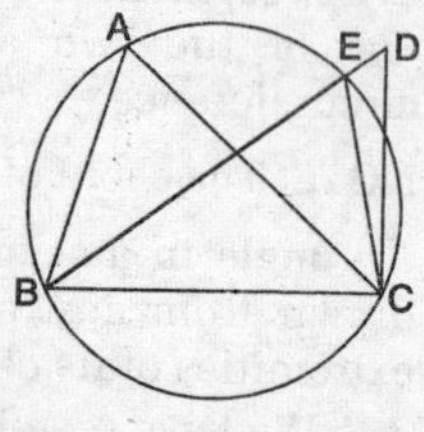

Let **BAC**, **BDC** be two equal angles standing on the same base **BC**, and on the same side of it.

It is required to prove that **A** *and* **D** *lie on an arc of a circle having* **BC** *as its chord.*

Let **ABC** be the circle which passes through the three points **A, B, C**; and suppose it cuts **BD** or **BD** produced at the point **E**.

Join **EC**.

Proof. Then the ∠**BAC** = the ∠**BEC** in the same segment.

But, by hypothesis, the ∠**BAC** = the∠**BDC**;

∴ the ∠**BEC** = the ∠**BDC**;

which is impossible unless **E** coincides with **D**;

∴ the circle through **B, A, C** must pass through **D**.

COROLLARY. *The locus of the vertices of triangles drawn on the same side of a given base, and with equal vertical angles, is an arc of a circle.*

EXERCISES ON THEOREM 39

1. In Fig. 1, if the angle **BDC** is 74°, find the number of degrees in each of the angles **BAC, BOC, OBC**.
2. In Fig. 2, let **BD** and **CA** intersect at **X**. If the angle **DXC** = 40°, and the angle **XCD** = 25°, find the number of degrees in the angle **BAC** and in the reflex angle **BOC**.
3. In Fig. 1, if the angles **CBD, BCD** are respectively 43° and 82°, find the number of degrees in the angles **BAC, OBD, OCD**.
4. Show that in Fig. 2 the angle **OBC** is always less than the angle **BAC** by a right angle.

[For further Exercises on Theorem 39 see page 155.]

THEOREM 40. [Euclid III. 22]

The opposite angles of any quadrilateral inscribed in a circle are together equal to two right angles.

Let **ABCD** be a quadrilateral inscribed in the ⊙**ABC**.

It is required to proved that

(i) *the* $\angle^s$ **ADC, ABC** *together = two rt. angles.*

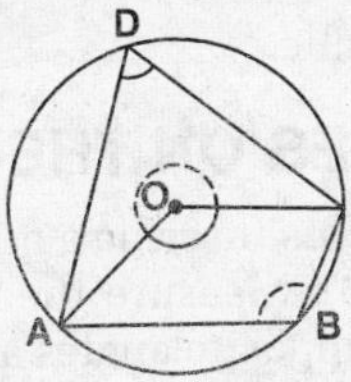

(ii) *the* $\angle^s$ **BAD, BCD** *together = two rt. angles.*

Suppose **O** is in the centre of the circle.

Join **OA, OC.**

Proof. Since the ∠**ADC** at the **O**ce = half the ∠**AOC** at the centre, standing on the same arc **ABC**; and the ∠**ABC** at the **O**ce = half the reflex ∠**AOC** at the centre, standing on the same arc **ADC**;

∴ The $\angle^s$ **ADC, ABC** together = half the sum of the ∠**AOC** and the reflex ∠**AOC.**

But these angles make up four rt. angles.

∴ the $\angle^s$ **ADC, ABC** together = two rt. angles.

Similarly the $\angle^s$ **BAD, BCD** together = two rt. angles. **Q.E.D.**

NOTE. The results of Theorems 39 and 40 should be carefully compared.

From Theorem 39 we learn that angles in the *same* segment are *equal.*

From Theorem 40 we learn that angles in *conjugate* segments are *supplementary.*

DEFINITION. A quadrilateral is called **cyclic** when a circle can be drawn through its four vertices.

CONVERSE OF THEOREM 40

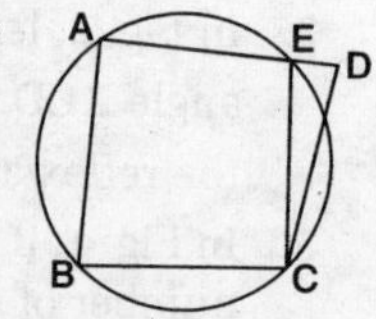

If a pair of opposite angles of a quadrilateral are supplementary, its vertices are concycle.

Let **ABCD** be a quadrilateral in which the opposite angles at **B** and **D** are supplementary.

It is required to prove that the points **A, B, C, D** *are concyclic.*

Let **ABC** be the circle which passes through the three points **A, B, C;** and suppose it cuts **AD** or **AD** produced in the point **E.**

Join EC.

Proof. Then since **ABCDE** is a cyclic quadrilateral,

∴ the **∠AEC** is the supplement of the **∠ABC.**

But, by hypothesis the **∠ADC** is the supplement of the **∠ABC**

∴ the **∠AEC** = the **∠ADC;**

which is impossible unless E coincides with **D.**

∴ the circle which passes through **A, B, C** must pass through **D;**

that is **A, B, C, D** are concyclic. **Q.E.D.**

EXERCISES ON THEOREM 40

1. In a circle of 3.2 cm. radius inscribe a quadrilateral **ABCD**, making the angle **ABC** equal to 126°. Measure the remaining angles, and hence verify in this case that opposite angles are supplementary.
2. Prove Theorem 40 by the aid of Theorems 39 and 16, after first joining the opposite vertices of the quadrilateral.
3. If a circle can be described about a parallelogram, the parallelogram must be rectangular.
4. **ABC** is an isosceles triangle, and **XY** is drawn parallel to the base **BC** cutting the sides in **X** and **Y**: show that the four points **B, C, X, Y** lie on a circle.
5. *If one side of a cyclic quadrilateral is produced, the exterior angle is equal to the opposite interior angle of the quadrilateral.*

THEOREM 41. [Euclid III. 31]

The angle in a semi-circle is a right angle.

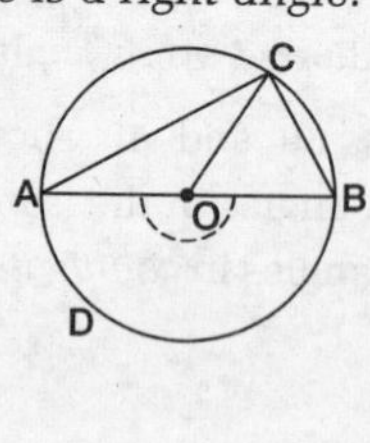

Let **ADB** be a circle of which **AB** is a diameter and **O** the centre; and let **C** be any point on the semi-circumference **ACB**.

It is required to prove that the ∠ACB is a rt. angle.

1st Proof. The ∠**ACB** at the $\mathbf{O}^{ce}$ is half the *straight angle* **AOB** at the centre, standing on the same arc **ADB**;

and a *straight angle* = two rt. angles:

∴ the ∠**ACB** is at rt. angle. **Q.E.D.**

2nd Proof. Join **OC**.

Then because **OA** = **OC**,

∴the ∠**OCA** = ∠**OAC** ***Theor.* 5.**

And because **OB** = **OC**,

∴the ∠**OCB** = the ∠**OBC**.

∴the whole ∠**ACB** = the ∠**OAC** + the ∠**OBC**.

But the three angles of the Δ**ACB** together = two rt. angles;

∴ the ∠**ACB** = one-half of two rt. angles

= one rt. angle. **Q.E.D.**

COROLLARY. *The angle in a segment greater than a semi-circle is acute; and the angle in a segment less than a semi-circle is obtuse.*

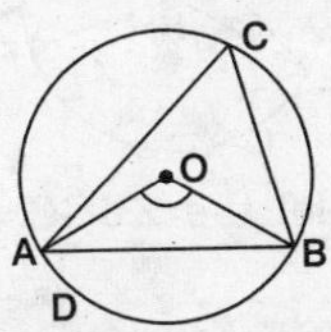

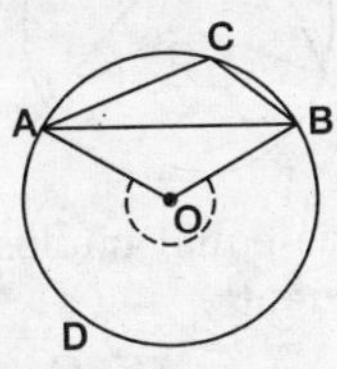

The ∠**ACB** at the $\mathbf{O}^{ce}$ is half the ∠**AOB** at the centre, on the same arc **ADB**.

(i) If the segment **ACB** is greater than a semi-circle, then ADB is a *minor* arc;

∴ the ∠**AOB** is *less* than two rt. angles;

∴ the ∠**ACB** is *less* than one rt. angle.

(ii) If the segment **ACB** is less than a semi-circle, then **ADB** is a *major*-arc;

∴ the ∠**AOB** is *greater* than two rt. angles;

∴ the ∠**ACB** is *greater* than one rt. angle.

EERCISES ON THEOREMS 41

1. *A circle described on the hypotenuse of a right-angled triangle as diameter, passes through the opposite angular point.*
2. Two circles interesect at **A** and **B**; and through **A** two diameters **AP**, **AQ** are drawn, one in each circle: show that the points **P**, **B**, **Q**, are collinear.

3. A circle is described on one of the equal sides of an isosceles triangle as diameter. Show that it passes through the middle point of the base.
4. Circles described on any two sides of a triangle as diameters intersect on the third side, or the third side produced.
5. A straight rod of given length slides between two straight rulers placed at right angles to one another; find the locus of its middle point.
6. *Find the locus of the middle points of chords a circle drawn through a fixed point. Distinguish between the cases when the given point is within, on, or without the circumference.*

DEFINITION.

A sector of a circle is a figure bounded by two radii and the arc intercepted between them.

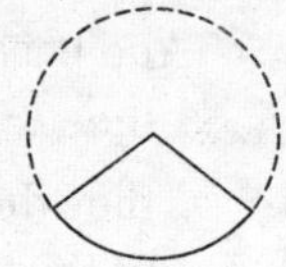

THEOREM 42. [Euclid III. 26]

In equal circles, arcs which subtend equal values, either at the centres or at the circumferences, are equal.

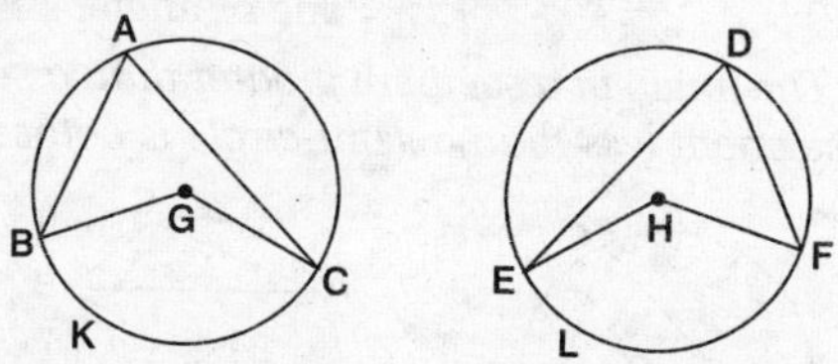

Let **ABC, DEF** be equal circles, and let the ∠**BGC** = the ∠**EHF** at the centres; and consequently

the ∠**BAC** = the ∠**EDF** at the **O**^{ces} *Theor.* 38.

It is required to prove that the arc **BKC** = *the arc* **ELF**.

Proof. Apply the ⊙**ABC** to the ⊙**DEF**, so that the centre **G** falls on the centre **H**, and **GB** falls along **HE**.

Then because the ∠**BGC** = the ∠**EHF**,

∴ **GC** will fall along **HF**.

And because the circles have equal radii, **B** will fall on **E**, and **C** on **F**, and the circumferences of the circles will coincide entirely.

∴ the arc **BKC** must coincide with the are **ELF**;

∴ the arc **BKC** the arc **ELF**.

∴ the arc **BKC** = the arc **ELF**. **Q.E.D.**

COROLLARY. *In equal circles sectors which have equal angles are equal.*

Obs. It is clear that any theorem relating to arcs, angles, and chords in *equal* circles must also be true in the *same* circle.

THEOREM 43. [Euclid III. 27]

In equal circles, angles, either at the centres or at the circumferences, which stand on equal arcs are equal.

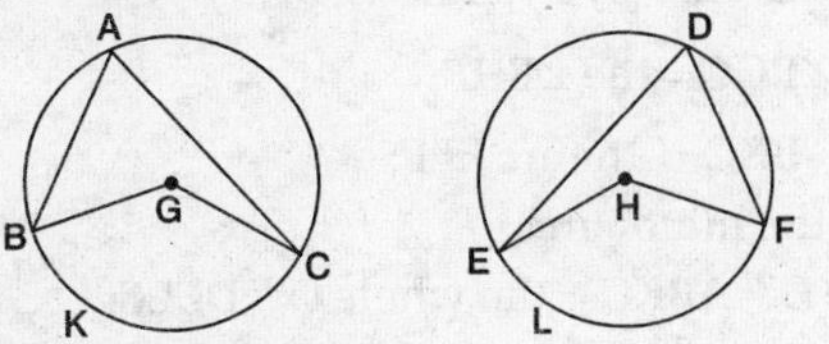

Let **ABC**, **DEF** be equal circles;

and let the arc **BKC** = the arc **ELF**.

It is required to prove that

the ∠**BGC** *= the* ∠**EHF** *at the centres;*

also the ∠**BAC** *= the* ∠**EDF** *at the* $\mathbf{O}^{ces}$.

Proof. Apply the ⊙**ABC** to the ⊙**DEF**, so that the centre **G** falls on the centre **H**, and **GB** falls along **HE**.

Then because the circles have equal radii,

∴ **B** falls on **E**, and the two $\mathbf{O}^{ces}$ coincide entirely.

And, by hypothesis, the arc **BKC** = the arc **ELF**.

∴**C** falls on **F**, and consequently **GC** on **HF**;

∴ the ∠**BGC** = ∠**EHF**.

And since the ∠**BAC** at the $\mathbf{O}^{ce}$ = half the ∠**BGC** at the centre;

and likewise the **EDF** = half the ∠**EHF**;

∴ the ∠**BAC** = the ∠**EDF**. **Q.E.D.**

THEOREM 44. [Euclid III. 28]

In equal circles, arcs which are cut off by equal chords are equal, the major arc equal to the major arc, and the minor to the mirnor.

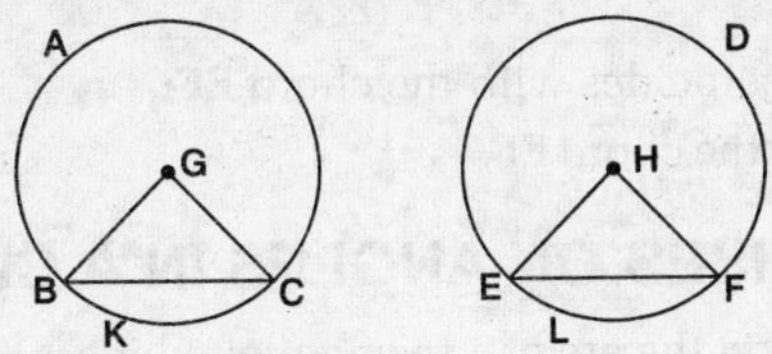

Let **ABC**, **DEF** be equal circles whose centres are **G** and **H**; and let the chord **BC** = the chord **EF**.

It is required to prove that

the major arc **BAC** *= the major arc* **EDF**,

and the minor arc **BKC** *= the minor arc* **ELF**.

Join **BG, GC, EH, HF**.

Proof. In the Δ^s **BGC, EHF,**

because $\begin{cases} \textbf{BG} = \textbf{EH}, \text{ being radii of equal circles,} \\ \textbf{GC} = \textbf{HF}, \text{ for the same reson,} \\ \text{and } \textbf{BC} = \textbf{EF}, \text{ by hypothesis;} \end{cases}$

∴ the ∠**BGC** = the ∠**EHF**; *Theor.* **7.**

∴ the arc **BKC** = the arc **ELF**; *Theor.* **42.**

and these are the minor arcs.

But the whole **O**ce **ABKC** = the whole **O**ce **DELF**;

∴ the remaining arc **BAC** = the remaining arc **EDF**:

and these are the major arcs. **Q.E.D.**

THEOREM 45. [Euclid III. 29]

In equal circles chords which cut off equal arcs are equal.

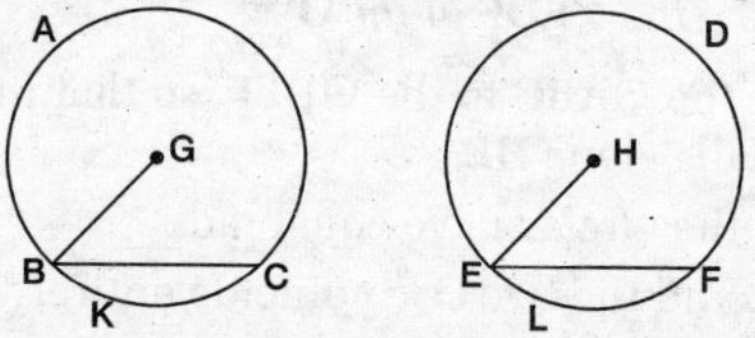

Let **ABC, DEF** be equal circles whose centres are **G** and **H**;
and let the arc **BKC** = the arc **ELF.**

It is required to prove that the chord **BC** = *the chord* **EF.**

Join **BG, EH.**

Proof. Apply the ○**ABC** to the ⊙**DEF**, so that **G** falls on **H** and **GB** along **HE.**

Then because the circles have equal radii,

∴ **B** falls on **E**, and the **O**ces coincide entirely.

And because the arc **BKC** = the arc **ELF**,

∴ **C** falls on **F.**

∴ the chord **BC** coincides with the chord **EF**;

∴ the chord **BC** = the chord **EF.** **Q.E.D.**

EXERCISES ON ANGLES IN A CIRCLE

1. **P** is any point on the arc of a segment of which **AB** is the chord. Show that the sum of the angles **PAB, PBA** is constant.
2. **PQ** and **RS** are two chords of a circle intersecting at **X**: prove that the triangles **PXS, RXQ** are equiangular to one another.
3. Two circles intersect at **A** and **B**; and through **A** any straight line **PAQ** is drawn terminated by the circumferences: show that **PQ** subtends a constant angle at **B.**

4. Two circles intersect at **A** and **B**; and through **A** any two straight lines **PAQ**, **XAY** are drawn terminated by the circumferences; show that the arcs **PX**, **QY** subtend equal angles at **B**.

5. **P** is any point on the arc of a segment whose chord is **AB**: and the angles **PAB**, **PBA** are bisected by straight lines which intersect at **O**. Find the locus of the point **O**.

6. *If two chords intersect within a circle, they form an angle equal to that at the centre, subtended by half the sum of the arcs they cut off.*

7. *If two chords intersect without a circle, they form an angle equal to that at the centre subtended by half the difference of the arcs they cut off.*

8. The sum of the arcs cut off by two chords of a circle at right angles to one another is equal to the semi-circumference.

9. *If* **AB** *is a fixed chord of a circle and* **P** *any point on one of the arcs cut off by it, then the bisector of the angle* **APB** *cuts the conjugate arc in the same point for all positions of* **P**.

10. **AB**, **AC** are any two chords of a circle; and **P**, **Q** are the middle points of the minor arcs cut off by them; if **PQ** is joined, cutting **AB** in **X** and **AC** in **Y**, show that **AX** = **AY**.

11. A triangle **ABC** is inscribed in a circle, and the bisectors of the angles meet the circumference at **X**, **Y**, **Z**. Show that the angles of the triangle **XYZ** are respectively

$$90° - \frac{A}{2},\ 90° - \frac{B}{2},\ 90° - \frac{C}{2}.$$

12. Two circles intersect at **A** and **B**; and through these points lines are drawn from any point **P** on the circumference of one of the circles: show that when produced they intercept on the other circumference an arc which is constant for all positions of **P**.

13. The straight lines which join the extremities of parallel chords in a circle (i) towards the same parts, (ii) towards opposite parts, are equal.

14. Through **A**, a point of intersection of two equal circles, two straight lines **PAQ**, **XAY** are drawn: show that the chord **PX** is equal to the chord **QY**.

15. Through the points of intersection of two circles two parallel straight lines are drawn terminated by the circumferences: show that the straight lines which join their extremities towards the same parts are equal.

16. Two equal circles intersect at **A** and **B**; and through **A** any straight line **PAQ** is drawn terminated by the circumferences: show that **BP** = **BQ**.

17. **ABC** is an isosceles triangle inscribed in a circle, and the bisectors of the base angles meet the circumference at **X** and **Y**. Show that the figure **BXAYC** must have four of its sides equal.

    What relation must subsist among the angles of the triangle **ABC**, in order that the figure **BXAYC** may be equilateral?

18. **ABCD** is a cyclic quadrilateral, and the opposite sides **AB, DC** are produced to meet at **P**, and **CB, DA** to meet at **Q**: if the circles circumscribed about the triangles **PBC, QAB** intersect at **R**, show that the points **P**, **R**, **Q** are collinear.

19. **P,Q,R** *are the middle points of the sides of a triangle, and* **X**, *is the foot of the perpendicular let fall from one vertex on the opposite side : show that the four points* **P**, **Q**, **R**, **X** *are concyclic.*

20. *Use the preceding exercise to show that the middle points of the sides of a triangle and the feet of the perpendiculars let fall from the vertices on the opposite sides, are concyclic.*

21. If a series of triangles are drawn standing on a fixed base, and having a given vertical angle, show that the bisectors of the vertical angles all pass through a fixed point.

22. **ABC** is a triangle inscribed in a circle, and **E** the middle point of the arc subtended by **BC** on the side remote from **A** : if through **E** a diameter **ED** is drawn, show that the angle **DEA** is half the difference of the angles at **B** and **C**.

TANGENCY

DEFINITIONS AND FIRST PRINCIPLES

1. Asecant of a circle is a straight line of indefinite length which cuts the circumference at two points.

2. If a secant moves in such a way that the two points in which it cuts the circle continually approach one another, then in the ultimate position when these two points become one, the secant becomes a **tangent** to the circle, and is said to touch it at the point at which the two intersections coincide. This point is called the **point of contact**.

For instance :

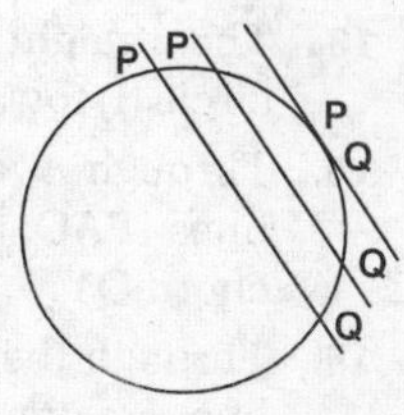

(i) Let a secant cut the circle at the points **P** and **Q**, and suppose it to recede from the centre, moving always parallel to its original position; then the two points **P** and **Q** will clearly approach one another and finally coincide.

In the ultimate position when **P** and **Q** become one point, the straight line becomes a tangent to the circle at that point.

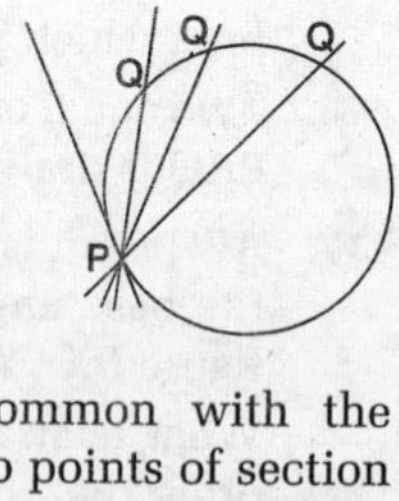

(ii) Let a secant cut the circle at the points **P** and **Q**, and suppose it to be turned about the point **P** so that while **P** remains fixed, **Q** moves on the circumference nearer and nearer to **P**. Then the line **PQ** in its ultimate position, when **Q** coincides with **P**, is a tangent at the point **P**.

Since a secant can cut a circle at *two* points only, it is clear that a tangent can have only one point in common with the circumference, namely the point of contact, at which two points of section coincide.

Hence we may define a tangent as follows :

3. A tangent to a circle is a straight line which meets the circumference at one point only; and though produced indefinitely does not cut the circumference.

4. Let two circles intersect (as in Fig. 1) in the points **P and Q**, and let one of the circles turn about the point **P**, which remains fixed, in such a way that **Q** continually approaches **P**. Then in the ultimate

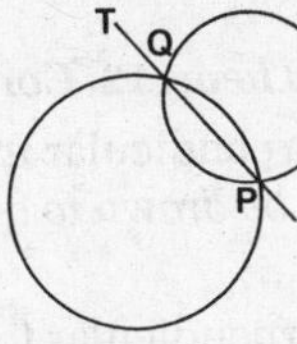

Fig. 1.

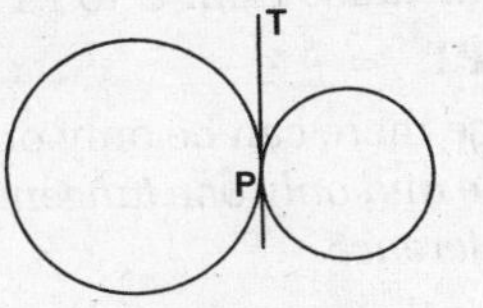

Fig. 2.

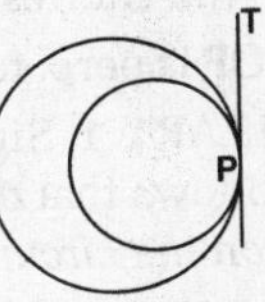

Fig. 3.

position, when **Q** coincides with **P** (as in Figs. 2 and 3), the circles are said to touch one another at **P**.

Since two circles cannot intersect in more than *two* points, two circles which touch one another cannot have more than *one* point in common, namely the point of contact at which the two points of section coincide. Hence circles are said to touch one another when they meet, but do not cut one another.

NOTE. When each of the circles which meet is *outside the other*, as in Fig. 2, they are said to touch one another **externally**, or to have **external contact**: when one of the circles is *within the other, as* in Fig. 3, the first is said to touch the other internally, or to have internal contact with it.

INFERENCE FROM DEFINITIONS 2 AND 4

If in Fig. 1, **TQP** is a common chord of two circles one of which is made turn about P, then when **Q** is brought into coincidence with **P**, the line **TP** passes through two coincident points on each circle, as in Figs. 2 and 3, and therefore becomes a tangent to each circle. Hence

Two circles which touch one another have a common tangent at their point of contact.

THEOREM 46

The tangent at any point of a circle is perpendicular to the radius drawn to the point of contact.

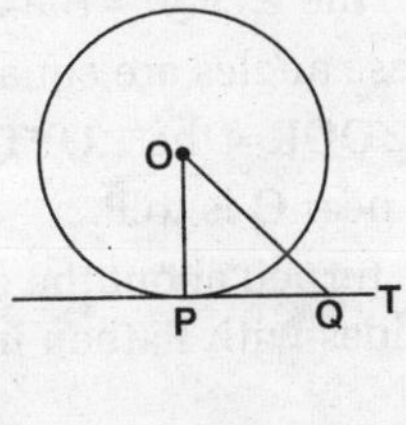

Let **PT** be a tangent at the point **P** to a circle whose centre is **O**.

It is required to prove that **PT** *is perpendicular to the radius* **OP**.

Proof. Take *any* point **Q** in **PT**, and join **OQ**.

Then since **PT** is a tangent, every point in it except **P** is outside the circle.

∴ **OQ** is greater than the radius **OP**.

And this is true for every point **Q** in **PT**;

∴ **OP** is the shortest distance from **O** to **PT**.

Hence **OP** is perp. to **PT**. ***Theor.* 12, *Cor.* 1. Q.E.D.**

COROLLARY 1. Since there can be only one perpendicular to **OP** at the point **P**, it follows that *one and only one tangent can be drawn to a circle at a given point on the circumference.*

COROLLARY 2. Since there can be only one perpendicular to **PT** at the point **P**, it follows that *the perpendicular to a tangent at its point of contact passes through the centre.*

COROLLARY 3. Since there can be only one perpendicular from **O** to the line **PT**, it follows that *the radius drawn perpendicular to the tangent passes through the point of contact.*

THEOREM 46. [By the Method of Limits]

The tangent at any point of a circle is perpendicular to the radius drawn to the point of contact.

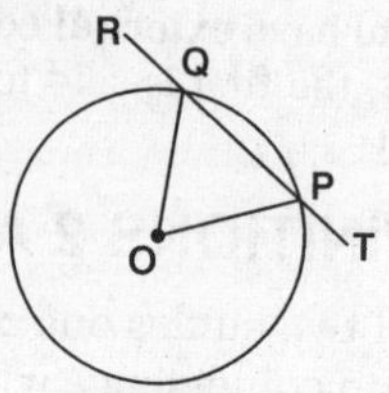

Fig. 1.

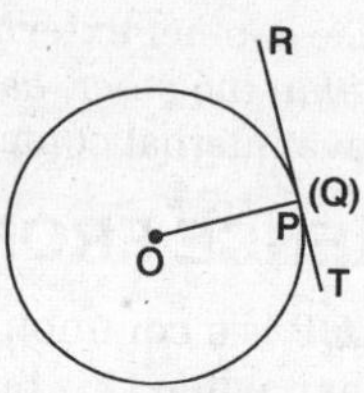

Fig. 2.

Let **P** be a point on a circle whose centre is **O**.

It is required to prove that the tangent at **P** *is perpendicular to the radius* **OP**.

Let **RQPT** (Fig. 1) be a secant cutting the circle at **Q** and **P**.

Join **OQ, OP**.

Proof. Because **OP** = **OQ**,

∴ the ∠**OQP** = the ∠**OPQ**;

∴ the supplements of these angles are equal,

that is, the ∠**OQR** = the ∠**OPT**,

and this is true however near **Q** is to **P**.

Now let the secant **OP** be turned about the point **P** so that **Q** continually approaches and finally coincides with **P**; then in the ultimate position,

(i) the secant **RT** becomes the tangent at P, }
(ii) **OQ**coincides with **OP**; } Fig. 2

and therefore the equal $\angle^s$**OQR, OPT** become adjacent,

∴ **OP** is perp. to **RT**. **Q.E.D.**

NOTE. The method of proof employed here is known as the **Method of Limits.**

THEOREM 47

Two tangents can be drawn to a circle from an external point.

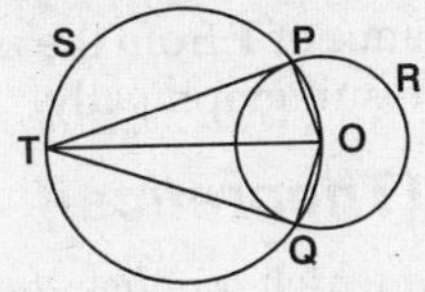

Let **PQR** be a circle whose centre is **O**, and let **T** be an external point.

It is required to prove that there can be two tangents drawn to the circle from **T**.

Join **OT**, and let **TSO** be the circle on **OT** as diameter.

This circle will cut the ⊙ **PQR** in two points, since **T** is without, and **O** is within, the. **PQR** ⊙ Let **P** and **Q** be these points.

Join **TP, TQ ; OP, OQ**.

Proof. Now each of the $\angle^s$**TPO, TQO** being in a semi-circle, is a rt. angle;

∴**TP, TQ** are perp. to the radii **OP, OQ** respectively.

∴**TP, TQ** are tangents at **P** and **Q**. ***Theor.*** 46. **Q.E.D.**

COROLLARY. *The two tangents to a circle from an external point are equal, and subtend equal angles at the centre.*

For in the Δ^s**TPO, TQO**,

because { the $\angle^s$**TPO, TQO** are *right angles*
the hypotenuse **TO** is common,
and **OP** = **OQ**, being radii;

∴ **TP** = **TQ**,

and the $\angle$**TOP** = the $\angle$**TOQ**. ***Theor.*** 18.

EXERCISES ON THE TANGENT

(*Numerical and Graphical*)

1. Draw two concentric circles with radii 5.0 cm. and 3.0 cm. Draw a series of chords of the former to touch the latter. Calculate and measure their lengths, and account for their being equal.
2. In a circle of radius 5 cm. draw a number of chords each 8 cm, in length. Show that they all touch a concentric circle, and find its radius.

3. The diameters of two concentric circles are respectively 10.0 cm. and 5.0 cm. : find to the nearest millimetre the length of any chord of the outer circle which touches the inner, and check your work by measurement.
4. In the figure of Theorem 47, if **OP** = 5 cm., **TO** = 13 cm., find the length of the tangents from **T**. Draw the figure (scale 1 cm. to 2 cm.), and measure to the nearest degree the angles subtended at **O** by the tangents.
5. The tangents from **T** to a circle whose radius is 1.4 cm, are each 4.8 cm. in length. Find the distance of **T** from the centre of the circle. Draw the figure and check your result graphically.

(*Theoretical*)

6. *The centre of any circle which touches two intersecting straight lines must lie on the bisector of the angle between them.*
7. **AB** and **AC** are two tangents to a circle whose centre is **O**; show that **AO** bisects the chord of contact **BC** at right angles.
8. If **PQ** is joined in the figure of Theorem 47, show that the angle **PTQ** is double the angle **OPQ**.
9. Two parallel tangents to a circle intercept on any third tangent a segment which subtends a right angle at the centre.
10. The diameter of a circle bisects all chords which are parallel to the tangent at either extremity.
11. *Find the locus of the centres of all circles which touch a given straight line at a given point.*
12. Find the locus of the centres of all circles which touch each of two parallel straight lines.
13. *Find the locus of the centres of all circles which touch each of two intersecting straight lines of unlimited length.*
14. *In any quadrilateral circumscribed about a circle, the sum of one pair of opposite sides is equal to the sum of the other pair.*
    State and prove the converse theorem.
15. If a quadrilateral is described about a circle, the angles subtended at the centre by any two opposite sides are supplementary.

THEOREM 48

If two circles touch one another, the centres and the point of contact are in one straight line.

Let two circles whose centres are **O** and **Q** touch at the point **P**. *It is required to prove that* **O**, **P** *and* **Q** *are in one straight line.*

Join **OP**, **QP**.

Proof. Since the given circles touch at **P**, they have a common tangent at that point. ***Page* 159.**

Suppose **PT** to touch both circles at **P**.

Then since **OP** and **QP** are radii drawn to the point of contact,

∴ **OP** and **QP** are both perp. to **PT**;

∴ **OP** and **QP** are in one st. line. ***Theor.* 2.**

That is, the points **O**, **P**, and **Q** are in one st. line. **Q.E.D.**

COROLLARIES. (i) *If two circles touch externally the distance between their centres is equal to the sum of their radii.*

(ii) *If two circles touch internally the distance between their centres is equal to the difference of their radii.*

EXERCISES ON THE CONTACT OF CIRCLES

(*Numerical and Graphical*)

1. From centres 5.2 cm. apart draw two circles with radii 3.4 cm. and 1.8 cm. respectively. Why and where do these circles touch one another? If circles of the above radii are drawn from centres 1.6 cm. apart, prove that they touch. How and why does the contact differ from that in the former case?
2. Draw a triangle **ABC** in which $a = 8$ cm., $b = 7$ cm., and $c = 6$ cm. From **A**, **B**, and **C** as centres draw circles of radii 2.5 cm., 3.5 cm., and 4.5 cm. respectively; and show that these circles touch in pairs.
3. In the triangle **ABC**, right-angled at **C**, $a = 8$ cm. and $b = 6$ cm.; and from centre **A** with radius 7 cm. a circle is drawn. What must be the radius of a circle drawn from centre **B** to touch the first circle?
4. **A** and **B** are the centres of two fixed circles which touch internally. If **P** is the centres of any circle which touches the larger circle internally and the smaller externally, prove that **AP** + **BP** is constant.

   If the fixed circles have radii 5.0 cm. and 3.0 cm. respectively, verify the general result by taking different positions for **P**.
5. **AB** is a line 8 cm. in length, and **C** is its middle point. On **AB**, **AC**, **CB** semicircles are described. Show that if a circle is inscribed in the space enclosed by the three semicircles its radius must be $1\frac{1}{3}$ cm.

(*Theoretical*)

6. *A straight line is drawn through the point of contact of two circles whose centres are* **A** *and* **B**, *cutting the circumferences at* **P** *and* **Q** *respecting; show that the* **AP** *and* **BQ** *are parallel.*

7. Two circles touch externally, and through the point of contact a .straight line is drawn terminated by the circumferences; show that the tangents at its extremities are parallel.
8. Find the locus of the centres of all circles
   (i) which touch a given circle at a given point;
   (ii) which are of given radius and touch a given circle.
9. From a given point as centre describe a circle to touch a given circle. How many solutions will there be?
10. Describe a circle of radius a to touch a given circle of radius b at a given point. How many solutions will there be?

THEOREM 49. [Euclid III. 32]

The angles made by a tangent to a circle with a chord drawn from the point of contact are respectively equal to the angles in the alternate segments of the circle.

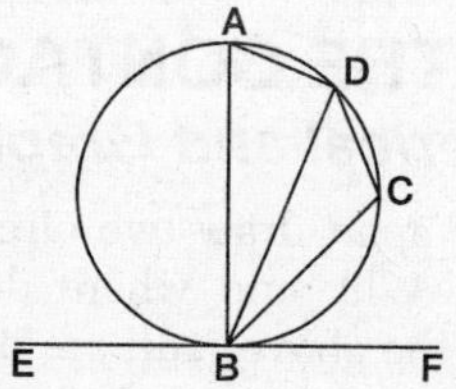

Let **EF** touch the ⊙ **ABC** at **B**, and let **BD** be a chord drawn from **B**, the point of contact.

It is required to prove that

(i) *the* ∠**FBD** = *the angle in the alternate segment* **BAD**;

(ii) *the* ∠**EBD** = *the angle in the alternate segment* **BCD**.

Let **BA** be the diameter through **B**, and **C** any point in the arc of the segment which does not contain **A**.

Join **AD, DC, CB**.

Proof. Because ∠**ADB** in a semicircle is a rt. angle,

∴ the ∠^s **DBA, BAD** together = a rt. angle.

But since **EBF** is a tangent, and **BA** a diameter,

∴ the ∠**FBA** is a rt. angle.

∴ the ∠**FBA** = the ∠^s **DBA, BAD** together

Take away the common ∠**DBA**,

then the ∠**FBD** = the ∠**BAD**, which is in the alternate segment.

Again because **ABCD** is a cyclic quadrilateral,

∴ the ∠**BCD** = the supplement of the ∠**BAD**

= the supplement of the ∠**FBD**

= the ∠**EBD**;

∴ the ∠**EBD** = the ∠**BCD**, which is in the alternate segment.

EXERCISES ON THEOREM 49

1. In the figure, of Theorem 49, if the ∠**FBD** = 72°, write down the values of the ∠^s **BAD, BCD, EBD.**
2. Use this theorem to show that tangents to a circle from an external point are equal.
3. Through **A**, the point of contact of two circles, chords **APQ**, **AXY** are drawn : show that **PX** and **QY** are parallel.

   Prove this (i) for internal, (ii) for external contact.
4. **AB** is the common chord of two circles, one of which passes through **O**, the centre of the other : prove that **OA** bisects the angle between the common chord and the tangent to the first circle at **A**.
5. Two circles intersect at **A** and **B** and through **P**, any point on one of them, straight lines **PAC**, **PBD** are drawn to cut the other at **O** and **D** : show that **CD** is parallel to the tangent at **P**.
6. If from the point of contact of a tangent to a circle a chord is drawn, perpendiculars dropped on the tangent and chord from the middle point of either arc cut off by the chord are equal

EXERCISES ON THE METHOD OF LIMITS

1. *Prove Theorem 49 by the Method of Limits.*

   Let **ACB** be a segment of a circle of which **AB** is the chord; and let **PAT′** be any *secant* through **A**. Join **PB**.

   Then the ∠**BCA** = the∠**BPA**; ***Theor.*** 39.

   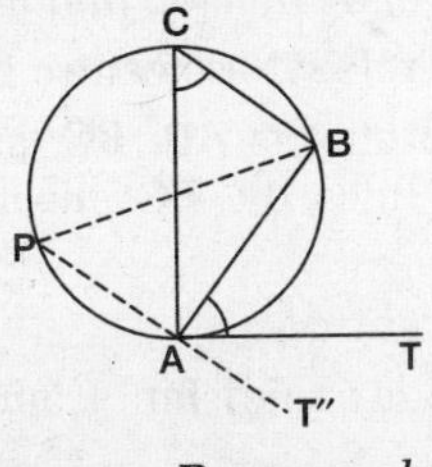

   and this is true *however near* **P** *approaches to* **A**.

   If **P** moves up to coincidence with **A**, then the secant **PAT′** becomes the tangent **AT**, and the ∠**BPA** becomes the ∠**BAT**.

   ∴ ultimately, the ∠**BAT** = the ∠**BCA**, in the alt. segment.
2. From Theorem 31, prove by the Method of Limits that

   The straight line drawn perpendicular to the diameter of a circle at its extremity is a tangent.
3. Deduce Theorem 48 from the property that *the line of centres bisects a common chord at right angles.*
4. Deduce Theorem 49 from Ex. 5, page 150.
5. Deduce Theorem 46 from Theorem 41.

PROBLEMS

GEOMETRICAL ANALYSIS

Hitherto the Propositions of this text-book have been arranged **Synthetically**, that is to say, by *building up known results* in order to obtain a *new* result.

But this arrangement, though convincing as an argument, in most cases affords little clue as to the way in which the construction or proof *was discovered*. We therefore draw the student's attention to the following hints.

In attempting to solve a problem begin" by *assuming* the required result; then by working backwards, trace the consequences of the assumption, and try to ascertain its dependence on some condition or known theorem which suggests the necessary construction. If this attempt is successful, the steps of the argument may in general be rearranged in reverse order, and the construction and proof presented in a synthetic form.

This unravelling of the conditions of a proposition in order to trace it back to some earlier principle on which it depends, is called **geometrical analysis** : it is the natural way of attacking the harder types of exercises, and it is especially useful in solving problems.

Although the above directions do not amount to a *method*, they often furnish a very effective mode of *searching for a suggestion*. The approach by analysis will be illustrated in some of the following problems.

[See Problems 23, 28, 29.]

PROBLEMS 20

Given a circle, or an arc of a circle, to find its centre,

Let **ABC** be an arc of a circle whose centre is to be found.

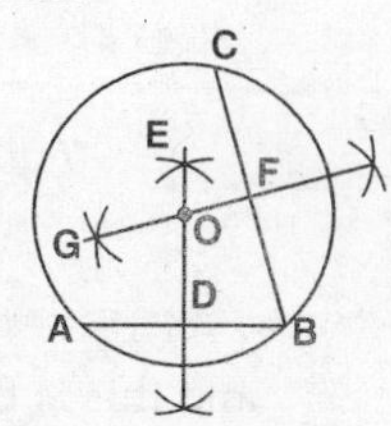

Construction. Take two chords **AB**, **BC**, and bisect them at right angles by the lines **DE**, **FG**, meeting at **O**. *Prob.* 2.

Then **O** is the required centre.

Proof. Every point in **DE** is equidistant from **A** and **B**. *Prob.* 14.

And every point in **FG** is equidistant from **B** and **C**.

∴ **O** is equidistant from **A**, **B**, **C**.

∴ **O** is the centre of the circle **ABC**. *Theor.* 33.

PROBLEM 21

To bisect a given arc.

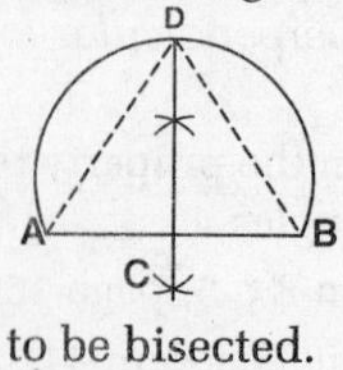

Let **ADB** be the given arc to be bisected.

Construction. Join **AB**, and bisect it at right angles by **CD** meeting the arc at **D**. ***Prob.*** 2.

Then the arc is bisected at **D**.

Proof. Join **DA, DB**.

Then every point on **CD** is equidistant from **A** and **B**; ***Prob.*** 14.

$\therefore$ **DA = DB**;

$\therefore$ the $\angle$**DBA** = the $\angle$**DAB**; ***Theor.*** 5.

$\therefore$ the arcs, which subtend these angles at the **O**^{ce}, are equal;

that is, the arc **DA** = the arc **DB**.

PROBLEM 22

To draw a tangent to a circle from a given external point.

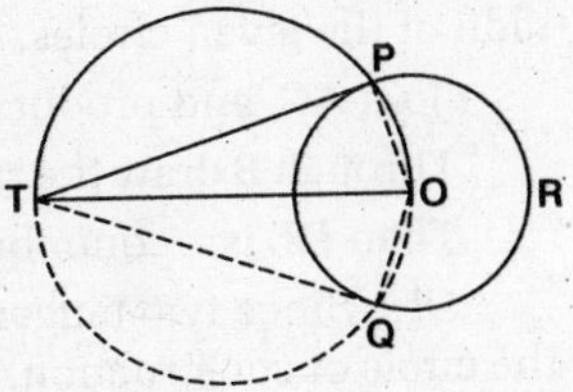

Let **PQR** be the given circle, with its centre at **O**; and let **T** be the point from which a tangent is to be drawn.

Construction. Join **TO**, and on it describe a semi-circle **TPO** to cut the circle at **P**.

Join **TP**.

Then **TP** is the required tangent.

Proof. Join **OP**.

Then since the $\angle$**TPO**, being in a semi-circle, is a rt. angle,

$\therefore$ **TP** is at right angles to the radius **OP**.

$\therefore$ **TP** is a tangent at **P**. ***Theor.*** 46.

Since the semi-circle may be described on either side of **TO**, a second tangent **TQ** can be drawn from T, as shown in the figure.

NOTE. Suppose the point **T** to approach the given circle, then the angle **PTQ** gradually increases. When **T** reaches the circumference, the angle **PTQ** becomes a *straight angle*, and the two tangents coincide. When T enters the circle, no tangent can be drawn.

PROBLEM 23

To draw a common tangent to two circles.

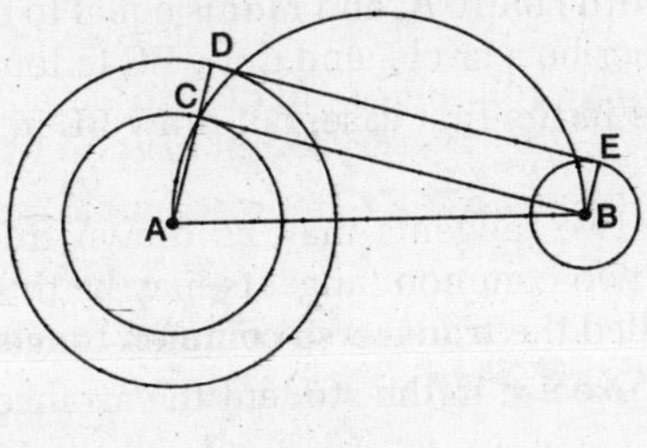

Let **A** be the centre of the greater circle, and a its radius; and let **B** be the centre of the smaller circle, and b its radius.

Analysis. Suppose **DE** to touch the circles at **D** and **E**. Then the radii **AD**, **BE** are both perp. to **DE**, then therefore par^l to one another.

Now if **BC** were drawn par^l to **DE**, then the fig. **DB** would be a rectangle, so that $\mathbf{CD} = \mathbf{BE} = b$.

And if **AD**, **BE** are *one the same side of* **AB**,

then $\mathbf{AC} = a - b$, and the $\angle\mathbf{ACB}$ is a rt. angle.

These hints enable us to draw **BC** *first*, and thus lead to the following construction.

Construction. With centre **A**, and radius equal to the *difference* of the radii of the given circles, describe a circle, and draw **BC** to touch it.

Join **AC**, and produce it to meet the circle (**A**) at **D**.

Through **B** draw the radius **BE** par^l to **AD** and in the *same sense*. Join **DE**.

Then **DE** is a common tangent to the given circles.

Obs. Since two tangents, such as **BC**, can in general be drawn from **B** to the circle of construction, the method will furnish two common tangents to the given circles. These are called the **direct common tangents.**

PROBLEM 23. *(Continued)*

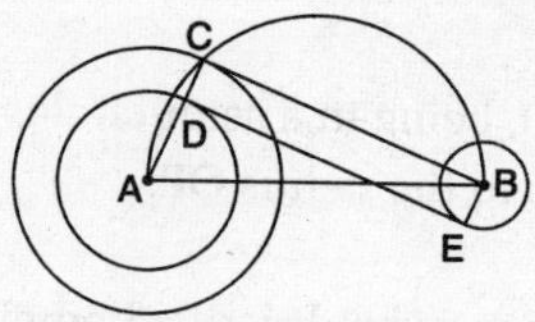

Again, if the circles are *external to one another* two more common tangents may be drawn.

Analysis. In this case we may suppose **DE** to touch the circles at **D** and **E** so that the radii **AD**, **BE** fall *on opposite side of* **AB**.

Then **BC**, drawn par^l to the supposed common tangent **DE**, would meet **AD** *produced* at **C**; and we should now have $\mathbf{AC} = \mathbf{AD} + \mathbf{DC} = a + b$; and, as before, the $\angle\mathbf{ACB}$ is rt. angle. Hence the following construction.

Construction. With centre **A**, and radius equal to the *sum* of the radii of the given circles, describe a circle, and draw **BC** to touch it.

Then proceed as in the first case, but draw **BE** in the sense *opposite* to **AD**.

Obs. As before, two tangents may be drawn from **B** to the circle of construction; hence two common tangents may be thus drawn to the given circles. These are called the **transverse common tangents.**

[We leave as an execise to the student the arrangement of the proof in synthetic form].

EXERCISES ONE COMMON TANGENTS

(*Numerical and Graphical*)

1. How many common tangents can be drawn in each of the following cases?
   (i) when the given circles intersect;
   (ii) when they have external contact;
   (iii) when they have internal contact.

   Illustrate your answer by drawing two circles of radii 2.8 cm. and 2.0 cm. respectively,
   (i) with 2 cm. between the centres;
   (ii) with 4.8 cm. between the centres;
   (iii) with 0.8 cm. between the centres;
   (iv) with 6 cm. between the centres.

   Draw the common tangents in each case, and note where the general construction fails, or modified.
2. Draw two circles with radii 4 cm. and 1.6 cm., placing their centres 2 cm. apart. Draw the common tangents, and find their lengths between the points of contact, both by calculation and by measurement.
3. Draw all the common tangents to two circles whose centres are 3.6 cm. apart and whose radii are 1.2 cm. and 2.4 cm. respectively. Calculate and measure the length of the direct common tangents.
4. Two circles of radii 3.4 cm. and 2 cm. have their centres 4.2 cm. apart. Draw their common tangents and find their lengths. Also find the length of the common chord. Produce the common chord and show by measurement that it bisects the common tangents.
5. Draw two circles with radii 4 cm. and 2.5 cm. and with their centres 7 cm. apart. Draw all their common tangents.
6. Draw the direct common tangents as two equal circles.

(*Theoretical*)

7. If the two direct, or the two transverse, common tangents are drawn to two circles, the parts of the tangents intercepted between the points of contact are equal.
8. If four common tangents are drawn to two circles external to one another, show that the two direct, and also the two transverse tangents intersect on the line of centres.
9. Two given circles have external contact at **A**, and a direct common tangent is drawn to touch them at **P** and **Q** : show that **PQ** subtends a right angle at the point **A**.

ON THE CONSTRUCTION OF CIRCLES

In order to draw a circle we must know

(i) the position of the centre, (ii) length of the radius.

(i) To find the position of the centre, two conditions are needed, each giving a locus on which the centre must lie; so that the one or more points in which the two loci intersect are possible positions of the required centre, as explained in part II

(ii) The position of the centre being thus fixed, the radius is determined if we know (or can find) any point on the circumference.

Hence in order to draw a circle *three* independent data are required.

For example, we may draw a circle if we are given

(i) *three* points on the circumference:

or (ii) *three* tangent lines;

or (iii) one point on the circumference, one tangent, and its point of contact.

It will however often happen that more than one circle can be drawn satisfying three given conditions.

Before attempting the constructions of the next Exercise the student should make himself familiar with the following loci.

(i) *The locus of the centres of circles which pass through two given points.*

(ii) *The locus of the centres of circles which touch a given straight line at a given point.*

(iii) *The locus of the centres of circles which touch a given circle at a given point.*

(iv) *The locus of the centres of circles which touch a given straight line, and have a given radius.*

(v) *The locus of the centres of circles which touch a given circle, and have a given radius,*

(vi) *The locus of the centres of circles which touch two given straight lines.*

EXERCISES

1. Draw a circle to pass through three given points.
2. If a circle touches a given line **PQ** at a point **A**, on what line must its centre lie?

   If a circle passes through two given points **A** and **B**, on what line must its centre lie?

   Hence draw a circle to touch a straight line **PQ** at the point **A**, and to pass through another given point **B**.
3. If a circle touches a given circle whose centre is **C** at the point **A**, on what line must its centre lie?

   Draw a circle to touch the given circle (**C**) at the point **A**, and to pass through a given point **B**.
4. A point P is 4.5 cm. distant from a straight line **AB**. Draw two circles of radius 3.2 cm. to pass through **P** and to touch **AB**.
5. Given two circles of radius 3.0 cm. and 2.0 cm. respectively, their centres being 6.0 cm. apart; draw a circle of radius 3.5 cm. to touch each of the given circles externally.

How many solutions will there be? What is the radius of the smallest circle that touches each of the given circles externally?

6. If a circle touches two straight lines **OA**, **OB**, on what line must its centre lie?

   Draw **OA**, **OB** making an angle of 76°, and describe a circle of radius 3 cm. to touch both lines.

7. Given a circle of radius 3.5 cm., with its centre 5.0 cm. from a given straight line **AB**; draw two circles of radius 2.5 cm. to touch the given circle and the line **AB**.

8. Devise a construction for drawing a circle to touch each of two parallel straight lines and a transversal.

   Show that two such circles can be drawn, and that they are equal.

9. Describe a circle to touch a given circle, and also to touch a given straight line at a given point.

10. Describe a circle to touch a given straight line, and to touch a given circle at a given point.

11. Show how to draw a circle to touch each of three given straight lines of which no two are parallel.

    How many such circles can be drawn?

    [Further Examples on the Construction of Circles will be found in coming parts.

PROBLEM 24

On a given straight line to describe a segment of a circle which shall contain an angle equal to a given angle.

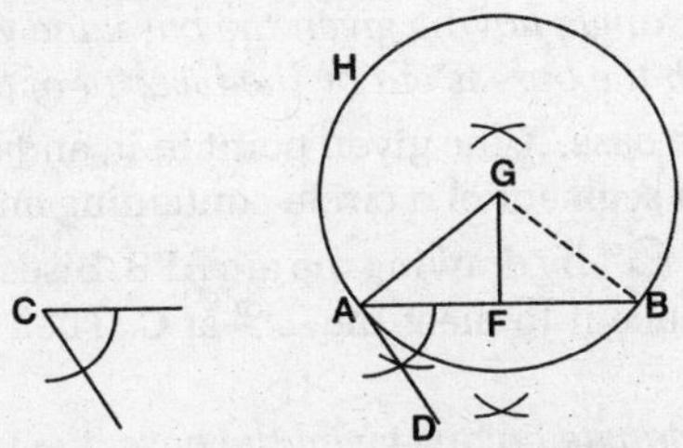

Let **AB** be the given st. line, and **C** the given angle.

It is required to describe on **AB** *a segment of a circle containing an angle equal to* **C**.

Construction. At **A** in **BA**, make the ∠**BAD** equal to the ∠**C**.

From **A** draw **AG** perp. to **AD**.

Bisect **AB** at rt. angles by **FG**, meeting **AG** in **G**. ***Prob.*** **2.**

Proof. Join **GB**.

Now every point in **FG** is equidistant from **A** and **B**; ***Prob.*** **14.**

∴ **GA = GB.**

With centre **G**, and radius **GA**, draw a circle, which must pass through **B**, and touch **AD** at **A**. ***Theor.*** 46.

Then the segment **AHB** , alternate to the ∠**BAD**, contains an angle equal to **C**. ***Theor.*** 49.

NOTE. In the particular case when the given angle is a rt. angle, the segment required will be the semi-circle on **AB** as diameter. [Theorem 41.]

COROLLARY. *To cut off from a given circle a segment containing a given angle, it is enough to draw a tangent to the circle, and from the point of contact to draw a chord making with the tangent an angle equal to the given angle.*

It was proved on page 148 that

The locus of the vertices of triangles which stand on the same base and have a given vertical angle, is the arc of the segment standing on this base, and containing an angle equal to the given angle.

The following Problems are derived from this result by the Method of Intersection of Loci.

EXERCISES

1. *Describe a triangle on a given base having a given vertical angle and having its vertex on a given straight line.*

2. *Construct a triangle having given the base, the vertical angle, and*

(i) one other side.

(ii) the altitude.

(iii) the length of the median which bisects the base.

(iv) the foot of the perpendicular from the vertex to the base.

3. *Construct a triangle having given the base; the vertical angle, and the point at which the bass is cut by the bisector of the vertical angle.*

[Let **AB** be the base, **X** the given point in it, and **K** the given angle. On **AB** describe a segment of a circle containing an angle equal to **K**; Complete the $\bigcirc^{ce}$ by drawing the arc **APB**. Bisect the arc **APB** at **P**: join **PX**, and produce it to meet the $\bigcirc^{ce}$ at **C**. Then **ABC** is the required, triangle.]

4. *Construct a triangle having given the base, the vertical angle, and the sum of the remaining sides.*

[Let **AB** be the given base, **K** the given angle, and **H** a line equal to the sum of the sides. On **AB** describe a segment containing an angle equal to **K**, also another segment containing an angle to half the ∠**K**. With centre **A**, and radius **H**, describe a circle cutting the arc of the latter segment at **X** and **Y**. Join **AX** (or **AY**) cutting the arc of the first segment at **C**. Then **ABC** is the required triangle.]

5. *Construct a triangle having given the base, the vertical angle, and the difference of the remaining sides.*

CIRCLES IN RELATION TO RECTILINEAL FIGURES

DEFINITIONS

1. A **Polygon** is a rectilineal figure bounded by more than four sides.

   A **Polygon** of *five* sides is called a **Pentagon**,

   " *six* sides " **Hexagon**,

   " *seven* sides " **Heptagon**,

   " *eight* sides " **Octagon**,

   " *ten* sides " **Decagon**,

   " *twelve* sides " **Dodecagon**,

   " *fifteen* sides is called a **Quindecagon**.

2. A Polygon is **Regular** when all its sides are equal, and all its angles are equal.

3. A rectilineal figure is said to be **inscribed** in a circle, when all its angular points are on the circumference of the circle; and a circle is said to be **circumscribed about** a rectilineal figure, when the circumference of the circle passes through all the angular points of the figure.

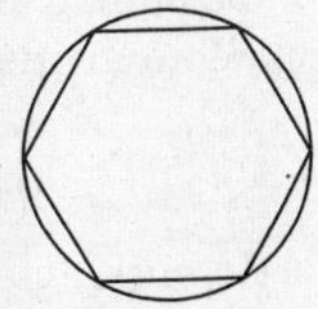

4. A circle is said to be **inscribed** in a rectilineal figure, when the circumference of the circle is touched by each side of the figure; and a rectilineal figure is said to be **circumscribed about** a circle, when each side of the figure is a tangent to the circle.

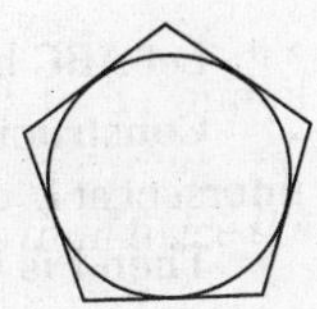

PROBLEM 25

To circumscribe a circle about a given triangle.

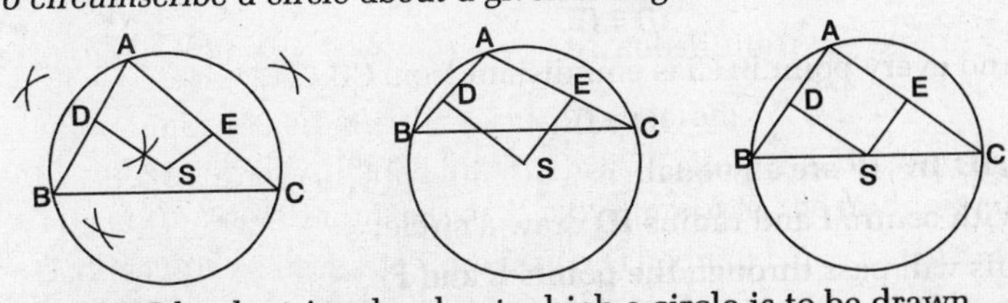

Let **ABC** be the triangle, about which a circle is to be drawn.

Construction. Bisect **AB** and **AC** at rt. angles by **DS** and **ES**, meeting at **S**. ***Prob.* 2.**

Then **S** is the centre of the required circle.

Proof. Now every point in **DS** is equidistant from **A** and **B**; ***Prob.* 14.**

and every point in **ES** is equidistant from **A** and **C**;

∴ **S** is equidistant from **A, B,** and **C.**

With centre **S**, and radius **SA** describe a circle; this will pass through **B** and **C**, and is, therefore, the required circumcircle.

Obs. It will be found that if the given triangle is acute-angled, the centre of the circum-circle falls within it: if it is a right-angled triangle, the centre falls on the hypotenuse: if it is an obtuse-angled triangle, the centre falls without the triangle.

NOTE. From page 94 it is seen that if **S** is joined to the middle point of **BC**, then the joining line is perpendicular to **BC**.

Hence the perpendiculars drawn to the sides of a triangle from their middle points are concurrent, the point of intersection being the centre of the circle circumscribed about the triangle.

PROBLEM 26

To inscribe a circle in a given triangle.

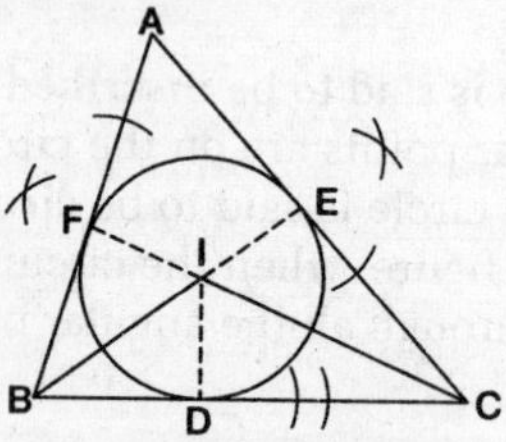

Let **ABC** be the triangle, in which a circle is to be inscribed.

Construction. Bisect the ∠ˢ**ABC, ACB** by the st. lines **BI, CI**, which intersect at **I**. ***Prob.* 1.**

Then **I** is the centre of the required circle.

Proof. From **I** draw **ID, IF, IF**, perp to **BC, CA, AB**.

Then every point in **BI** is equidistant from **BC, BA**; ***Prob.* 15.**

∴ **ID = IF.**

And every point in CI is equidistant from **CB, CA**;

∴ **ID = IE.**

∴ **ID, IE , IF** are all equal.

With centre **I** and radius **ID** draw a circle;

this will pass through the points **E** and **F**.

Also the circle will touch the sides **BC, CA, AB**,

because the angles at **D, E, F** are right angles.

∴ The ⊙**DEF** is inscribed in the Δ**ABC**.

NOTE. From II., p 84, it is seen that if joined, then **AI** bisects the angle **BAC** : hence it follows that

The bisectors of the angles of a triangle are concurrent, the point of intersection being the centre of the inscribed circle.

DEFINITION

A circle which touches one side of a triangle and the other two sides produced is called an escribed circle of the triangle.

PROBLEM 27

To draw an escribed circle of a given triangle.

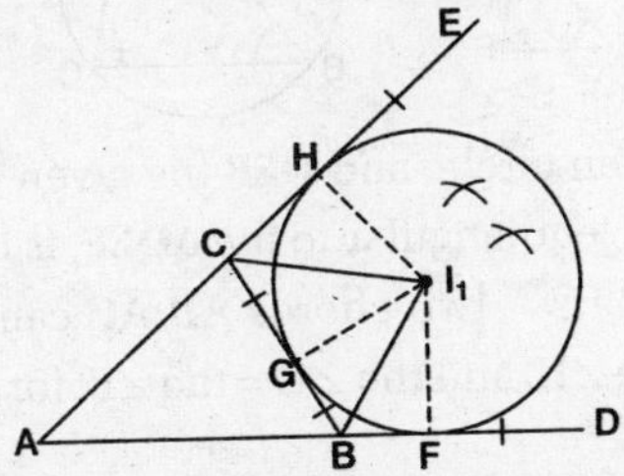

Let **ABC** be the given triangle of which the sides **AB**, **AC** are produced to **D** and **E**.

It is required to describe a circle touching **BC**, *and* **AB**, **AC** *produced.*

Construction. Bisect the $\angle^s$**CBD, BCF** by the st. lines BI_1, CI_1 which intersect at I_1.

Then I_1 is the centre of the required circle.

Proof. From I_1 draw I_1F, I_1G, I_1H perp. to **AD, BC, AE**.

Then every point in BI_1 is equidistant from **BD, BC**. ***Prob.* 15.**

$\therefore$ $$I_1F = I_1G.$$

Similarly $$I_1G = I_1H.$$

$\therefore$ I_1F, I_1G, I_1H are all equal.

With centre I_1 and radius I_1F describe a circle;

this will pass through the points **G** and **H**.

Also the circle will touch **AD, BC,** and **AE,**

because the angles at **F, G, H** are rt. angles.

$\therefore$ the ⊙**FGH** is an escribed circle of the Δ**ABC**.

NOTE 1. It is clear that every triangle has three escribed circles. Their centres are known as the **Ex-centres.**

NOTE 2. It may be shown, as in II., page 84, that if AI_1 is joined then AI_1 bisects the angle BAC : hence it follows that

The bisectors of two exterior angles of a triangle and the bisector of the third angle are concurrent, the point of intersection being the centre of an escribed circle.

PROBLEM 28

In a given circle to inscribe a triangle equiangular to a given triangle.

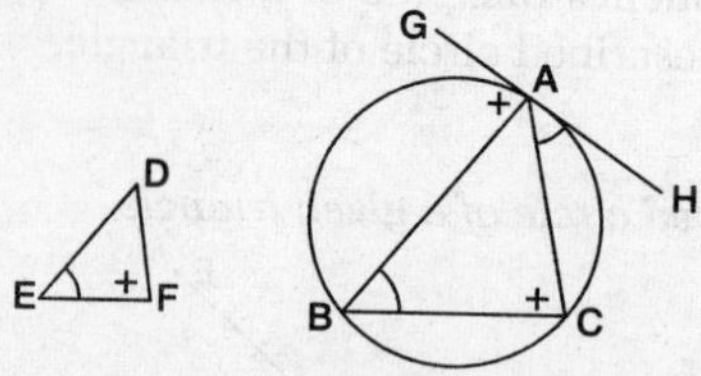

Let **ABC** be the given circle, and **DEF** the given triangle.

Analysis. A **ΔABC**, equiangular to the **ΔDEF**, is inscribed in the circle, if from any point **A** on the ○^{ce} two chords **AB, AC** can be so placed that, on joining **BC**, the **∠B** = the **∠E**, and the **∠C** = the **∠F**; for then the **∠A** = the **∠D**.

***Theor.* 16.**

Now the **∠B**, in the segment **ABC**, suggests the *equal* angle between the chord **AC** and the tangent at its extremity (Theor. 49); so that, if at A we draw the tangent **GAH**,

then the **∠HAC** = the **∠E**;
and similarly, the **∠GAB** = the **∠F**

Reversing these steps, we have the following construction

Construction. At any point A on the ○^{ce} of the **⊙ABC** draw the tangent GAH.

***Prob.* 22.**

At A make the **∠GAB** equal to the **∠F**,
and make the **∠HAC** equal to the **∠E**.
Join **BC**.
Then **ABC** is the required triangle.

NOTE. In drawing the figure on a larger scale the student should show the construction lines for the tangent **GAH** and for the angles **GAB**, HAC. A similar remark applies to the next Problem.

PROBLEM 29

About a given circle to circumscribe a triangle equiangular to a given triangle.

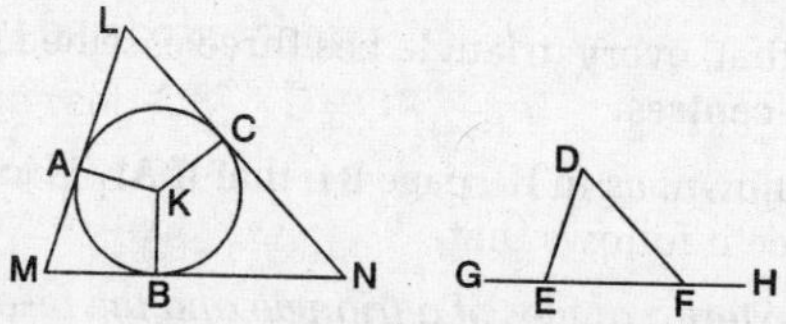

Let **ABC** be the given circle, and **DEF** the given triangle.

Analysis. Suppose **LMN** to be a circumscribed triangle in which the **∠M** = the **∠E**, the **∠N** = the **∠F**, and consequently, the **∠L** = the **∠D**.

Let us consider the radii **KA, KB, KC**, drawn to the points of contact of the sides; for the tangents **LM, MN, NL** could be drawn if we know the relative positions of **KA, KB, KC**, that is, if we know the **∠^{s}BKA, BKC**.

Now from the quad[l] **BKAM**, since the $\angle^s$**B** and **A** are rt. $\angle^s$,

the $\angle$**BKA** = 180° – **M** = 180°– **E**;

similarly the $\angle$**BKC** = 180°– **N** = 180°– **F**.

Hence we have the following construction.

Construction. Produce EF both ways to **G** and **H**.

Find **K** the centre of the ⊙**ABC**,

and draw any radius **KB**.

At **K** make the $\angle$**BKA** equal to the $\angle$**DEG**;

and make the $\angle$**BKC** equal to the $\angle$**DFH**.

Through **A**, **B**, **C** draw **LM**, **MN**, **NL** perp. to **KA**, **KB**, **KC**.

Then **LMN** is the required triangle.

[The student should now arrange the proof synthetically.]

EXERCISES

ON CIRCLES AND TRIANGLES

(Inscriptions and Circumscriptions)

1. In a circle of radius 5 cm. inscribe an equilateral triangle; and about the same circle circumscribe a second equilateral triangle. In each case state and justify your construction.
2. Draw an equilateral triangle on a side of 8 cm., and find by calculation and measurement (to the nearest millimetre) the radii of the inscribed, circumscribed, and escribed circles.

   Explain why the second and third radii are respectively double and treble of the first.
3. Draw triangles from the following data:

   (i) a = 2.5 cm., **B** = 66°, **C** = 50°;

   (ii) a = 2.5 cm., **B** = 72°, **C** = 44°;

   (iii) a = 2.5 cm., **B** = 41°, **C** = 23°.

   Circumscribe a circle about each triangle, and measure the radii to the nearest hundredth of an inch. Account for the three results being the same, by comparing the vertical angles.
4. In a circle of radius 4 cm. inscribe an equilateral triangle. Calculate the length of its side to the nearest millimetre; and verify by measurement.

   Find the area of the inscribed equilateral triangle, and show that it is one quarter of the circumscribed equilateral triangle.
5. In the triangle **ABC**, if **I** is the centre, and r the length of the radius of the in-circle, show that

   $$\Delta IBC = \frac{1}{2}ar;\ \Delta ICA = \frac{1}{2}br;\ \Delta IAB = \frac{1}{2}cr.$$

Hence prove that $\Delta ABC = \frac{1}{2}(a+b+c)r$.

Verify this formula by measurements for a triangle whose sides are 9 cm., 8 cm., and 7 cm.

6. If r_1 is the radius of the ex-circle opposite to **A**, prove that

$$\Delta ABC = \frac{1}{2}(b + c - a)r_1.$$

If $a = 5$ cm., $b = 4$ cm., $c = 3$ cm., verify this result by measurement.

7. Find by measurement the circum-radius of the triangle **ABC** in which $a = 6.3$ cm., $b = 3.0$ cm., and $c = 5.1$ cm.

Draw and measure the perpendiculars from **A, B, C** to the opposite sides. In their lengths are represented by p_1, p_2, p_3, verify the following statement:

circum-radius

$$\frac{bc}{2p_1} = \frac{ca}{2p_2} = \frac{ab}{2p_3}.$$

EXERCISES

ON CIRCLES AND SQUARES
(Inscriptions and Circumscriptions)

1. Draw a circle of radius 4.2 cm., and find a construction for inscribing a square in it.

Calculate the length of the side to the nearest cm., and verify by measurement.

Find the area of the inscribed square.

2. Circumscribe a square about a circle of radius 3.5 cm., showing all lines of construction.

Prove that the area of the square circumscribed about a circle is double that of the inscribed square.

3. Draw a square on a side of 7.5 cm., and state a construction for inscribing a circle in it.

Justify your construction by considerations of symmetry.

4. Circumscribe a circle about a square whose side is 6 cm.

Measure the diameter to the nearest millimetre, and test your drawing by calculation.

5. In a circle of radius 3.6 cm. inscribe a rectangle of which one side measures 6 cm. Find the approximate length of the other side.

Of all rectangles inscribed in the circle show that the square has the greatest area.

6. A square and an equilateral triangle are inscribed in a circle. If a and b denote the lengths of their sides, show that $3a^2 = 2b^2$.

7. **ABCD** is a square inscribed in a circle, and **P** is any point on the arc **AD**: show that the side **AD** subtends at **P** an angle three times as great as that subtended at **P** by any one of the other sides.

(*Problems. State your construction and give a theoretical proof.*)

8. Circumscribe a rhombus about a given circle.
9. Inscribe a square in a given square **ABCD**, so that one of its angular points shall be at a given point **X** in **AB**.
10. In a given square inscribe the square of minimum area.
11. Describe (i) a circle, (ii) a square about a given rectangle.
12. Inscribe (i) a circle, (ii) a square in a given quadrant.

ON CIRCLES AND REGULAR POLYGONS

PROBLEM 30

To draw a regular polygon (i) **in** (ii) **about** *a given circle.*

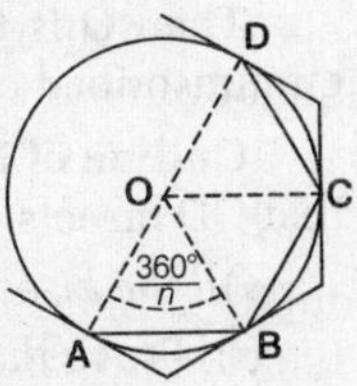

Let **AB, BC, CD**, ... be consecutive sides of a regular polygon inscribed in a circle whose centre is **O**.

Then **AOB, BOC, COD**, ... are congruent isosceles triangles. And if the polygon has n sides, each of the $\angle^s$ **AOB, BOC, COD**, ... $= \frac{360°}{n}$.

(i) Thus to **inscribe** a polygon of n sides in a given circle, draw an angle **AOB** at the centre equal to $\frac{360°}{n}$. This gives the length of a side **AB**; and chords equal to **AB** may now be set off round the circumference. The resulting figure will clearly be equilateral and equiangular.

(ii) To **circumscribe** a polygon of n sides about the circle, the points **A, B, C, D**,... must be determined as before, and tangents drawn to the circle at these points. The resulting figure may readily be proved equilateral and equiangular.

Note. The method gives a *strict geometrical construction* only when the angle $\frac{360°}{n}$ can be drawn with ruler and compasses.

EXERCISES

1. Give strict constructions for inscribing in a circle (radius 4 cm.) (i) a regular hexagon, (ii) a regular octagon; (iii) a regular dodecagon.
2. About a circle of radius 4.5 cm. circumscribe

   (i) a regular hexagon;

   (ii) a regular octagon.

   Test the constructions by measurement, and justify them by proof.

3. An equilateral triangle and a regular hexagon are inscribed in a given circle, and a and b denote the lengths of their sides : prove that

(i) area of triangle $= \frac{1}{2}$ (area of hexagon); (ii) $a^2 = 3b^2$.

4. By means of your protractor inscribe a regular heptagon in a circle of radius 4 cm. Calculate and measure one of its angles; and measure the length of a side.

PROBLEM 31

To draw a circle (i) **in** (ii) **about** *a regular polygon.*

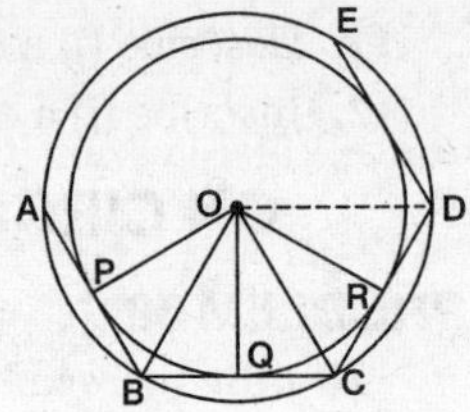

Let **AB, BC, CD, DE**, ... be consecutive sides of a regular polygon of n sides.

Bisect the $\angle^s$ **ABC, BCD** by **BO, CO** meeting at **O**.

Then **O** is the centre both of the inscribed and circumscribed circle.

Outline of Proof. Join **OD**; and from the congruent Δ^s**OCB, OCD**, show that OD bisects the $\angle$**CDE**. Hence we conclude that

All the bisectors of the angles of the polygon meet at **O**.

(i) Prove that **OB = OC = OD**; from Theorem 6.

Hence **O** is the circum-centre.

(ii) Draw **OP, OQ, OR** =...; perp. to **AB, BC, CD**, ...

Prove that **OP = OQ = OR** = ...; from the congruent Δ^s**OBP, OBQ**, ...

Hence O is the in-centre

EXERCISES

1. Draw a regular hexagon on a side of 4 cm. Draw the inscribed and circumscribed circles. Calculate and measure their diameters to the nearest centimetre.
2. Show that the area of a regular hexagon inscribed in a circle is three-fourths of that of the circumscribed hexagon.

   Find the area of a hexagon inscribed in a circle of radius 10 cm. to the nearest tenth of a sq. cm.
3. If **ABC** is an isosceles triangle inscribed in a circle, having each of the angles **B** and **C** double of the angle **A**; show that **BC** is a side of a regular pentagon inscribed in the circle.
4. On a sides of 4 cm. construct (without protractor)

   (i) a regular hexagon;

   (ii) a regular octagon.

   In each case find the approximate area of the figure.

THE CIRCUMFERENCE OF A CIRCLE

By experiment and measurement it is found that the length of the circumference of a circle is roughly $3\frac{1}{7}$ times the length of its diameter: that is to say

$$\frac{circumference}{diameter} = 3\frac{1}{7} \text{ nearly;}$$

and it can be proved that this is the same for all circles.

A more correct value of this ratio is found by theory to be 3.1416; while correct to 7 places of decimals it is 3.1415926. Thus the value $3\frac{1}{7}$ (or 3.1428) is too great, and correct to 2 places only.

The ratio which the circumference of any circle bears to its diameter is denoted by the Greek letter π; so that

$$circumference = diameter \times \pi.$$

Or, if r denotes the radius of the circle,

$$circumference = 2r \times \pi = 2\pi r;$$

where to π we are to give one of the values $3\frac{1}{7}$, 3.1416, or 3.1415926, according to the degree of accuracy required in the final result.

NOTE. The theoretical methods by which π is evaluated to any required degree of accuracy cannot be explained at this stage, but its value may be easily verified by experiment to two decimal places.

For example: round a cylinder wrap a strip of paper so that the ends overlap. At any point in the overlapping area prick a pin through both folds. Unwrap and straighten the strip, then measure the distance between the pin holes: this gives the length of the circumference. Measure the diameter, and divide the first result by the second.

Ex. 1. From these data find and record the value of π.

CIRCUMFERENCE.	DIAMETER.	VALUE OF π
16.0 cm.	5.1 cm.	
8.8 cm.	2.8 cm.	
13.5 cm.	4.3 cm.	

Find the mean of the three results.

Ex.2. A fine thread is wound evenly round a cylinder, and it is found that the length required for 20 complete turns is 75.4 cm. The diameter of the cylinder is 1.2 cm: find roughly the value of π.

Ex. 3. A bicycle wheel, 56 cm. in diameter, makes 400 revolutions in travelling over 40 m. 32 cm. From this result estimate the value of π.

THE AREA OF A CIRCLE

Let **AB** be a side of a polygon of n sides circumscribed about a circle whose centre is **O** and radius r. Then we have

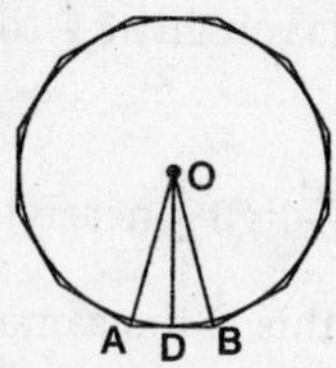

$$\text{Area of polygon} = n \cdot \Delta \mathbf{AOB}$$
$$= n \cdot \frac{1}{2} \mathbf{AB} \times \mathbf{OD}$$
$$= \frac{1}{2} \cdot n\mathbf{AB} \times r$$
$$= \frac{1}{2} (\text{perimeter of polygon}) \times r;$$

and this is true however many sides the polygon may have.

Now if the number of sides is increased without limit, the perimeter and area of the polygon may be made to differ from the circumference and area of the circle by quantities smaller than any that can be named; hence ultimately

$$\text{Area of circle} = \frac{1}{2} \cdot \text{Circumference} \times r$$
$$= \frac{1}{2} \cdot 2\pi r \times r$$
$$= \pi r^2.$$

ALTERNATIVE METHOD

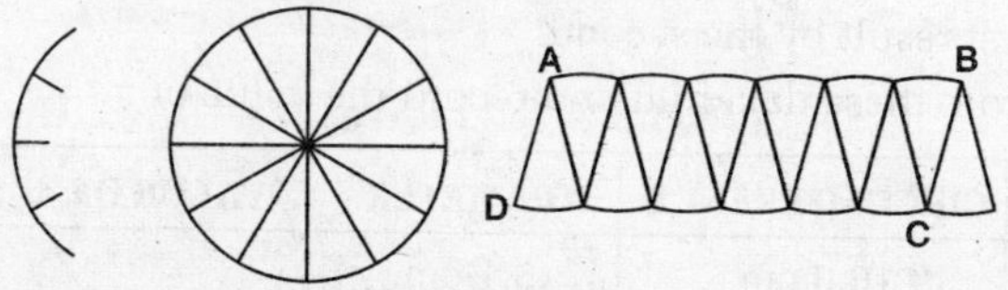

Suppose the circle divided into any even number of sectors having equal angles: denote the number of sectors by n.

Let the sectors be placed side by side as represented in the diagram; then the area of the circle = the area of the fig. **ABCD**;

and this is true however great n may be.

Now as the number of sectors is increased, each arc is decreased; so that

(i) the outlines **AB**, **CD** tend to become *straight*, and

(ii) the angles at **D** and **B** tend to become rt. angles.

Thus when n is increased without limit, the fig. **ABCD** ultimately becomes a rectangle, whose length is the *semi-circumference of the circle*, and whose breadth is its *radius*.

$$\therefore \text{Area of circle} = \frac{1}{2} \cdot \text{circumference} \times \text{radius}$$

$$= \frac{1}{2} \cdot 2\pi r \times r = \pi r^2.$$

THE AREA OF A SECTOR

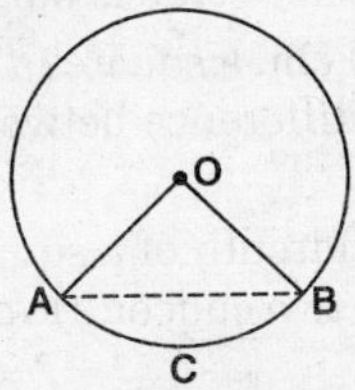

If two radii of a circle make an angle of 1°, they cut off

(i) an arc whose length $= \frac{1}{360}$ of the circumference;

and (ii) a sector whose area $= \frac{1}{360}$ of the circle;

∴ if the angle **AOB** contains **D** degrees, then

(i) *the arc* **AB** $= \frac{D}{360}$ *of the circumference,*

(ii) *the sector* **AOB** $= \frac{D}{360}$ *of the area of the circle*

$$= \frac{D}{360} \text{ of} \left(\frac{1}{2} \text{ circumference} \times \text{radius}\right)$$

$$= \frac{1}{2} \cdot \text{arc AB} \times \text{radius}.$$

THE AREA OF A SEGMENT

The area of a minor segment is found by subtracting from the corresponding sector the area of the triangle formed by the chord and the radii. Thus

Area of segment **ABC** = *sector* **OACB** – *triangle* **AOB**.

The area of a major segment is most simply found by subtracting the area of the corresponding minor segment from the area of the circle.

EXERCISES

In each case choose the value of π so as to give a result of the assigned degree of accuracy.

1. Find to the nearest millimetre the circumference of the circles whose radii are (i) 4.5 cm. (ii) 100 cm.
2. Find to the nearest hundredth of a square centimetre the areas of the circles whose radii are (i) 2.3 cm. (ii) 10.6 cm.
3. Find to two places of decimals the circumference and area of a circle inscribed in a square whose side is 3.6 cm.
4. In a circle of radius 7.0 cm. a square is described: find to the nearest square centimetre the difference between the areas of the circle and the square.
5. Find to the nearest hundredth of a square centimetre the area of the circular ring formed by two concentric circles whose radii are 5.7 cm. and 4.3 cm.
6. Show that the area of a ring lying between the circumferences of two concentric circles is equal to the area of a circle whose radius is the length of a tangent to the inner circle from any point on the outer.
7. A rectangle whose sides are 8.0 cm. and 6.0 m. is inscribed in a circle. Calculate to the nearest tenth of a square centimetre the total area of the four segments outside the rectangle.
8. Find to the nearest tenth of a centimetre the side of a square whose area is equal to that of a circle of radius 5 cm.
9. A circular ring is formed by the circumference of two concentric circles. The area of the ring is 44 sq. cm., and its width is 2 cm; taking π at $\frac{22}{7}$, find approximately the radii of the two circles.
10. Find to the nearest hundredth of a square centimetre the difference between the areas of the circumscribed and inscribed circles of an equilateral triangle each of whose sides is 4 cm.
11. Draw on squared paper two circles whose centres are at the points (3 cm., 0) and (0, 1.6 cm.), and whose radii are respectively 1.4 cm. and 2 cm. Prove that the circles touch one another, and find approximately their circumference and areas.
12. Draw a circle of radius 2 cm. having the point (3.2 cm., 2.4 cm.) as centre. Also draw two circles with the origin as centre and of radii 2 cm. and 6 cm. respectively. Show that each of the last two circles touches the first.

EXERCISES

ON THE INSCRIBED, CIRCUMSCRIBED, AND ESCRIBED CIRCLES OF A TRIANGLE

(*Theoretical*)

1. Describe a circle to touch two parallel straight lines and a third straight line which meets them. Show that two such circles can be drawn, and that they are equal.
2. *Triangles which have equal bases and equal vertical angles have equal circumscribed angles.*
3. **ABC** is a triangle, and **I**, **S** are the centres of the inscribed and circumscribed circles; if **A**, **I**, **S** are collinear, show that **AB** = **AC**.
4. The sum of the diameters of the inscribed and circumscribed circles of a right-angled triangle is equal to the sum of the sides containing the right angle.
5. If the circle inscribed in the triangle **ABC** touches the sides at **D**, **E**, **F**; show that the angles of the triangle **DEF** are respectively
$$90-\frac{A}{2}, 90-\frac{B}{2}, 90-\frac{C}{2}.$$
6. If I is the centre of the circles inscribed in the triangle **ABC**, and I_1 the centre of the escribed circle which touches **BC**; show that
I, **B**, I_2, **C** are concyclic.
7. In any triangle the difference of two sides is equal to the difference of the segments into which the third side is divided at the point of contact of the inscribed circle.
8. In the triangle **ABC**, **I** and **S** are the centres of the inscribed and circumscribed circles; show that **IS** subtends at **A** an angle equal to half the difference of the angles at the base of the triangle.

   Hence show that if **AD** is drawn perpendicular to **BC**, then **AI** is the bisector of the angle **DAS**.
9. The diagonals of a quadrilateral **ABCD** intersect at **O**: show that the centres of the circles circumscribed about the four triangles **AOB**, **BOC**, **COD**, **DOA** are at the angular points of a parallelogram.
10. In any triangle **ABC**, if **I** is the centre of the inscribed circle, and if **AI** is produced to meet the circumscribed circle at **O**; show that **O** is the centre of the circle circumscribed about the triangle **BIC**.
11. Given the base, altitude, and the radius of the circumscribed circle; construct the triangle.
12. Three circles whose centres are **A**, **B**, **C** touch one another externally two by two at **D**, **E**, **F**: show that the inscribed circle of the triangle **ABC** is the circumscribed circle of the triangle **DEF**.

THEOREMS AND EXAMPLES ON CIRCLES AND TRIANGLES

THE ORTHOCENTRE OF A TRIANGLE

I. *The perpendiculars drawn from the vertices of a triangle to the apposite sides are concurrent.*

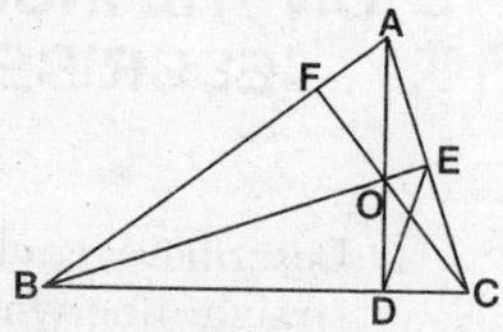

In the Δ**ABC**, let **AD**, **BE** be the perp^s drawn from **A** and **B** to the opposite sides; and let them intersect at **O**.

Join **CO**; and produce it to meet **AB** at **F**.

It is required to show that **CF** *is perp. to* **AB**.

Join **DE**.

Then, because the $\angle^s$**OEC**, **ODC** are rt. angles,

$\therefore$ the points **O**, **E**, **C**, **D** are concyclic:

$\therefore$ the $\angle$**DEC** = the $\angle$**DOC**, in the same segment;

= the vert. opp. $\angle$**FOA**.

Again, because the $\angle^s$**AEB**, **ADB** are rt. angles,

$\therefore$ the points **A**, **E**, **D**, **B** are concyclic :

$\therefore$ the $\angle$**DEB** = the $\angle$**DAB**, in the same segment.

$\therefore$ the sum of the $\angle^s$**FOA**, **FAO** = the sum of the $\angle^s$**DEC**, **DEB**

= a rt. angle.

$\therefore$ the remaining $\angle$**AFO** = a rt. angle : ***Theor.* 16.**

that is, **CF** is perp. to **AB**.

Hence the three perp^s **AD**, **BE**, **CF** meet at the point **O**. **Q.E.D.**

DEFINITIONS

(i) The intersection of the perpendiculars drawn from the vertices of a triangle to the opposite sides is called its **orthocentre.**

(ii) The triangle formed by joining the feet of the perpendiculars is called the **pedal** or **orthocentric triangle.**

II. *In an acute-angled triangle the perpendiculars drawn from the vertices to the opposite sides bisect the angles of the pedal triangle through which they pass*

In the acute-angled Δ**ABC**, let **AD**, **BE**, **CF** be the perp^s drawn from the vertices to the opposite sides, meeting at the orthocentre **O**; and let **DEF** be the pedal triangle.

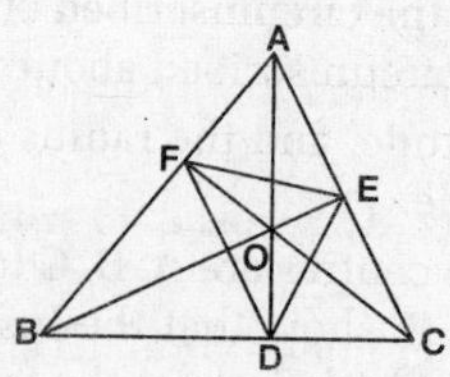

It is required to prove that **AD, BE, CF** *bisect respectively the* $\angle^s$ **FDE, DEF, EFD**.

It may be shown, as in the last theorem, that the points **O, D, C, E** are concyclic;

∴ the ∠**ODE** = the ∠**OCE**, in the same segment.

Similarly the points **O, D, B, F** are concyclic;

∴ the ∠**ODF** = the ∠**OBF**, in the same segment.

But the ∠**OCE** = the ∠**OBF**, each being the comp^t of the ∠**BAC**.

∴ the ∠**ODE** = the ∠**ODF**.

Similarly it may be shown that the $\angle^s$ **DEF, EFD** are bisected by **BE** and **CF**. **Q.E.D.**

COROLLARY. (i) *Every two sides of the pedal triangle are equally inclined to that side of the original triangle in which they meet.*

For the ∠**EDC** = the comp^t of the ∠**ODE**

= the comp^t of the ∠**OCE**

= the ∠**BAC**.

Similarly it may be shown that the ∠**FDB** = the ∠**BAC**,

∴ the ∠**EDC** = the ∠**FDB** = the ∠**A**.

In like manner it may be proved that

the ∠**DEC** = the ∠**FEA** = the ∠**B**

and the ∠**DFB** = the ∠**EFA** = the ∠**C**.

COROLLARY. (ii) *The triangles* **DEC, AEF, DBF** *are equiangular to one another and to the triangle* **ABC**.

NOTE. If the angle **BAC** is *obtuse*, then the perpendiculars **BE, CF** bisect *externally* the corresponding angles of the pedal triangle.

EXERCISES

1. *If* **O** *is the orthocentre of the triangle* **ABC** *and if the perpendicular* **AD** *is produced to meet the circum-circle in* **G**, *prove that* **OD = DG**.
2. *In an acute-angled triangle the three sides are the external bisectors of the angles of the pedal triangle : and in an obtuse-angled triangle the sides containing the obtuse angle are the internal bisectors of the corresponding angles of the pedal triangle.*
3. *If* **O** *is the orthocentre of the triangle* **ABC**. *show that the angles* **BOC, BAC** *are supplementary.*
4. *If* **O** *is the orthocentre of the triangle* **ABC**, *then any one of the four points* **O, A, B, C** *is the orthocentre of the triangle whose vertices are the other three.*
5. *The three circles which pass through two vertices of a triangle and its orthocentre are each equal to the circum-circle of the triangle.*

6. D, E are taken on the circumference of a semi-circle described on a given straight line **AB** : the chords **AD**, **BE** and **AE**, **BD** intersect (produced if necessary) at **F** and **G** : show that **FG** is perpendicular to **AB**.

7. **ABC** is a triangle, **O** is its orthocentre, and **AK** a diameter of the circum-circle : show that **BOCK** is a parallelogram.

8. The orthocentre of a triangle is joined to the middle point of the base, and the joining line is produced to meet the circum-circle : prove that it will meet it at the same point as the diameter which passes through the vertex.

9. The perpendicular from the vertex of a triangle on the base, and the straight line joining the orthocentre to the middle point of the base, are produced to meet the circum-circle at **P** and **Q** : show that **PQ** is parallel to the base.

10. *The distance of each vertex of a triangle from the orthocentre is double of the perpendicular drawn from the centre of the circum-circle to the opposite side.*

11. Three circles are described each passing through the orthocentre of a triangle and two of its vertices : show that the triangle formed by joining their centres is equal in all respects to the original triangle.

12. Construct a triangle, having given a vertex, the orthocentre, and the centre of the circum-circle.

LOCI

III. *Given the base and vertical angle of a triangle, find the locus of its orthocentre.*

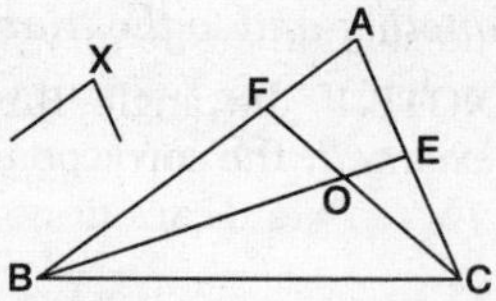

Let **BC** be the given base, and **X** the given angle; and let **BAC** be any triangle on the base **BC**, having its vertical ∠**A** equal to the ∠**X**.

Draw the perp^s **BE**, **CF**, intersecting at the orthocentre **O**.

It is required to find the locus of **O**.

Proof. Since the ∠^{s}**OFA**, **OEA** are rt. angles,

∴ the points **O**, **F**, **A**, E are concyclic;

∴ the ∠**FOE** is the supplement of the ∠**A** :

∴ the vert.opp. ∠**BOC** is the supplement of the ∠**A**.

But the ∠**A** is constant, being always equal to the ∠**X**;

∴ its supplement is constant;

that is, the Δ**BOC** has a fixed base, and constant vertical angle; hence the locus of its vertex **O** is the arc of a segment of which **BC** is the chord.

IV. *Given the base and vertical angle of a triangle, find the locus of the in-centre.*

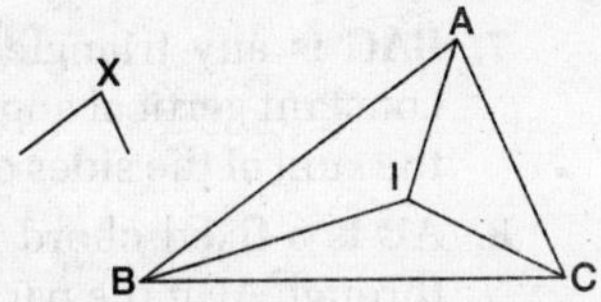

Let **BAC** be any triangle on the given base **BC**, having its vertical angle equal to the given $\angle$**X** and let **AI**, **BI**, **CI** be the bisectors of its angles. Then **I** is the incentre.

It is required to find the locus of **I**.

Proof. Denote the angles of the Δ**ABC** by **A**, **B**, **C**; and let the $\angle$**BIC** be denoted by **I**.

Then from the Δ**BIC**,

(i) $I + \frac{1}{2}B + \frac{1}{2}C =$ two rt. angles; ***Theor.* 16.**

and from the Δ**ABC**,

$A + B + C =$ two rt. angles;

(ii) so that $\frac{1}{2}A + \frac{1}{2}B + \frac{1}{2}C =$ one rt. angle.

$\therefore$ taking the differences of the equals in (i) and (ii),

$$I - \frac{1}{2}A = \text{one rt. angle :}$$

or,

$$I = \text{one rt. angle} + \frac{1}{2}A.$$

But A is constant, being always equal to the $\angle$**X**;

$\therefore$ **I** is constant:

$\therefore$ the locus of **I** is the arc of a segment on the fixed chord **BC**.

EXERCISES ON LOCI

1. Given the base **BC** and the vertical angle **A** of a triangle; find the locus of the ex-centre opposite **A**.
2. Through the extremities of a given straight line **AB** any two parallel straight lines **AP**, **BQ** are drawn; find the locus of the intersection of the bisectors of the angles **PAB**, **QBA**.
3. Find the locus of the middle points of chords of a circle drawn through a fixed point.

   Distinguish between the cases when the given point is within, on, or without the circumference.
4. Find the locus of the points of contact of tangents drawn from a fixed point to a system of concentric circles.
5. Find the locus of the intersection of straight lines which pass through two fixed points on a circle and intercept on its circumference an arc of constant length.
6. **A** and **B** are two fixed points on the circumference of a circle, and **PQ** is any diameter: find the locus of the intersection of **PA** and **QB**.

7. **BAC** is any triangle described on the fixed base **BC** and having a constant vertical angle: and **BA** is produced to **P**, so that BP is equal to the sum of the sides containing the vertical angle: find the locus of **P**.
8. **AB** is a fixed chord of a circle, and **AC** is a movable chord passing through **A** : if the parallelogram **CB** is completed, find the locus of the intersection of its diagonals.
9. A straight rod **PQ** slides between two rulers placed at right angles to on another, and from its extremities **PX**, **QX** are drawn perpendicular to the rulers : find the locus of **X**.
10. Two circles intersect at **A** and **B**, and through **P**, any point on the circumference of one of them, two straight lines **PA**, **PB** are drawn, and produced if, necessary, to cut the other circle at **X** and **Y** : find the locus of the intersection of **AY** and **BX**.
11. Two circles intersect at **A** and **B**; **HAK** is a fixed straight line drawn through **A** and terminated by the circumferences, and **PAQ** is any other straight line similarly drawn: find the locus of the intersection of **HP** and **QK**.

SIMSON'S LINE

V. *The feet of the perpendiculars drawn to the three sides of a triangle from any point on its circum-circle are collinear.*

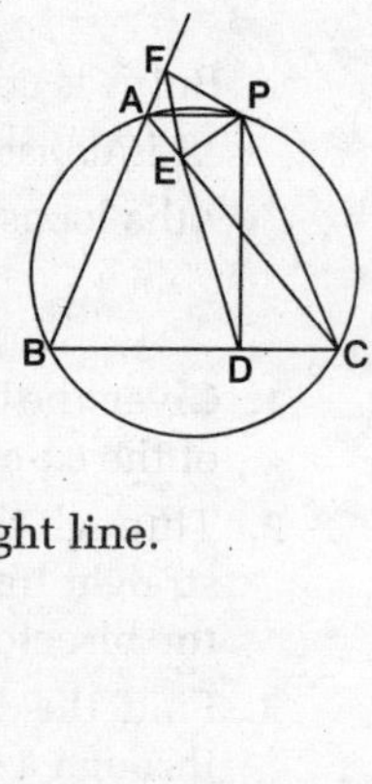

Let **P** be any point on the circum-circle of the Δ**ABC**; and let **PD**, **PE**, **PF** be the perp^s. drawn from P to the sides.

It is required to prove that the points **D**, **E**, **F** *are collinear.*

Join **FE** and **ED** :

then FE and ED will be shown to be in the same straight line.

Join **PA**, **PC**.

Proof. Because the ∠^{s}**PEA**, **PFA** are rt. angles,

∴ the points **P**, **E**, **A**, **F** are concyclic :

∴ the ∠**PEF** = the ∠**PAF**, in the same segment

= the supp^t of the ∠**PAB** = the ∠**PCD**,

since the points **A**, **P**, **C**, **B** are concyclic.

Again because the ∠^{s}**PEC**, **PDC** are rt. angles,

∴ the points **P**, **E**, **D**, **C** are concyclic,

∴ the ∠**PED** = the supp^t of the ∠**PCD**

= the supp^t of the ∠**PEF**.

∴ **FE** and **ED** are in one st. line.

Obs. The line **FED** is known as the Pedal or Simson's Line of the triangle **ABC** for the point P.

EXERCISES

1. From any point **P** on the circum-circle of the triangle **ABC**, perpendiculars **PD**, **PF** are drawn to **BC** and **AB**: if **FD**, or **FD** produced, cuts **AC** at **E**, show that **PE** is perpendicular to **AC**.
2. Find the locus of a point which moves so that if perpendiculars are drawn from it to the sides of a given triangle, their feet are collinear.
3. **ABC** and **AB'C'** are two triangles with a common angle, and their circum-circles meet again at **P**; show that the feet of perpendiculars drawn from **P** to the lines **AB**, **AC**, **BC**, **B'C'** are collinear.
4. A triangle is inscribed in a circle, and any point **P** on the circumference is joined to the orthocentre of the triangle: show that this joining line is bisected by the pedal of the point **P**.

THE TRIANGLE AND ITS CIRCLES

VI. **D**, **E**, **F** *are the points of contact of the inscribed circle of the triangle* **ABC** *and* $\mathbf{D_1}$, $\mathbf{E_1}$, $\mathbf{F_1}$ *the points of contact of the escribed circle, which touches* **BC** *and the other sides produced*: a, b, c *denote the length of the sides* **BC**, **CA**, **AB**; s *the semi-perimeter of the triangle, and* r, r_1 *the radii of the inscribed and escribed circles.*

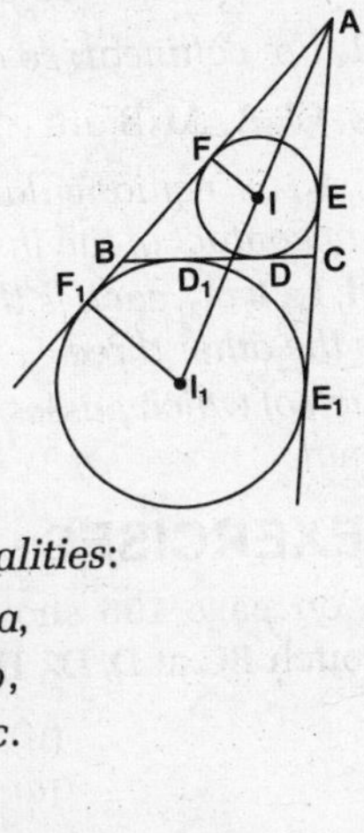

Prove the following equalities:

(i) $\mathbf{AE} = \mathbf{AF} = s - a$,

$\mathbf{BD} = \mathbf{BF} = s - b$,

$\mathbf{CD} = \mathbf{CE} = s - c$.

(ii) $\mathbf{AE_1} = \mathbf{AF_1} = s$.

(iii) $\mathbf{CD_1} = \mathbf{CE_1} = s - b$, $\mathbf{BD_1}, = \mathbf{BF_1}, = s - c$.

(iv) $\mathbf{CD} = \mathbf{BD_1}$, and $\mathbf{BD} = \mathbf{CD_1}$.

(v) $\mathbf{EF_1} = \mathbf{EF_1} = a$

(vi) The area of the $\Delta\mathbf{ABC} = rs = r_1(s - a)$.

(vii) Draw the above figure in the case when **C** is a right angle, and prove that

$$r = s - c;\ r_1 = s - b.$$

VII. *In the triangle* **ABC**, **I** *is the centre of the inscribed circle, and* $\mathbf{I_1}$, $\mathbf{I_2}$, $\mathbf{I_3}$ *the centres of the escribed circles touching respectively the sides* **BC**, **CA**, **AB** *and the other sides produced.*

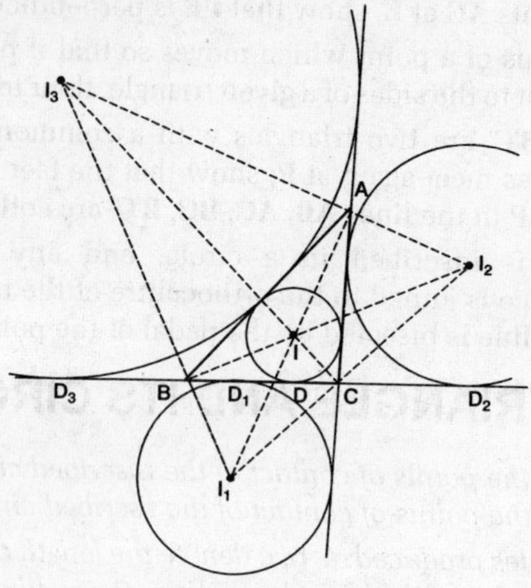

Prove the following properties :

(i) *The points* **A**, **I**, $\mathbf{I_1}$ *are collinear : so are* **B**, **I**, $\mathbf{I_2}$; *and* **C**, **I**, Is,

(ii) The points $\mathbf{I_2}$, **A**, $\mathbf{I_3}$ *are collinear; so are* $\mathbf{I_3}$, **B**, $\mathbf{I_1}$; and $\mathbf{I_1}$, **C**, $\mathbf{I_2}$.

(iii) *The triangles* $\mathbf{BI_1C}$, $\mathbf{CI_2A}$, $\mathbf{AI_3B}$ *are equiangular to one another.*

(iv) *The triangle* $\mathbf{I_1}$, $\mathbf{I_2}$, $\mathbf{I_3}$, *is equiangular to the triangle formed by joining the points of contact of the inscribed circle.*

(v) *Of the four points* **I**, $\mathbf{I_1}$, $\mathbf{I_2}$, $\mathbf{I_3}$, *each is the orthocentre of the triangle whose vertices are the other three.*

(vi) *The four circles, each of which passes through three of the points* **I**, $\mathbf{I_1}$, $\mathbf{I_2}$, $\mathbf{I_3}$, *are all equal.*

EXERCISES

1. With the figure given on page 196 show that if the circles whose centres are **I**, $\mathbf{I_1}$, $\mathbf{I_2}$, $\mathbf{I_3}$ touch **BC** at **D**, $\mathbf{D_1}$, $\mathbf{D_2}$, $\mathbf{D_3}$, then

   (i) $\mathbf{DD_2} = \mathbf{D_1}, \mathbf{D_3} = b$. (ii) $\mathbf{DD_3} = \mathbf{D_1D_2} = c$.

   (iii) $\mathbf{D_2D_3} = b + c$. (iv) $\mathbf{DD_1} = b \sim c$.

2. *Show that the orthocentre and vertices of a triangle are the centres of the inscribed and escribed circles of the pedal triangle.*

3. *Given the base and vertical angle of a triangle, find the locus of the centre of the escribed circle which touches the base.*

4. *Given the base and vertical angle of a triangle, show that the centre of the circum-circle is fixed.*

5. Given the base **BC**, and the vertical angle **A** of the triangle, find the locus of the centre of the escribed circle which touches **AC**.

6. Given the base, the vertical angle, and the point of contact with the base of the in-circle; construct the triangle.
7. Given the base, the vertical angle, and the point of contact with the base, or base produced, of an escribed circle; construct the triangle.
8. **I** *is the centre of the circle inscribed in a triangle, and* I_1, I_2, I_3 *the centres of the escribed circles; show that* II_1, II_2, II_3 *are bisected by the circumference of the circum-circle.*
9. **ABC** is a triangle, and I_2, I_3 the centres of the escribed circles which touch **AC**, and **AB** respectively : show that the points **B**, **C**, I_2, I_3 lie upon a circle whose centre is on the circumference of the circum-circle of the triangle **ABC**.
10. With three given points as centres describe three circle touching one another two by two. How many solutions will there be?
11. Given the centres of the three escribed circles; construct the triangle.
12. Given the centre of the inscribed circles, and the centres of two escribed circles: construct the triangle.
13. Given the vertical angle, perimeter, and radius of the inscribed circle; construct the triangle.
14. Given the vertical angle, the radius of the inscribed circle, and the length of the perpendicular from the vertex to the base; construct the triangle.
15. In a triangle **ABC**, **I** is the centre of the inscribed circle; show that the centres of the circles circumscribed about the triangles **BIC**, **CIA**, **AIB** lie on the circumference of the circle circumscribed about the given triangle.

THE NINE-POINTS CIRCLE

VIII. *In any triangle the middle points of the sides, the feet of the perpendiculars from the vertices to the opposite sides, and the middle points of the lines joining the orthocentre to the vertices are concyclic.*

In the ΔABC, let **X**, **Y**, **Z** be the middle points of the sides **BC**, **CA**, **AB**; let D, E, F be the feet of the perp[s] to these sides from **A**, **B**, **C**; let **O** be the orthocentre, and α, β, γ the middle points of **OA**, **OB**, **OC**.

It is required to prove that the nine points **X, Y, Z, D, E, F,** α, β, γ are *concyclic.*

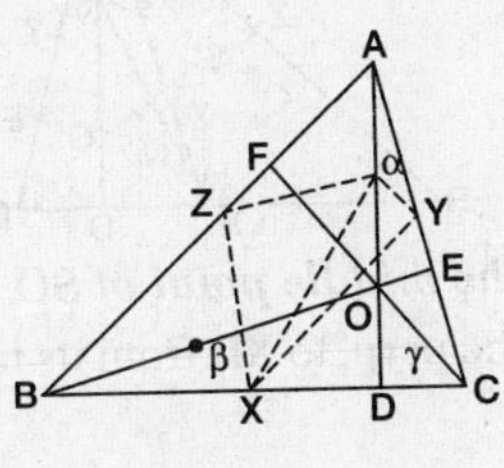

Join **XY**, **XZ**, **X**α, **Y** α, **Z** α.

Now from the Δ**ABO**,

since **AZ** = **ZB**, and **A**α = α**O**,

$\therefore$ **Z**α par[l] to **BO**. Ex. 2, p. 64.

And from the Δ**ABC**, since **BZ** = **ZA**, and **BX** = **XC**,

$\therefore$ **ZX** is par[l] to **AC**.

But **BO** produced makes a rt. angle with **AC**;

$\therefore$ the $\angle$**ZX**α is a rt. angle.

Similarly, the $\angle$**XY**α is a rt. angle.

$\therefore$ the points **X**, **Z**, α, **Y** are concyclic:

that is, α lies on the $\bigcirc^{ce}$ of the circle which passes through **X**, **Y**, **Z**; and **X**α is a diameter of this circle.

Similarly if may be shown that β and γ lie on the $\bigcirc^{ce}$ of this circle.

Again, since α**DX** is a rt. angle,

$\therefore$ the circle on **X**α as diameter passes through **D**.

Similarly it may be shown that **E** and **F** lie on the $\bigcirc^{ce}$ of the circle;

$\therefore$ the points **X**, **Y**, **Z**, **D**, **E**, **F**, α, β, γ are concylic. **Q.E.D.**

Obs. From this property the circle which passes through the middle points of the sides of a triangle is called the **Nine-Points Circle**; many of its properties may be derived from the fact of its being the circum-circle of the **pedal triangle.**

To prove that

(i) *the centre of the nine-points circle is the middle point of the straight line which joins the orthocentre to the circum-centre.*

(ii) *the radius of the nine-points circle is half the radius of the circum-circle.*

(iii) *the centroid is collinear with the circum-centre, the nine-points* centre, and the orthocentre.

In the Δ**ABC**, let **X**, **Y**, **Z** be the middle points of the sides; **D**, **E**, **F** the feet of the perp[s]; **O** the orthocentre; **S** and **N** the centres of the circumscribed and nine-points circles respectively.

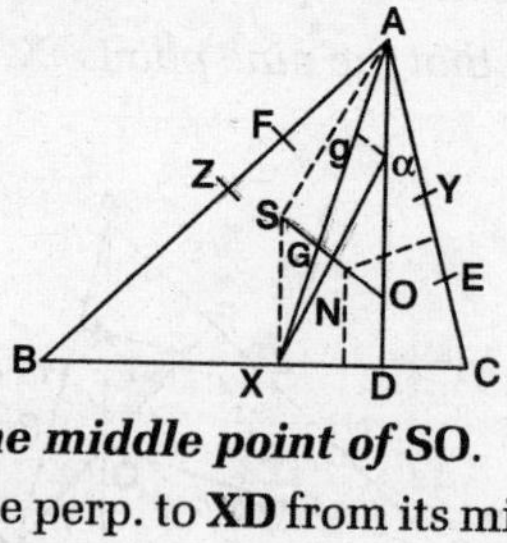

(i) *To prove that* **N** ***is the middle point of*** **SO**.

It may be shown that the perp. to **XD** from its middle point bisects **SO**; ***Theor.* 22.**

Similarly the perp. to **EY** at its middle point bisects **SO**:

that is, these perp[s] intersect at the middle point of **SO**:

And since **XD** and **EY** are chords of the nine-points circle,

∴ the intersection of the lines which bisect **XD** and **EY** at rt. angles is its centre: ***Theor.* 31, *Cor.* 1.**

∴the centre **N** is the middle point of **SO**. **Q.E.D.**

(ii) *o prove that the radius of the nine-points circle is half the radius of the circum-circle.*

By the last Proposition **X**α is a diameter of the nine-points circle.'

∴the middle points of **X**α is its centre:

but the middle point of **SO** is also the centre of the nine-points circle. *(Proved.)*

Hence **X**α and **SO** bisect one another at **N**.

Then from the Δ^s **SNX, ON**α,

$$\text{because}\begin{cases} \mathbf{SN = ON} \\ \text{and } \mathbf{NX = N}\alpha \\ \text{and the } \angle\mathbf{SNX} = \text{the } \angle\mathbf{ON}\alpha \end{cases}$$

$$\therefore \quad \mathbf{SX = O}\alpha = \mathbf{A}\alpha$$

And **SX** is also par[l] to **A**α,

$$\therefore \quad \mathbf{SA = X}\alpha.$$

But **SA** is a *radius* of the circum-circle;

and **X** α is a *diameter* of the nine-points circle;

∴ the radius of the nine-points circle is half the radius of the circum-circle. **Q.E.D.**

(iii) *To prove that the centroid is collinear with points* **S, N, O**. Join **AX** and draw *ag par*[l] to **SO**.

Let **AX** meet **SO** at **G**.

Then from the Δ**AGO**, since **A** α = α **O** and αg is par[l] to **OG**,

∴ **A***g* = *g***G**. Ex. l, p. 57 And from the Δ**X**αg,

since α**N** = **NX**, and **NG** is par[l] to αg,

$$\therefore \quad g\mathbf{G} = \mathbf{GX}.$$

$$\therefore \quad \mathbf{AG} = \frac{2}{3} \text{ of } \mathbf{AX};$$

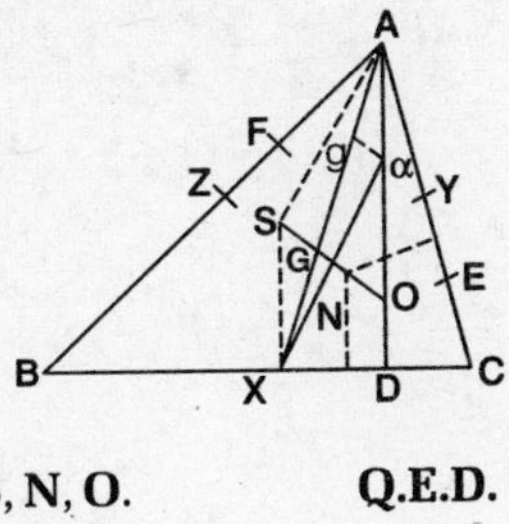

∴ **G** is the centroid of the triangle **ABC**.

Theor. III, *Cor.*, p. 85.

That is, the centroid is collinear with the points **S, N, O**. **Q.E.D.**

EXERCISES

1. *Given the base and vertical angle of a triangle, find the locus of the centre of the nine-points circle.*
2. The nine-points circle of any triangle **ABC**, whose orthocentre is **O**, is also the nine-points circle of each of the triangles **AOB**, **BO C**, **COA**.
3. If $\mathbf{I}$, $\mathbf{I_1}$, $\mathbf{I_2}$, $\mathbf{I_3}$ are the centres of the inscribed and escribed circles of a triangle **ABC**, then the circle circumscribed about **ABC** is the nine-points circle of each of the four triangles formed by joining three of the points $\mathbf{I}$, $\mathbf{I_1}$, $\mathbf{I_2}$, $\mathbf{I_3}$.
4. All triangles which have the same orthocentre and the same circumscribed circle, have also the same nine-points circle.
5. Given the base and vertical angle of a triangle, show that one angle and one side of the pedal triangle are constant.
6. Given the base and vertical angle of a triangle, find the locus of the centre of the circle which passes through the three escribed centres.

NOTE. For some other important properties of the Nine-points Circle see Ex. 54, in part V.

PART IV

ON SQUARES AND RECTANGLES IN CONNECTION WITH THE SEGMENTS OF A STRAIGHT LINE

THE GEOMETRICAL EQUIVALENTS OF CERTAIN ALGEBRAICAL FORMULAE

DEFINITIONS

1. A rectangle **ABCD** is said to be contained by two adjacent sides, **AB**, **AD**; for these sides fix its size and shape.

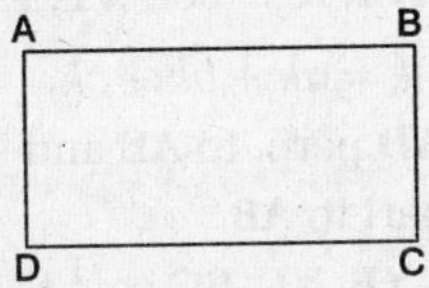

A rectangle whose adjacent sides are **AB**, **AD** is denoted by *the rect.* **AB**, **AD**; this is equivalent to the product **AB**, **AD**.

Similarly a square drawn on the side **AB** is denoted by *the sq. on* **AB**, or AB^2.

2. If a point **X** is taken in a straight line **AB**, or in **AB** produced, then **X** is said to divide **AB** into the two **segments AX**, **XB**; the segments being in either case *the distances of the dividing point* **X** *from the extremities of the given line* **AB**.

Fig. 1.

Fig. 2.

In Fig. 1, **AB** is said to be divided **internally** at **X**.

In Fig. 2, **AB** .... divided **externally** at **X**.

Obs. In internal division the given line **AB** is the *sum* of the segments **AX**, **XB**.

In external division the given line **AB** is the *difference* of the segments **AX**, **XB**.

THEOREM 50. [Euclid II. 1]

If of two straight lines, one is divided into any number of parts, the rectangle contained by the two lines is equal to the sum of the rectangles contained by the undivided line and the several parts of the divided line.

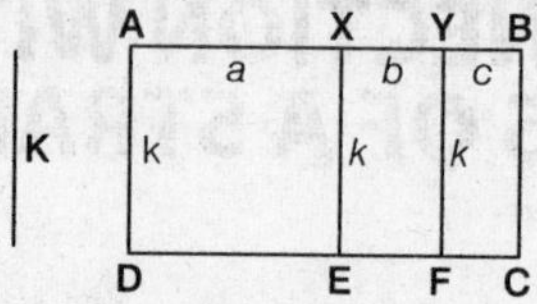

Let **AB** and **K** be the two given st. lines, and let **AB** be divided into any number of parts **AX**, **XY**, **YB**, which contain respectively a, b and c units of length; so that **AB** contains $a + b + c$ units.

Let the line **K** contain k units of length.

It is required to prove that

the rect. **AB**, **K** = rect. **AX**, **K** + rect. **XY**, **K** + rect. **YB**, **K**;

namely that $(a + b + c)k = ak + bk + ck$.

Construction. Draw **AD** perp. to **AB** and equal to **K**.

Through **D** draw **DC** parl to **AB**.

Through **X**, **Y**, **B** draw **XE**, **YF**, **BC** par[l] to **AD**.

Proof. The fig. **AC** = the fig. **AE** + the fig. **XF** + the fig. **YC**; and of these, by construction,

fig. **AC** = rect. **AB**, **K**; and contains $(a + b + c)k$ units of area;

fig. **AE** = rect. **AX**, **K**; and contains ak units of area;
fig. **XF** = rect. **XY**, **K**;.... .....bk ....;
fig. **YC** = rect. **YB**, **K**; ....ck ....

Hence

the rect. **AB**, **K** = rect. **AX**, **K** + rect. **XY**, **K** + rect. **YB**, **K**;

or, $(a + b + c)k = ak + bk + ck$. **Q.E.D.**

*COROLLARIES. [Euclid II. 2 and 3]

Two special cases of this Theorem deserve attention.

(i) When **AB** is divided only at one point **X**, and when the undivided line **AD** is equal to **AB**.

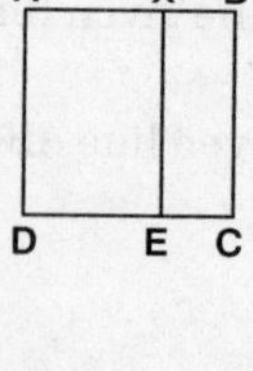

Then the sq. on **AB** = the rect. **AB, AX** + the rect. **AB, XB.**

That is,
The square on the given line is equal to the sum of the rectangles contained by the whole line and each of the segments.

Or thus:

$$\begin{aligned} AB^2 &= AB \cdot AB \\ &= AB\,(AX + XB) \\ &= AB \cdot AX + AB \cdot XB. \end{aligned}$$

(ii) When **AB** is divided at one point **X**, and when the undivided line **AD** is equal to one segment **AX**.

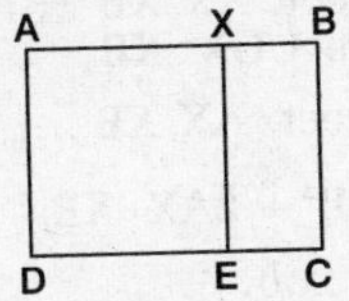

Then the rect. **AB, AX** = the sq. on **AX** + the rect. **AX, XB.**

That is,
The rectangle contained by the whole line and one segment is equal to the square on that segment with the rectangle contained by the two segments.

Or thus: $BA \cdot AX = (AX + XB)AX$
$= AX^2 + AX \cdot XB.$

THEOREM 51. [Euclid II. 4]

If a straight line is divided **internally** *at any point, the square on the given line is equal to the sum of the squares on the two segments* **together** *with twice the rectangle contained by the segments.*

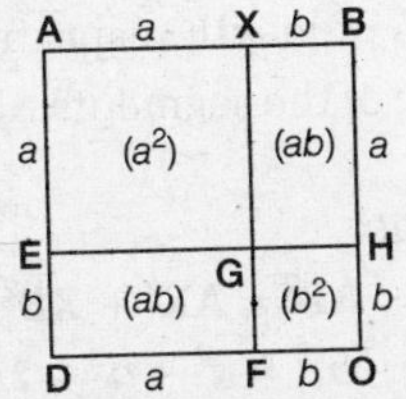

Let **AB** be the given st. line divided *internally* at **X**; and let the segments **AX, XB** contain a and b units of length respectively.

Then **AB** is the *sum* of the segments **AX, XB**, and therefore contains $a + b$ units.

It is required to prove that

$$AB^2 = AX^2 + XB^2 + 2AX \cdot XB;$$

namely that $$(a + b)^2 = a^2 + b^2 + 2ab.$$

Construction. On **AB** describe a square **ABCD**. From **AD** cut off **AE** equal to **AX**, or a. Then **ED** = **XB** = b. Through **E** and **X** draw **EG**, **XF** par[l] respectively to **AB**, **AD** and meeting at **G**.

Proof. Then the fig. **AC** = the figs. **AG**, **GC** + the figs. **EF**, **XH**.

And of these, by construction,

fig. **AC** is the sq. on **AB**, and contains $(a+b)^2$ units of area;

fig. **AG** = sq. on **AX**, and contains a^2 units of area;
fig. **GC** = sq. on **XB**, ...b^2 ....;
fig. EF = rect. **EG**, **ED**
= rect. **AX**, **XB** .... ab ....,
fig. **XH** = rect. **GX**, **XB**
= rect. **AX**, **XB** .... ab ....

Hence $\quad AB^2 = AX^2 + XB^2 + 2AX \cdot XB;$

that is, $(a+b)^2 = a^2 + b^2 + 2ab.$ **Q.E.D.**

THEOREM 52 [Euclid II. 7]

If a straight line is divided **externally** *at any point, the square on the given line is equal to the sum of the squares on the two segments* **diminished by** *twice the rectangle contained by the segments.*

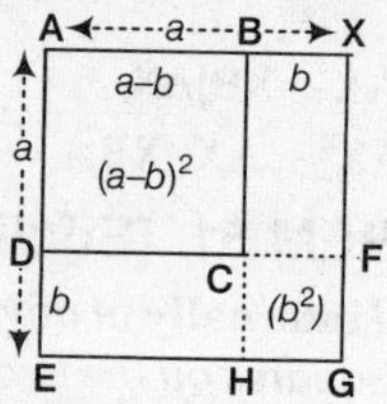

Let **AB** be the given st. line divided *externally* at **X**; and let the segments **AX**, **XB** contain a and b units of length respectively.

Then **AB** is the *difference* of the segments **AX**, **XB**, and therefore contains $a-b$ units.

It is required to prove that

$$AB^2 = AX^2 + XB^2 - 2AX \cdot XB;$$

namely that $\quad (a-b)^2 = a^2 + b^2 - 2ab.$

Construction. On **AX** describe a square **AXGE**. From **AE** cut off **AD** equal to **AB**, or $a-b$. Then **ED** = **XB** = b. Through **D** and **B** draw **DF**, **BH** par[l] respectively to **AX**, **AE**, meeting at **C** .

Proof. Then the fig. **AC** = the figs. **AG**, **CG** – the figs. **EF**, **XH**.

And of these, by construction,

fig. AC is the sq. on **AB**, and contains $(a-b)^2$ units of area;

fig. **AG** = sq. on **AX**, and contains a^2 units of area;
fig. **CG** = sq. on **XB**, ...b^2 ....;
fig. **EF** = rect. **EG, ED**
= rect. **AX, XB** .... ab ......,
fig. **XH** = rect. **GX**, XB
= rect. **AX, XB** .... ab ....

Hence $\quad AB^2 = AX^2 + XB^2 - 2AX \cdot XB;$

that is, $\quad (a-b)^2 = a^2 + b^2 - 2ab.$ **Q.E.D.**

THEOREM 53. [Euclid II. 5 and 6]

The difference of the squares on two straight lines is equal to the rectangle contained by their sum and difference.

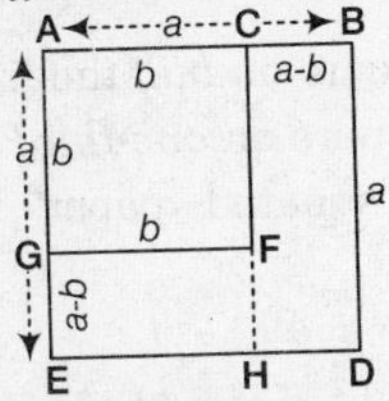

Let the given lines **AB**, **AC** be placed in the same st. line, and let them contain a and b units of length respectively.

It is required to prove that

$$AB^2 - AC^2 = (AB + AC)(AB - AC);$$

namely that $\quad a^2 - b^2 = (a+b)(a-b).$

Construction. On **AB** and **AC** draw the squares **ABDE, ACFG**; and produce **CF** to meet **ED** at **H**.

Then **GE** = **CB** = $a - b$ units.

Proof. Now $AB^2 - AC^2$ = the sq. **AD** – the sq. **AF**
= the rect. **CD** + the rect. **GH**
= **DB · BC** + **GF · GE**
= **AB · CB** + **AC · CB**
= **(AB + AC) CB**
= **(AB + AC) (AB – AC)**.

That is,

$$a^2 - b^2 = (a+b)(a-b).$$ **Q.E.D.**

COROLLARY. *If a straight line is bisected, and also divided (internally or externally) into two unequal segments, the rectangle contained by these segments is equal to the difference of the squares on half the line and on the line between the points of section.*

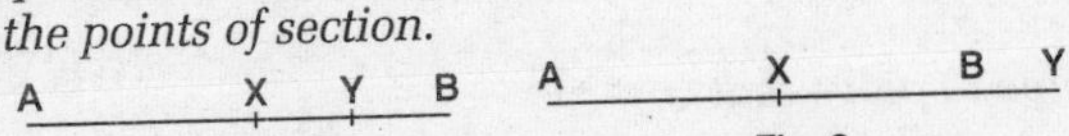

Fig. 1. Fig. 2.

That is, if **AB** is bisected at **X** and also divided at **Y**, internally in Fig. 1, and externally in Fig. 2, then

in Fig. 1, $\mathbf{AY \cdot YB = AX^2 - XY^2}$;

in Fig. 2, $\mathbf{AY \cdot YB = XY^2 - AX^2}$.

For in the first case, $\mathbf{AY \cdot YB = (AX + XY)(XB - XY)}$

$$\mathbf{= (AX + XY)(AX - XY)}$$

$$\mathbf{= AX^2 - XY^2}.$$

The second case may be similarly proved.

EXERCISES

1. Draw diagrams on squared paper to show that the square on a straight line is
   (i) *four*-times the square on *half* the line;
   (ii) *nine*-times the square on *one-third* of the line.
2. Draw diagrams on squared paper to illustrate the following algebraical formulae:
   (i) $(x + 7)^2 = x^2 + 14x + 49$.
   (ii) $(a + b + c)^2 = a^2 + b^2 + c^2 + 2bc + 2ca + 2ab$.
   (iii) $(a + b)(c + d) = ac + ad + bc + bd$.
   (iv) $(x + 7)(x + 9) = x^2 + 16x + 63$.
3. In Theor. 50, Cor. (i) if **AB** = 4 cm., and the fig. **AE** = 9.6 sq. cm., find the area of the fig. **XC**.
4. In Theor. 50, Cor. (ii), if **AX** = 2.1 cm., and the fig. **XC** = 3.36 sq. cm., find **AB**.
5. In Theor. 51, if the fig. **AG** = 36 sq. cm., and the rect. **AX, XB** = 24 sq. cm., find **AB**.
6. In Theorem 52, if the fig. **AG** = 9.61 sq. cm., and the fig. **DG** = 6.51 sq. m., find **AB**.

[For further Examples on Theorems 50-53 see. p. **210**.]

THEOREM 54. [Euclid II. 12]

In an obtuse-angled triangle, the square on the side subtending the obtuse angle is equal to the sum of the squares on the sides containing the obtuse angle **together with** *twice the rectangle contained by one of those sides and the* **projection of the other side** *upon it.*

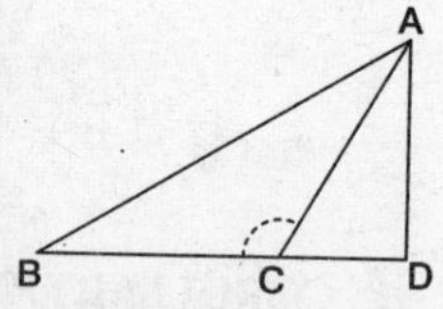

Let **ABC** be a triangle obtuse-angled at **C**; and let **AD** be drawn perp. to *BC* produced, so that **CD** is the projection of the side **CA** on **BC**.

[See Def. p. **56**.]

It is required to prove that

$$\mathbf{AB^2 = BC^2 + CA^2 + 2BC \cdot CD}.$$

Proof. Because **BD** is the *sum* of the lines **BC; CD.**

$\therefore$ $$BD^2 = BC^2 + CD^2 + 2BC \cdot CD.$$ ***Theor.* 51.**

To each of these equals add DA^2.

Then $$BD^2 + DA^2 = BC^2 + (CD^2 + DA^2) + 2BC \cdot CD.$$

$$\left.\begin{array}{l}\text{But } BD^2 + DA^2 = AB^2 \\ \text{and } CD^2 + DA^2 = CA^2\end{array}\right\}, \text{ for the } \angle D \text{ is a rt. } \angle.$$

Hence $$AB^2 = BC^2 + CA^2 + 2BC \cdot CD$$ **Q.E.D.**

THEOREM 55. [Euclid II. 13]

In every triangle the square on the side subtending an acute angle is equal to the sum of the squares on the sides containing that angle **diminished by** *twice the rectangle contained by one of those sides and the* **projection of the other side** *upon it.*

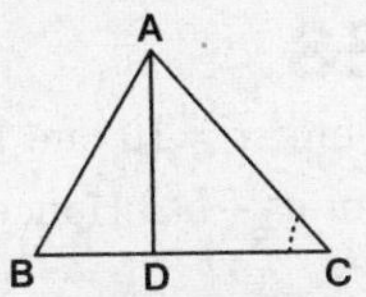

Fig. 1.

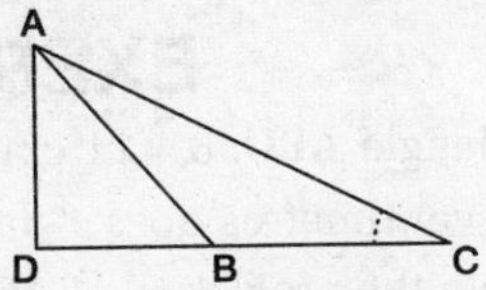

Fig. 2.

Let **ABC** be a triangle in which the $\angle$**C** is acute and let **AD** be drawn perp. to **BC**, or **BC** produced; so that **CD** is the projection of the side **CA** on **BC**.

It is required to prove that

$$AB^2 = BC^2 + CA^2 - 2BC \cdot CD.$$

Proof. Since in both figures **BD** is the *difference* of the lines **BC, CD,**

$\therefore$ $$BD^2 = BC^2 + CD^2 - 2BC \cdot CD.$$ ***Theor.* 52.**

To each of these equals add DA^2.

Then $$BD^2 + DA^2 = BC^2 + (CD^2 + DA^2) - 2BC \cdot CD. \quad \text{...(i)}$$

$$\left.\begin{array}{l}\text{But } BD^2 + DA^2 = AB^2 \\ \text{and } CD^2 + DA^2 = CA^2\end{array}\right\}, \text{ for the } \angle D \text{ is a rt. } \angle.$$

Hence $$AB^2 = BC^2 + CA^2 - 2BC \cdot CD.$$ **Q.E.D.**

SUMMARY OF THEOREMS 29, 54 and 55

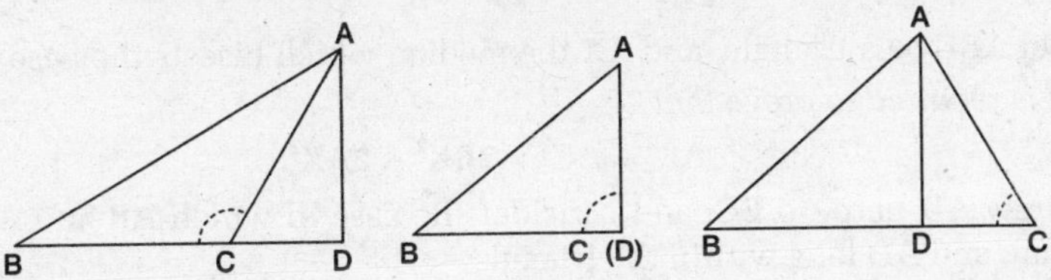

(i) If the $\angle$ACB is *obtuse*,

$$AB^2 = BC^2 + CA^2 + 2BC \cdot CD$$ ***Theor.* 54.**

(ii) If the $\angle$**ACB** is *a right angle*,

$$AB^2 = BC^2 + CA^2. \qquad \textit{Theor. 29.}$$

(iii) If the $\angle$**ACB** is *acute*,

$$AB^2 = BC^2 + CA^2 - 2BC \cdot CD. \qquad \textit{Theor. 55.}$$

Observe that in (ii), when the $\angle$**ACB** is *right*, **AD** coincides with **AC**, so that **CD** (the projection of **CA**) vanishes;

hence, in this case, $2BC \cdot CD = 0$.

Thus the three results may be collected in a single enunciation:

The square on a side of a triangle is greater than, equal to, or less than the sum of the squares on the other sides, according as the angle contained by those sides is obtuse, a right angle, or acute; the difference in cases of inequality being twice the rectangle contained by one of the two sides and the projection on it of the other.

EXERCISES

1. In a triangle **ABC**, $a = 21$ cm., $b = 17$ cm., $c = 10$ cm. By how many square centimetres does c^2 fall short of $a^2 + b^2$? Hence or otherwise calculate the projection of **AC** on **BC**.
2. **ABC** is an isosceles triangle in which **AB** = **AC**; and **BE** is drawn perpendicular to **AC**. Show that $BC^2 = 2AC \cdot CE$.
3. In the ΔABC, show that
   (i) if the $\angle C = 60°$, then $c^2 = a^2 + b^2 - ab$;
   (ii) if the $\angle C = 120°$, then $c^2 = a^2 + b^2 + ab$.

THEOREM 56

In any triangle the sum of the squares on two sides is equal to twice the square on half the third side together with twice the square on the median which bisects the third side.

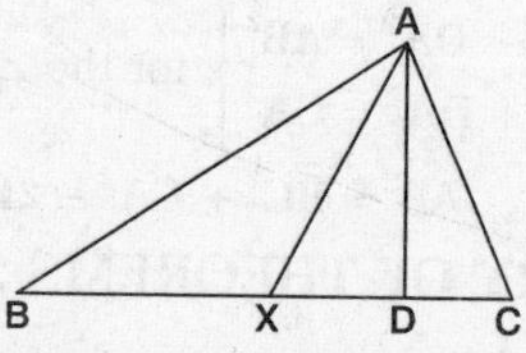

Let **ABC** be a triangle, and **AX** the median which bisects the base **BC**.

It is required to prove that

$$AB^2 + AC^2 = 2BX^2 + 2AX^2.$$

Draw **AD** perp. to **BC**; and consider the case in which **AB** and **AC** are unequal, and **AD** falls within the triangle.

Then of the $\angle^s$ **AXB**, **AXC**, one is obtuse, and the other acute. Let the $\angle$**AXB** be obtuse.

Then from the Δ**AXB**,

$$AB^2 = BX^2 + AX^2 + 2BX \cdot XD. \qquad \textit{Theor. 54.}$$

And from the Δ**AXC**,

$$AC^2 = XC^2 + AX^2 - 2XC \cdot XD. \qquad \textit{Theor. 55.}$$

Adding these results, and remembering that XC = BX, we have

$$AB^2 + AC^2 = 2BX^2 + 2AX^2. \qquad \text{Q.E.D.}$$

NOTE.–The proof may easily be adapted to the case in which the perpendicular **AD** falls outside the triangle.

ExERCISE

In any triangle the difference of the squares on two sides is equal to twice the rectangle contained by the base and the intercept between the middle point of the base and the foot of the perpendicular drawn from the vertical angle to the base.

EXERCISES ON THEOREMS 50-53

1. Use the Corollaries of Theorem 50 to show that if a straight line **AB** is divided internally at **X**, then
$$AB^2 = AX^2 + XB^2 + 2AX \cdot XB.$$
2. If a straight line **AB** is bisected at **X** and produced to **Y**, and if **AY** · **YB** = 8**AX**^{2}, show that **AY** = 2**AB**.
3. *The sum of the squares on two straight lines is never less than twice the rectangle contained by the straight lines.*
Explain this statement by reference to the diagram of Theorem 52. Also deduce it from the formula $(a - b)^2 = a^2 + b^2 - 2ab$.
4. In the formula $(a + b)(a - b) = a^2 - b^2$, substitute $a = \dfrac{x + y}{2}, b = \dfrac{x - y}{2}$, and enunciate verbally the resulting theorem.
5. If a straight line is divided internally at Y, show that the rectangle **AY**, **YB** continually diminishes as **Y** moves from **X**, the midpoint of **AB**.
Deduce this (i) from the Corollary of Theorem 53;
(ii) from the formula $ab = \left(\dfrac{a+b}{2}\right)^2 - \left(\dfrac{a-b}{2}\right)^2$.
6. *If a straight line* **AB** *is bisected at* **X**, *and also divided* (i) *internally*, (ii) *externally into two unequal segments at* Y, *show that in either case*
$$AY^2 + YB^2 = 2(AX^2 - XY^2). \qquad \textbf{[Eulcid 11.9, 10.]}$$

[*Proof of case (i).*

$$AY^2 + YB^2 = AB^2 - 2AY \cdot YB \qquad \textit{Theor. } 51.$$
$$= 4AX^2 - 2(AX + XY)(AX - XY)$$
$$= 4AX^2 - 2(AX^2 - XY^2) \qquad \textit{Theor. } 53.$$
$$= 2AX^2 + 2XY^2.$$

Case (ii) may be derived from Theorem 52 in a similar way.]

7. If **AB** is divided internally at **Y**, use the result of the last example to trace the changes in the value of $AY^2 + YB^2$, as **Y** moves from **A** to **B**.

8. *In a right-angled triangle, if a perpendicular is drawn from the right angle to the hypotenuse, the square on this perpendicular is equal to the rectangle contained by the segments of the hypotenuse.*

9. **ABC** is an isosceles triangle, and **AY** is drawn to cut the base **BC** internally or externally at **Y**. Prove that

$$AY^2 = AC^2 - BY \cdot YC \text{ , for internal section;}$$
$$AY^2 = AC^2 - BY \cdot YC \text{ , for external section.}$$

EXERCISES ON THEOREMS 54-56

1. **AB** is a straight line 8 cm. in length, and from its middle point **O** as centre with radius 5 cm. a circle is drawn; if **P** is any point on the circumference, show that

$$AP^2 + BP^2 = 82 \text{ sq. cm.}$$

2. In a triangle **ABC**, the base **BC** is bisected at **X**. If $a = 17$ cm., $b = 15$ cm., and $c = 8$ cm., calculate the length of the median **AX**, and deduce the $\angle A$.

3. The base of a triangle = 10 cm., and the sum of the squares on the other sides = 122 sq. cm.; find the locus of the vertex.

4. Prove that the sum of the squares on the sides of a parallelogram is equal to the sum of the squares on its diagonals.

   The sides of a rhombus and its shorter diagonal each measure 3 cm.; find the longer diagonal to within a hundredth of a centimetre.

5. In any quadrilateral the squares on the diagonals are together equal to twice the sum of the squares on the straight lines joining the middle points of opposite sides. [See Ex. 7, p. 57.]

6. **ABCD** is a rectangle, and **O** any point with in it: show that

$$OA^2 + OC^2 = OB^2 + OD^2.$$

   If $AB = 6$ cm., $BC = 2.5$ cm., and $OA^2 + OC^2 = 21\frac{1}{4}$ sq. cm., find the distance of **O** from the intersection on the diagonals.

7. The sum of the squares on the sides of a quadrilateral is greater than the sum of the squares on its diagonals by four times the square on the straight line which joins the middle points of the diagonals.

8. In a triangle **ABC**, the angles at **B** and **C** are acute; if **BE**, **CF** are drawn perpendicular to **AC**, **AB** respectively, prove that

$$BC^2 = AB \cdot BF + AC \cdot CE.$$

9. Three times the sum of the squares on the sides of a triangle is equal to four times the sum of the squares on the medians.

10. **ABC** is a triangle, and **O** the point of intersection of its medians: show that

$$AB^2 + BC^2 + CA^2 = 3(OA^2 + OB^2 + OC^2).$$

11. If a straight line **AB** is bisected at **X**, and also divided (internally or externally) at **Y**, then

$$AY^2 + YB^2 = 2(AX^2 + XY^2).$$ [See p. 210 Ex. 6.]

Prove this from Theorem 56, by considering a triangle **CAB** in the limiting position when the vertex **C** falls at **Y** in the base **AB**.

12. In a triangle **ABC**, if the base **BC** is divided at **X** so that m**BX** = n**XC**, show that

$$mAB^2 + nAC^2 = mBX^2 + nXC^2 + (m+n)AX^2.$$

RECTANGLES IN CONNECTION WITH CIRCLES

THEOREM 57. [Euclid III. 35.]

If two chords of a circle cut at a point within it, the rectangles contained by their segments are equal.

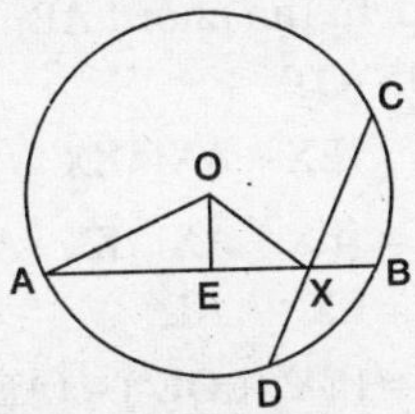

In the. **ABC**, let **AB**, **CD** be chords cutting at the internal point **X**.

It is required to prove that

the rect. **AX, XB** = *the rect.* **CX, XD**.

Let **O** be the centre, and r the radius, of the given circle.

Supposing **OE** drawn perp. to the chord **AB**, and therefore bisecting it.

Join **OA, OX**.

Proof. The rect. **AX, XB** = (**AE** + **EX**) (**EB** − **EX**)

$$= (AE + EX)(AE - EX)$$

$$= AE^2 - EX^2$$ ***Theor.* 53.**

$$= (AE^2 + OE^2) - (EX^2 + OE^2)$$

$$= r^2 - OX^2,$$

since the $\angle^s$ at E are rt.$\angle^s$.

Similarly it may be shown that

the rect. **CX, XD** = r^2 − **OX**^{2}.

∴ the rect. **AX, XB** = the rect. **CX, XD**. **Q.E.D.**

COROLLARY. *Each rectangle is equal to the square on half the chord which is bisected at the given point* **X**.

THEOREM 58. (Euclid III. 36]

If two chords of a circle, when produced, cut at a point outside it, the rectangles contained by their segments are equal. And each rectangle is equal to the square on the tangent from the point of intersection.

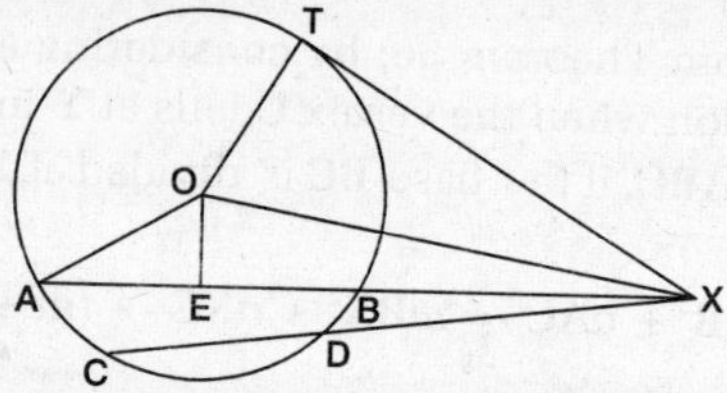

In the ○**ABC**, let **AB**, **CD** be chords cutting, when produced, at the external point **X**; and let **XT** be a tangent drawn from that point.

It is required to prove that

the rect. **AX, XB** = *the rect.* **CX, XD** = *the sq. on* **XT**.

Let **O** be the centre, and r the radius of the given circle.

Suppose **OE** drawn perp. to the chord **AB**, and therefore bisecting it.

Join **OA, OX·OT**.

Proof. The rect. **AX, XB** = (**EX** + **AX**) (**EX** − **EB**)

= (**EX** + **AX**) (**EX** − **AE**)

= **EX**^{2} − **AE**^{2} ***Theor.* 53.**

= (**EX**^{2} + **OE**^{2}) − (**AE**^{2} + **OE**^{2}) = **OX**^{2} − r^2,

since the $\angle^s$ at E are rt. $\angle^s$.

Similarly it may be shown that

the rect. **CX, XD** = **OX**^{2} − r^2.

And since the radius **OT** is perp. to the tangent **XT**,

∴ **OX**^{2} = **OX**^{2} − r^2. ***Theor.* 29.**

∴the rect. **AX, XB** = the rect. **CX, XD** = the sq. on **XT**. **Q.E.D.**

THEOREM 59. [Euclid III. 37]

If from a point outside a circle two straight lines are drawn, one of which cuts the circle, and the other meets it; and if the rectangle contained by the whole line which cuts the circle and the part of it outside the circle is equal to the square on the line which meets the circle, then the line which meets the circle is a tangent to it.

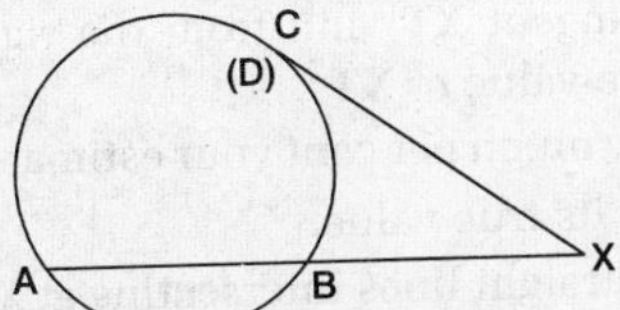

From **X** a point outside the ⊙ **ABC**, let two straight lines **XA**, **XC** be drawn, of which **XA** cuts the circle at A and B, and **XC** meets it at **C**;

and let the rect. **XA · XB** = the sq. on **XC**.

It is required to prove that **XC** *touches the circle at* **C**.

Proof. Suppose **XC** meets the circle again at **D**:

then $XA \cdot XB = XC \cdot XD$. ***Theor*. 58.**

But by hypothesis, $XA \cdot XB = XC^2$;

∴ $XC \cdot XD = XC^2$;

∴ $XD = XC$.

Hence **XC** cannot meet the circle again unless the points of section coincide;

that is, **XC** is a tangent to the circle **Q.E.D.**

NOTE ON THEOREMS 57, 58

Remembering that the segments into which the chord **AB** is divided at **X**, internally in Theorem 57, and externally in Theorem 58, are in each case **AX**, **XB**, we may include both Theorems in a single enunciation.

If any number of chords of a circle are drawn through a given point within or without a circle, the rectangles contained by the segments of the chords are equal.

EXERCISES ON THEOREMS 57-59

(*Numerical and Graphical*)

1. Draw a circle of radius 5 cm., and within it take a point **X** 3 cm. from the centre **O**. Through **X** draw any two chords **AB**, **CD**.

(i) Measure the segments of **AB** and **CD**; hence find approximately the areas of the rectangles **AX · XB** and **CX · XD**, and compare the results.

(ii) Draw the chord **MN** which is bisected at **X**; and from the right-angled triangle **OXM** calculate the value of XM^2.

(iii) Find by how much per cent your estimate of the rect. **AX · XB** differs from its true value.

2. Draw a circle of radius 3 cm., and take an external point **X** 5 cm. from the centre **O**. Through **X** draw any two secants **XAB**, **XCD**.

(i) Measure **XA**, **XB** and **XC**, **XD**; hence find approximately the rectangles $XA \cdot XB$ and $XC \cdot XD$, and compare the results.

(ii) Draw the tangent **XT**; and from the right-angled triangle **XTO** calculate the value of XT^2.

(iii) Find by how much per cent your estimate of the rect. $AX \cdot XB$ differs from its true value.

3. **AB**, **CD** are two straight lines intersecting at $X \cdot AX = 3.6$ cm., $XB = 2.4$ cm., and $CX = 5.4$ cm. If **A**, **C**, **B**, **D** are concyclic, find the length of **XD**.

Draw a circle through **A**, **C**, **B**, and check your result by measurement.

4. A secant **XAB** and a tangent **XT** are drawn to a circle from an external point **X**.

(i) If $XA = 1.2$ cm., and $XB = 4.8$ cm, find **XT**.

(ii) If $XT = 7.5$ cm., and $XA = 4.5$ cm., find **XB**.

5. A semi-circle is drawn on a given line **AB**; and from **X**, any point in **AB**, a perpendicular **XM** is drawn to **AB** cutting the circumference at **M**: show that $AX \cdot XB = MX^2$.

(i) If $AX = 5$ cm., and $MX = 4$ cm., find **XB**; hence find the diameter of the semi-circle.

(ii) If the radius of the semi-circle $= 3.7$ cm., and $AX = 4.9$ cm., find **MX**.

6. A point **X** moves within a circle of radius 4 cm., and **PQ** is any chord passing through **X**; if in all positions $PX \cdot XQ = 12$ sq. cm., find the locus of **X**.

What will the locus be if **X** moves outside the same circle, so that $PX \cdot XQ = 20$ sq. cm.?

EXERCISES ON THEOREMS 57-59

(Theoretical)

1. **ABC** is a triangle right-angled at **C**, and from **C** a perpendicular **CD** is drawn to the hypotenuse : show that

$$AD \cdot DB = CD^2.$$

2. If two circles intersect, and through any point **X** in their common chord two chord AB, CD are drawn, one in each circle, show that

$$AX \cdot XB = CX \cdot XD.$$

3. Deduce from Theorem 58 that the tangents drawn to a circle from any external point are equal.

4. If two circles intersect, tangents drawn to them from any point in their common chord produced are equal.

5. If a common tangent **PQ** is drawn to two circles which cut at **A** and **B**, show that **AB** produced bisects **PQ**.

6. If two straight lines **AB, CD** intersect at **X** so that $AX \cdot XB = CX \cdot XD$, deduce from Theorem 57 (*by reductio ad absurdum) that the points* **A, B, C, D** are concyclic.
7. In the triangle **ABC**, perpendiculars **AP, BQ** are drawn from **A** and **B** to the opposite sides, and intersect at **O** : show that
$$AO \cdot OP = BO \cdot OQ.$$
8. **ABC** is a triangle right-angled at **C**, and from **C** a perpendicular **CD** is drawn to the hypotenuse; show that
$$AB \cdot AD = AC^2.$$
9. Through A, a point of intersection of two circles, two straight lines **CAE; DAF** are drawn, each passing through a centre and terminated by the circumferences; show that
$$CA \cdot AE = DA \cdot AF.$$
10. If from any external point **P** two tangents are drawn to a given circle whose centre is **O** and radius r ; and if **OP** meets the chord of contact at **Q**; show that
$$OP \cdot OQ = r^2.$$
11. **AB** is a fixed diameter of a circle, and **CD** is perpendicular to **AB** (or **AB** produced); if *any* straight line is drawn from **A** to cut **CD** at P and the circle at **Q** show that
$AP \cdot AQ$ is constant.
12. **A** is a fixed point, and **CD** a fixed straight line; **AP** is *any* straight line drawn **A** to meet **CD** at P ; if in **AP** a point **Q** is taken so that $AP \cdot AQ$ is constant, find the locus of **Q**.

EXERCISES ON THEOREMS 57 - 59

(*Miscellaneous*)

1. The chord of an arc of a circle = $2c$, the height of the arc = h, the radius = r. Show by theorem 57 that
$$h(2r - h) = c^2.$$
Hence find the diameter of a circle in which a chord 24 cm. long cuts off a segment 8 cm. in height.
2. The radius of a circular arch is 50 m., and its height is 36 m: find the span of the arch.
If the height is reduced by 16 m., the radius remaining the same, by how much will the span be reduced?
Check your calculated results graphically by a diagram in which 1 cm. represents 5 m.
3. Employ the equation $h(2r - h) = c^2$ to find the height of an arc whose chord is 16 cm., and radius 17 cm.
Explain the double result geometrically.

4. If d denotes the shortest distance from an external point to a circle, and t the length of the tangent of the same point show by Theorem 58 that

$$d(d+2r)=t^2.$$

Hence find the diameter of the circle when $d=2.4$ cm., and $t=4.8$ cm.; and verify your result graphically.

5. If the horizon visible to an observer on a cliff 10.06 m. above the sea-level is 36 km. distant, find roughly the diameter of the earth.

Hence find the approximate distance at which a bright light raised 20.12 m. above the sea is visible at the sea-level.

6. If h is the height of an arc of radius r, and b the chord of half the arc, prove that

$$b^2=2rh.$$

7. A semi-circle is described on **AB** as diameter, and any to chords **AC**, BD are drawn intersecting at P : show that

$$\mathbf{AB^2=AC\cdot AP+BD\cdot BP}.$$

8. Two circles intersect at **B** and **C**, and the two direct common tangents **AE** and **DF** are drawn : if the common chord is produced to meet the tangents at **G** and **H**, show that

$$\mathbf{GH^2=AE^2+BC^2}.$$

9. If from an external point **P** a secant **PCD** is drawn to a circle, and **PM** is perpendicular to a diameter **AB**, show that

$$\mathbf{PM^2=PC\cdot PD-AM\cdot MB}.$$

PROBLEMS

PROBLEM 32

To draw a square equal in area to a given rectangle.

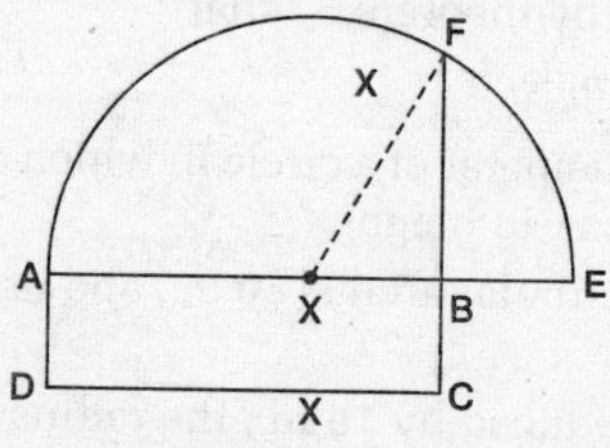

Let **ABCD** be the given rectangle.

Construction. Produce **AB** to **E**, making **BE** equal to **BC**. On **AE** draw a semi-circle; and produce **CB** to me et the circumference at **F**.

Then **BF** is a side of the required square.

Proof. Let **X** be the mid-point of **AE**, and r the radius of the semi-circle. Join **XF**.

Then the rect. $AC = AB \cdot BE$

$$= (r + XB)(r - XB)$$
$$= r^2 - XB^2$$
$$= FB^2, \text{ from the rt. angled } \Delta FBX.$$

COROLLARY. *To describe a square equal in area to any given rectilinear figure.*

Reduce the given figure to a triangle of equal area *Prob.* 18.

Draw a rectangle equivalent to this triangle. *Prob.* 17.

Apply to the rectangle the construction given above.

EXERCISES

1. Draw a rectangle 8 cm. by 2 cm., and construct a square of equal area. What is the length of each side?
2. Find graphically the side of a square equal in area to a rectangle whose length and breadth are 6 cm. and 3 cm. Test your work by measurement and calculation.
3. Draw any rectangle whose area is 24.2 sq. cm.; and construct a square of equal area. Find by measurement and calculation the length of each side.
4. Draw an equilateral triangle on a side of 8 cm., and construct a rectangle of equal area [Problem 17]. Hence find by construction and measurement the side of an equal square.
5. Draw a quadrilateral **ABCD** from the following data: $A = 65°$; $AB = AD = 9$ cm.; $BC = CD = 5$ cm. Reduce this figure to a triangle [Problem 18], and hence to a rectangle of equal area. Construct an equal square, and measure the length of its side.
6. Divide **AB**, a line 9 cm. in length, internally at **X**, so that $AX \cdot XB =$ the square on a side of 4 cm.

   Hence give a graphical solution, correct to the first decimal place, of the simultaneous equations:

   $$x + y = 9, \; xy = 16.$$
7. Taking 0.2 cm. as your unit of length, solve the following equations by a graphical construction, correct to one decimal figure:

   $$x + y = 40, \; xy = 169.$$
8. The area of a rectangle is 25 sq. cm., and the length of one side is 7.2 cm; find graphically the length of the other side to the nearest millimetre, and test your drawing by calculation.
9. Divide **AB**, a line 8 cm. in length, *externally* at **X**, so the $AX \cdot XB =$ the square on a side of 6 cm. [See p. 245.]

Hence find a graphical solution, correct to the first decimal place, of the equations:

$$x - y = 8, \; xy = 36.$$

10. On a straight line **AB** draw a semi-circle, and from any point **P** on the circumference draw **PX** perpendicular to **AB**. Join **AP**, **PB**, and denote these lines by x and y.

Noticing that (i) $x^2 + y^2 = AB^2$; (ii) $xy = 2\,\Delta APB = AB \cdot PX$; devise a graphical solution of the equations:

$$x^2 + y^2 = 100 \; ; \; xy = 25.$$

PROBLEM 33

To divide a given straight line so that the rectangle contained by the whole and one part may be equal to the square on the other part.

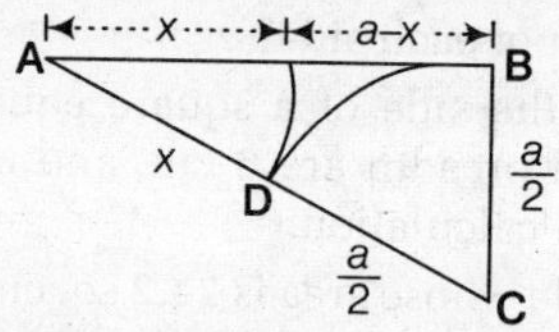

Let **AB** be the st. line to be divided at a point **X** in such a way that

$$AB \cdot BX = AX^2.$$

Construction. Draw **BC** perp. to **AB**, and make **BC** equal to half **AB**. Join **AC**.

From **CA** cut off **CD** equal to **CB**.

From **AB** cut off **AX** equal to **AD**.

Then **AB** is divided as required at **X**.

Proof. Let **AB** = a units of length, and let **AX** = x.

Then $BX = a - x$; $AD = x$; $BC = CD = \frac{a}{2}$.

Now $AB^2 = AC^2 - BC^2$, from the rt. angle ΔABC;

$$= (AC - BC)\,(AC + BC);$$

that is, $a^2 = x\,(x + a)$

$$= x^2 + ax.$$

From each of these equals take ax;

then $a^2 - ax = x^2$;

or, $a\,(a - x) = x^2$,

that is, $AB \cdot BX = AX^2$.

EXERCISES

Let **AB** be divided as above at **X**. On **AB · AX**, and on opposite sides of **AB**, draw the squares **AB**EF, **AXGH**; and produce **GX** to meet **FE** at **K**. In this diagram name rectangular figures equivalent to a^2, $x^2 \cdot x(x+a) \cdot ax$ and $a(a-x)$. Hence illustrate the above proof graphically.

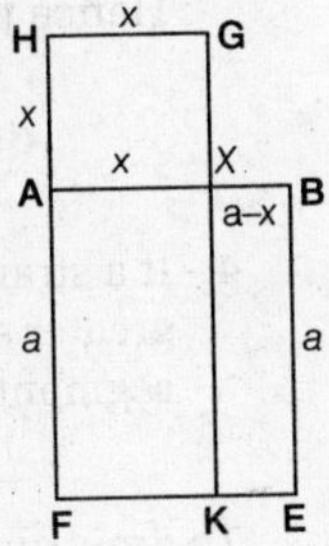

NOTE. A straight line is said to be divided in Medial Section when the rectangle contained by the given line and one segment is equal to the square on the other segment.

This division may be *internal* or *external*: that is to say, **AB** may be divided internally at **X**, and externally at **X′**, so that

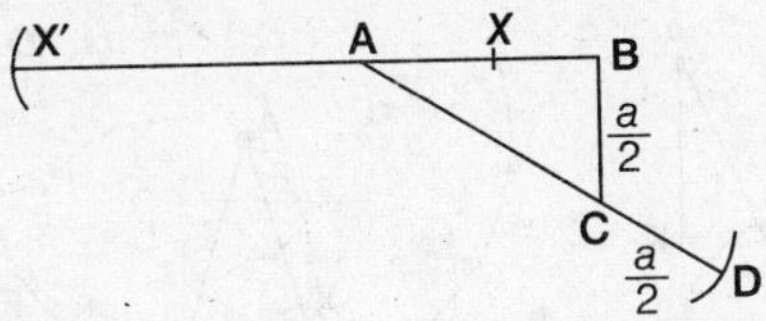

(i) $\mathbf{AB \cdot BX = AX^2}$,

(ii) $\mathbf{AB \cdot BX' = AX'^2}$.

To obtain **X′**, the construction of p. 220 must be modified thus: **CD** is to be cut off from **AC** *produced*;

AX′.............. from **BA** *produced*, in the *negative* sense.

ALGEBRAICAL ILLUSTRATION

If a st. line **AB** is divided at **X**, internally or externally, so that

$$\mathbf{AB \cdot BX = AX^2}.$$

and if **AB** = a, **AX** = x, and consequently **BX** = $a - x$, then

$$a(a-x) = x^2$$

or,
$$x^2 + ax - a^2 = 0,$$

and the roots of this quadratic, namely, $\dfrac{a\sqrt{5}}{2} - \dfrac{a}{2}$ and $-\left(\dfrac{a\sqrt{5}}{2} + \dfrac{a}{2}\right)$, are the lengths of **AX** and **AX′**.

EXERCISES

1. Divide a straight line 8 cm. long internally in medial section. Measure the greater segment, and find its length algebraically.
2. Divide **AB**, a line 4 cm. long, externally in medial section at **X′**. Measure **AX′**, and obtain its length algebraically, explaining the geometrical meaning of the negative sign.

3. In the figure of Problem 33, show that $AC = \frac{a\sqrt{5}}{2}$. [Theor. 29.]

Hence prove (i) $AX = \frac{a\sqrt{5}}{2} - \frac{a}{2}$;

(ii) $AX' = -\left(\frac{a\sqrt{5}}{2} + \frac{a}{2}\right)$.

4. If a straight line is divided internally in medial section, and from the greater segment a part is taken equal to the less, show that the greater segment is also divided in medial section.

PROBLEM 34

To draw an isosceles triangle having each of the angles at the base double of the vertical angle.

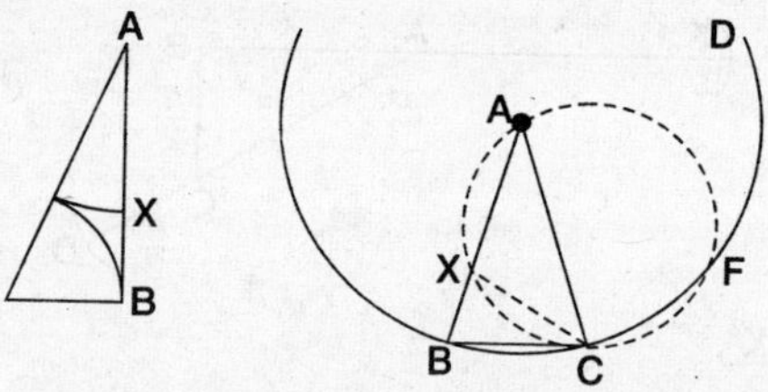

Construction. Take any line **AB**, and divide it at **X**, so that

$$AB \cdot BX = AX^2. \qquad \textit{Prob. 33.}$$

(This construction is shown separately on the left.)

With centre **A**, and radius **AB**, draw the ⊙**BCD**; and in it place the chord **BC** equal to **AX**.

Join **AC**.

Then **ABC** is the triangle required.

Proof. Join **XC**, and suppose a circle drawn through **A**, **X** and **C**. Now, by construction, $BA \cdot BX = AX^2 = BC^2$;

∴ **BC** touches the ⊙**AXC** at **C**; *Theor.* 59.

∴ the ∠**BCX** = the ∠**XAC**, in the alt. segment.

To each add the ∠**XCA**;

then the ∠**BCA** = the ∠**XAC** + the ∠**XCA**

= the ext.∠**CXB**.

And the ∠**BCA** = the ∠**CBA**, for **AB** = **AC**.

∴ the ∠**CBX** = the ∠**CXB**;

∴ **CX** = **CB** = **AX**,

∴ the ∠**XAC** = the ∠**XCA**;

∴ the ∠**XAC** + the ∠**XCA** = twice the ∠**A**.

But the ∠**ABC** = the ∠**ACB** = the ∠**XAC** + the ∠**XCA** ***Proved.***

= twice the ∠**A**.

EXERCISES

1. How many degrees are there in the vertical angle of an isosceles triangle in which each angle at the base is double of the vertical angle?
2. Show how a right angle may be divided into five equal parts by means of Problem 34.
3. In the figure of Problem 34 point out a triangle whose vertical angle is three times either angle at the base.

   Show how such a triangle may be constructed.
4. If in the triangle **ABC**, the $\angle$**B** = the $\angle$**C** = twice the $\angle$**A**, show that

$$\frac{\mathbf{BC}}{\mathbf{AB}} = \frac{\sqrt{5}-1}{2}.$$

5. In the figure of Problem 34, if the two circles intersect at **F**, show that
   (i) **BC** = **CF**;
   (ii) the circle **AXC** = the circum-circle of the triangle **ABC**;
   (iii) **BC**, **CF** are sides of a regular decagon inscribed in the circle **BCD**;
   (iv) **AX**, **XC**, **CF** are sides of a regular pentagon inscribed in the circle **AXC**.
6. In the figure of Problem 34, show that the centre of the circle circumscribed about the triangle **CBX** is the middle point of the arc **XC**.
7. In the figure of Problem 34, if **I** is the in-centre of the triangle **ABC**, and **I′**, **S′** the in-centre and circum-centre of the triangle **CBX**, show that **S′ I** = **S′ I′**.
8. If a straight line is divided in medial section, the rectangle contained by the sum and difference of the segments is equal to the rectangle contained by the segments.
9. If a straight line **AB** is divided internally in medial section at **X**, show that

$$\mathbf{AB}^2 + \mathbf{BX}^2 = 3\,\mathbf{AX}^2.$$

   Also verify this result by substituting the values given on page 222.

THE GRAPHICAL SOLUTION OF QUADRATIC EQUATIONS

From the following constructions, which depend on Problem 32, a graphical solution of easy quadratic equations may be obtained.

I. *To divide a straight line* **internally** *so that the rectangle contained by the segments may be equal to a given square.*

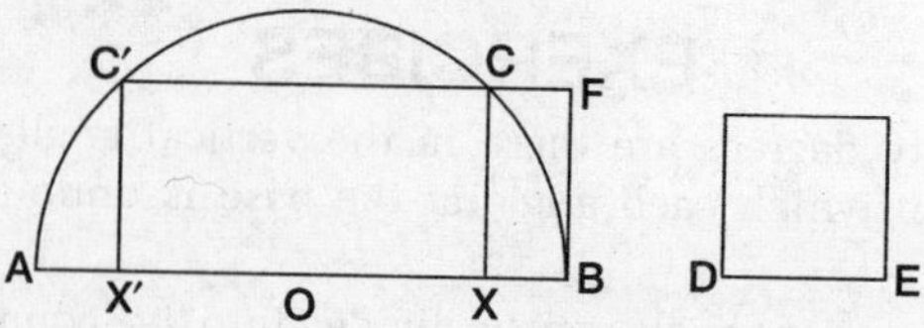

Let **AB** be the st. line to be divided, and **DE** a side of the given square;

Construction. On **AB** draw a semicircle; and from **B** draw **BF** perp. to **AB** and equal to **DE**.

From **F** draw **FCC′** par[1] to **AB**, cutting the ○[ce] at **C** and **C′**.

From C, C′ draw **CX**, **C′ X′** perp. to **AB**.

Then **AB** is divided as required at **X**, and also at **X′**.

Proof. $\mathbf{AX \cdot XB = CX^2}$ ***Prob*. 32.**

$$= \mathbf{BF}^2$$

$$= \mathbf{DE}^2.$$

Similarly $\mathbf{AX' \cdot X'B = DE^2}.$

Application. The purpose of this construction is to find two straight lines **AX**, **XB**, having given their *sum*, viz. **AB**, and their *product*, viz. the square on **DE**.

Now to solve the equation $x^2 - 13x + 36 = 0$, we have to find two numbers whose *sum* is 13, and whose *product* is 36, or 6^2.

To do this graphically, perform the above construction, making **AB** equal to 13 cm., and **DE** equal to $\sqrt{36}$ or 6 cm. The segments **AX**, **XB** represent the roots of the equation, and their values may be obtained by measurement.

NOTE. If the last term of the equation is not a perfect square, as $x^2 - 7x + 11 = 0$. $\sqrt{11}$ must be first got by the arithmetical rule, or graphically by means of Problem 32.

II. *To divide a straight line* **externally** *so that the rectangle contained by the segments may be equal to a given square.*

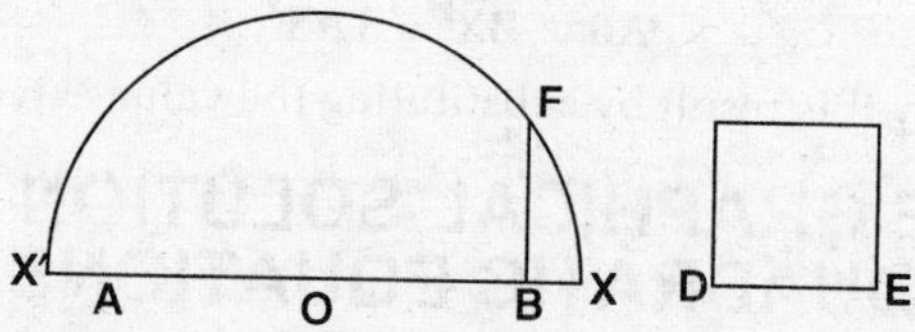

Let **AB** be the st. line to be divided externally, and **DE** the side of the given square.

Construction. From B draw BF perp. to **AB**, and equal to **DE**. Bisect **AB** at **O**.

With centre **O**, and radius **OF** draw a semi-circle to cut **AB** produced at **X** and **X′**.

Then **AB** is divided externally as required at **X**, and also at **X′**.

Proof. $\mathbf{AX \cdot XB = X'B \cdot BX}$, since $\mathbf{AB = X'B}$,

$= \mathbf{BF}^2$ *Prob.* 32.

$= \mathbf{DE}^2$.

Application. Here we find two lines **AX**, **XB**, having given their *difference*, viz. **AB**, and their *product*, viz. the square on **DE**.

Now to solve the equation $x^2 - 6x - 16 = 0$, we have to find two numbers whose numerical *difference* is 6, and whose product is 16, or 4^2.

To do this graphically, perform the above construction, making **AB** equal to 6 cm., and **DE** equal to $\sqrt{16}$ or 4 cm. The segments **AX**, **XB** represent the roots of the equation, and their values, as before, may be obtained by measurement.

EXERCISES

Obtain approximately the roots of the following quadratics by means of graphical construction; and test your results algebraically.

1. $x^2 - 10x + 16 = 0$.
2. $x^2 - 14x + 49 = 0$.
3. $x^2 - 12x + 25 = 0$.
4. $x^2 - 5x - 36 = 0$.
5. $x^2 - 7x - 49 = 0$.
6. $x^2 - 10x + 20 = 0$.

EXERCISES FOR SQUARED PAPER

1. A circle passing through the points (0, 4), (0, 9) touches the x-axis at **P**. Calculate and measure the length of **OP**.

2. With centre at the point (9, 6) a circle is drawn to touch the y-axis. Find the rectangle of the segments of any chord through **O**. Also find the rectangle of the segments of any chord through the point (9, 12).

3. Draw a circle (showing all lines of construction) through the points (6, 0), (24, 0), (0, 9). Find the length of the other intercept on the y-axis, and verify by measurement. Also find the length of a tangent to the circle from the origin.

4. Draw a circle through the points (10, 0), (0, 5), (0, 20); and prove by Theorem 59 that it touches the x-axis.

Find (i) the coordinates of the centre, (ii) the length of the radius.

5. If a circle passes through the points (16, 0), (18, 0), (0, 12) show by Theorem 58 that it also passes through (0, 24).

Find (i) the coordinates of the centre, (ii) the length of the tangent from the origin.

6. Plot the points **A**, **B**, **C**, **D** from the coordinates (12, 0), (– 6, 0), (0, 9), (0 – 8); and prove by Theorem 57 that they are concyclic.

If r denotes the radius of the circle, show that

$$\mathbf{OA}^2 + \mathbf{OB}^2 + \mathbf{OC}^2 + \mathbf{OD}^2 = 4r^2.$$

7. Draw a circle (showing all lines of construction) to touch the y-axis at the point (0, 9), and to cut the x-axis at (3,0).
Prove that the circle must cut the x-axis again at the point (27, 0); and find its radius. Verify your results by measurement.
8. Show that two circles of radius 13 may be drawn through the point (0, 8) to touch the x-axis; and by means of Theorem 58, find the length of their common chord.
9. Given a circle of radius 15, the centre being at the origin, show how to draw a second circle of the same radius touching the given circle and also touching the x-axis.
How many circles can be so drawn? Measure the coordinates of the centre of that in the first quadrant.
10. **A**, **B**, **C**, **D** are four points on the x-axis at distances 6, 9, 15, 25 from the origin **O**. Draw two intersecting circles, one through **A**, **B**, and the other through **C**, **D**, and hence determine a point P in the x-axis such that

$$\mathbf{PA \cdot PB = PC \cdot PD}.$$

Calculate and measure **OP**.
If the distances of **A**, **B**, **C**, **D** from **O** are a, b, c, d respectively, prove that

$$\mathbf{OP} = (ab - cd) / (a + b - c - d).$$

Answers to Numerical Exercises

Since the utmost care cannot ensure absolute accuracy in graphical work, results so obtained are likely to be only approximate. The answers here given are those found by calculation, and being true so far as they go, furnish a standard by which the student may test the correctness of his drawing and measurement. Results within one per cent of those given in the Answers may usually be considered satisfactory.

Exercises. Page 123.

1. 5 cm. **2.** 24 cm. **3.** 3 cm., 4 cm.
4. $\sqrt{7} = 2{\cdot}6$ cm. **5.** 12 cm. **6.** 12 sq. cm.
7. 2·4 cm.

Exercises. Page 125.

1. 3·4 cm. **2.** $3\sqrt{2} = 4{\cdot}2$ cm. **3.** $2\sqrt{3} = 3{\cdot}5$ cm.
4. 17 m. **6.** 5 cm.

Exercises. Page 127.

6. 4 cm. **7.** 1·3 cm.

Exercises. Page. 129.

2. 3·7 cm. **3.** 3·25 cm.
5. 1·7 cm.; (4·2 cm., 4·2 cm.); 6 cm.

Exercises. Page 130.

5. 51 cm. **6.** 3·2 cm.; 3 cm.; 1·2 cm.

Exercises. Page 132.

4. (8, 11). **5.** 17; 10; (0, – 8).

Exercises. Page 135.

1. 74°, 148°, 16°. **2.** 115°, 230°. **3.** 55°, 8°, 47°.

Exercises. Page 145.

1. 8·0 cm. **2.** 3 cm. **3.** 8·7 cm.
4. 12 cm., 67° **5.** 5 cm.

Exercises. Page 147.

3. 3 cm. and 17 cm.

Exercises. Page 149.

1. 72°, 108°, 108°.

Exercises. Page 153.

2. 3·2 cm. **3.** 4 cm. **4.** 4 cm.; 3·2 cm.

Exercises. Page 161.

2. 2·3 cm., 4·6 cm. 6·9 cm. **3.** 1·39 cm.
4. 6·9 cm.; 20·78 sq. cm. **7.** 3·2 cm.

Exercises. Page 162.

1. 6 cm.; 36 sq. cm. **4.** 8·5 cm. **5.** 4 cm.

Exercises. Page 163.

4. $128\frac{4^\circ}{7}$; 3·5 cm.

Exercises. Page 164.

1. 7 cm.; 8 cm. **2.** 259 · 8 sq. cm.
4. (i) 41 · 57 sq. cm.;
(ii) 77 · 25 sq. cm.

Exercises. Page 168.

1. (ii) 28 · 3 cm.; (ii) 628 · 3 cm.
2. (i) 16 · 62 sq. cm.; (ii) 352 · 99 sq. cm.
3. 11 · 31 cm.; 10 ·18 sq. cm.
4. 56 sq. cm. **5.** 43 · 98 sq. cm.
7. 30 · 5 sq. cm. **8.** 8 · 9 cm.
9. 4 · 5 cm.; 2·5 cm. **10.** 12 · 57 sq. cm.
11. Circumferences, 8 · 8 cm.; 12 · 6 cm. Areas, 6 · 16 sq. cm,; 12 · 6 sq. cm.

Exercises. Page 186.

3. 6 · 4 sq. cm. **4.** 3 · 7 cm.

5. 10 cm. **6.** 1 cm.

Exercises. Page 188.

1. 630 sq. cm. 15 cm.

Exercises. Page 190.

2. 8 · 5 cm. 90°, **3.** A circle of rad. 6 cm.

4. 5 · 20 cm. **6.** 0 · 25 cm.

Exercises. Page 193.

1. (i) 16 sq. cm. (ii) 16 sq. cm. **2.** (i) 16 sq. cm. (ii) 16 sq. cm

3. (i) 1 · 6 cm. **4.** (i) 2 · 4 cm. (ii) 12 · 5 cm.

5. (i) 3 · 2 cm.; 8 · 2 cm. (ii) 3 · 5 cm

6. Two concentric circles, radii 2 cm. and 6 cm.

Exercises. Page 195.

1. 26 cm. **2.** 96 m.; 16 m.

3. 2 cm.; 32 cm. **4.** 7·2 cm.

5. 12,960 km.; 16 km.

Exercises. Page 197.

1. 4 cm. **2.** 4 · 24 cm.

3. 5 cm. **5.** 6 · 6 cm.

6. 6 · 6, 2 · 4. **7.** 35 · 2, 4 · 8.

8. 3 · 5 cm. **9.** 11 · 2, 3 · 2.

10. 9 · 6, 2 · 6

Exercises. Page 199.

1. 4 · 14 cm. **2.** 6 · 48 cm.

Exercises. Page 203.

1. 8, 2. **2.** 7, 7.

3. 9 · 3, 2 · 7. **4.** 9, – 4.

5. 11·32 –4·32. **6.** 7 · 24, 2 · 76.

Exercises. Page 203-204.

1. 6. **2.** 36, 45.

3. 16, 12. **4.** $(10, 12\frac{1}{2})$; $12\frac{1}{2}$.

5. (17, 18); $12\sqrt{2} = 16\cdot97$. **7.** 15.

8. 10. **9.** Four. (26, 15).

10. 12 · 84.